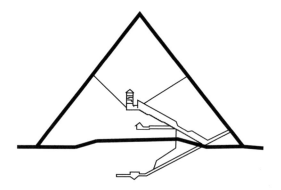

Bernard Tschumi, "Questions of Space: The Pyramid and the Labyrinth (or the Architectural Paradox)" (1975)

EVENT-CITIES 5

© 2024 Bernard Tschumi

All rights reserved. No part of this book may be reproduced in any form by any electronic or mechanical means (including photocopying, recording, or information storage and retrieval) without permission in writing from the publisher.

Event-Cities, published in 1994 on the occasion of Bernard Tschumi's exhibition at The Museum of Modern Art in New York, is an expanded version of *Praxis Villes-Evenements* (Le Fresnoy and Massimo Riposati, Editeurs, Paris). *Event-Cities 2* includes work from 1994 to 1999, and also features the 1982–98 Parc de la Villette. *Event-Cities 3* gathers work from 1999 to 2004. *Event-Cities 4* covers 2004 to 2009, as well as the 2002 Alésia MuséoParc. *Event-Cities 5* documents work from 2010 to 2024, along with the 1979–82 20th-Century Follies.

Book design and production: Bernard Tschumi and Greg Barton
Copy editor: Lisa Palmer
Printer: Musumeci S.p.A, Valle d'Aosta - Italy

Library of Congress Control Number: 2023945846

ISBN: 978-0-262-54937-0

Printed and bound in Italy

BERNARD TSCHUMI

EVENT-CITIES 5
Poetics

The MIT Press
Cambridge, Massachusetts
London, England

Acknowledgements

I wish to thank our teams at the New York and Paris offices of Bernard Tschumi Architects for the curiosity, ingenuity, and critical thinking that power the projects presented in this book, particularly Joel Rutten with Christopher Lee, Kate Scott, and Kim Starr in New York and Véronique Descharrières with Rémy Cointet and Vincent Prunier in the Paris office, Bernard Tschumi urbanistes Architectes. The following individuals also deserve special thanks: In New York: Christopher Ball, Cecil Barnes, Karen Berberyan, Kai Blatt, Pedro Camara, Sebastian Cilloniz, Dora Felekou, Eleonora Flammini, Jocelyn Froimovich, Sonia Grobelny, Jerome Haferd, Paul-Arthur Heller, Olga Jitariouk, Violaine Joessel, Gizem Karagoz, Pierre-Yves Kuhn, Clement Laurencio, Alissa Lopez Serfozo, Tina Marinaki, Jake Matatyaou, Alison McIlvride, Jess Myers, Nate Oppenheim, Valeria Paez-Cala, Clinton Peterson, Bart-Jan Polman, Ashley Simone, Susan Steinfield, Emma Sumrow, Ida Yazdi, Wenjun Yu, and Nianlai Zhong. In Paris: Emilie Bilan, Emmanuel Desmazières, Thomas Ducher, Florence Festa, Catherine Rambourg, and Thomas Sanson. I also thank Aleksandr Bierig, Sarah Rafson, and Colin Spoelman, who helped with earlier publications.

Among consultants and collaborators, particular gratitude is due to Hugh Dutton, Michel Desvigne and Sophie Mourthé, as well as Ray Quinn, David Farnsworth, and Michelle Roelofs of Arup. I am indebted to our many local partners, including Denis Bouvier and Nathalie Pierre of Groupe-6; Serge Fehlmann with Christophe Faini; Tianjin Urban Planning and Design Institute; ArchiFED; HHDesign; iDEA; Yves Dessuant; Alfonso Giancotti; Jean-Jacques Hubert and Antoine Santiard of h2o; and Glauco Lombardi. I thank the photographers who documented our projects, including Iwan Baan, Peter Mauss, Christian Richters, Fred Delangle, and Kris Provoost.

I deeply appreciate the support and confidence of clients who approached us for new projects years after our initial buildings for them: Philippe Gudin and Christophe Gudin at Institut Le Rosey, Juan Carlos Torres at Vacheron Constantin, Didier Fusillier at Parc de la Villette, Alain Fleischer at Le Fresnoy, and François Sauvadet at Alésia. I also extend my thanks to Sylvie Retailleau with Maxime Jourdain at Paris-Saclay University, Vincenzo Marini Marini at Fondazione Carisap in Grottammare, Tedros Adhanom Ghebreyesus and Gaudenz Silberschmidt at the World Health Organization, and Spiro Latsis in Monaco. Gratitude is due to many individuals at institutions that exhibited our work, particularly Frédéric Migayrou at the Centre Pompidou, Hubertus Adam at Swiss Architecture Museum, and Gong Yan at Power Station of Art, as well as Marie-Ange Brayer at Frac Centre and Stéphanie Quantin-Biancalani at the Cité de l'Architecture et du Patrimoine.

Event-Cities 5 benefited from the close attention of Greg Barton, who oversaw its content and production. I especially thank the MIT Press for publishing the *Event-Cities* series, from Roger Conover, who first encouraged its development, to Thomas Weaver, who shepherded along this final volume. Thanks are due to my students and colleagues at Columbia University in New York, in particular Mark Wigley, Amale Andraos, Andrés Jaque, and Enrique Walker, and to Kenneth Frampton and the late Anthony Vidler for their constant intellectual support.

Credit is due to my esteemed colleague, Luca Merlini, for his unique insights and to Colin Fournier for his architectural acumen. Finally, I wish to thank Kate Linker, whose advice and contributions over many years have played an invaluable role in my work.

Contents

Introduction: *Poetics*   **013**
Prologue: *Advertisements & Transcripts*   **023**
20th-Century Follies, 1979–1982: *Abstract Constructions*   **028**

A. Circular Autonomy & Dialogue
Carthage, Carthage National Museum, 2022: *Gardens and Crowns*   **048**
Alésia, MuséoParc, 2002–12 (revision 2015): *Dual Panoramic Fortification*   **060**
Geneva, World Health Museum, 2018: *Compositions*   **088**
Shenzhen, Finance Culture Center, 2020: *Chance Encounters over Nature*   **104**
Rolle, Center for Science and Entrepreneurship, 2017–25: *Twin Circles*   **120**

B1. Abstract Superpositions (Concepts)
Doha, Presidential Hotel, 2013: *Suspended Volumes*   **156**
Monaco, Tour Honoria, 2016: *Tripartite Articulations*   **164**
Luxembourg, ArcelorMittal Headquarters, 2017: *Autonomous Parts*   **176**

B2. Site-Specific Superpositions (Contexts)
Anyang, Yinxu Ruins Museum, 2019: *The River and the Ruins*   **204**
Lausanne, Musée Cantonal des Beaux-Arts, 2010: *Hovering Vista*   **216**
Shenzhen, OCT-LOFT Master Plan, 2011: *Insertion/Densification*   **228**
Guangzhou, Guangzhou Museum, 2014: *Directed Dialogue*   **240**

C. Analogical Reference
Paris, Cité Musicale, Ile Seguin, 2012: *Ship, Lantern, Passage, Garden*   **264**
Tianjin, Binhai Science Museum, 2013–19: *Industrial Cones*   **280**
Geneva, Caran d'Ache Headquarters, 2021: *Colored Pencil Allusions*   **324**
Grottammare, A.N.I.M.A. Cultural Center, 2012–14: *Courts and Facades*   **340**

D. Typological Urbanisms
Shenzhen, Xiangmihu Area, 2018: *Singular Towers on Hanging Garden*   **376**
Beijing, 100KM2 City, 2018: *Cluster Grid*   **388**
Budapest, Museum of Ethnography, 2016: *Architectural Landscape*   **400**
Paris-Saclay, Biology-Pharmacy-Chemistry Center, 2015–22: *Interlinked Chain*   **416**

E. Self-Preservation
Geneva, Vacheron Constantin Headquarters Extension, 2011–15: *Thematic Variation*   **484**
Tourcoing, Le Fresnoy Extension, 2019: *Material Continuations*   **504**
Paris, Folie P7 Café, Parc de la Villette, 2011: *Material Hypervigilance*   **516**
Paris, Folie L4 HyperTent, Parc de la Villette, 2021: *Material Difference*   **524**
France, Micro-folies, 2015–: *Combinatory Games*   **536**

F. Retrospective Concepts
New York, Thresholds, Museum of Modern Art, 1994: *Architecture and Event*   **548**
Orléans, Chronomanifestes 1950–2010, Frac Centre, 2013–14: *Avant-Garde Timeline*   **556**
Paris, Retrospective, Centre Pompidou, 2014: *Concept and Notation I*   **564**
Basel, Retrospective, Swiss Architecture Museum, 2015: *Concept and Notation II*   **580**
Shanghai, Retrospective, Power Station of Art, 2016: *Concept and Notation III*   **584**

Project Chronology (1974–2024), Project Teams, Project List, Bibliography   **591**

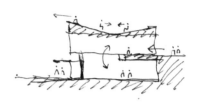

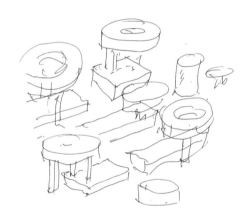
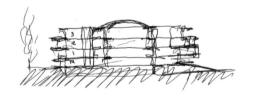
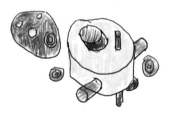

POETICS

Introduction

This is the fifth and final volume of the *Event-Cities* series. Conceived as a "project discourse," four volumes were published in 1994, 2000, 2005, and 2010.

The expression "project discourse" is from Roger Conover, the legendary executive editor of MIT Press and a lasting influence on numerous writers. When first presented with the idea of a book that would address the making of mostly unbuilt architectural projects as an evolving thought process, Roger's reaction was, "But MIT Press publishes books of words, not drawings." I also told him that the volume was intended to accompany the collection of my writings that MIT Press was preparing at the time. As it happened, *Architecture and Disjunction* was scheduled to appear in 1994, in conjunction with my retrospective exhibition, *Space and Event*, at New York's Museum of Modern Art. During our phone conversation, Roger finally ventured, "MIT Press does books about textual discourse, so why not try a book about a 'project discourse?'" With those words, the 640-page book was under way. Published with great speed, this early *Event-Cities* volume was one of the first "thick" architectural books of the time. Soon books of architecture that deal with project discourses became important, documenting the direction of thought rather than serving as personal propaganda or client seduction, in the manner of traditional monographs.

I found the format congenial to a potential series documenting aspects of architectural thinking during a particular era, my own. Reminders of Le Corbusier's *Complete Works 1910-1965*, published in eight volumes by Girsberger, inevitably came to mind, but the intent behind *Event-Cities* was different: The series was conceived as an exploration of the questions raised by architecture rather than promoting the certainties of a "heroic" modernist era. If anything, the series was about uncertainties, the irresolute questions that accompany nearly every aspect of the design process.

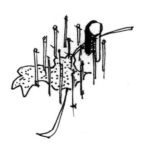

"Why" Concepts

The first *Event-Cities* was soon followed by the three other volumes. They addressed the theoretical issues of program and event, the materialization of concepts, and the relationships of concept to context and concept to form. Simply put, they were about the "What," "Where," "When," and "How" of architecture, in no particular order, and used my work as the basis for the experiment. While every issue discussed remains valid today, one was rarely addressed, and necessarily came last: "Why?" Why architecture? What differentiates architecture from building? In my early writings, I had proposed that architectural concepts made the difference, noting that "a cathedral without a concept is just a building, a bicycle shed with a concept is architecture," in an ironic reworking of the historian Nikolaus Pevsner's esthetic proposition that "a bicycle shed is a building; Lincoln Cathedral is a piece of architecture." Pevsner's provocation had already been questioned, including by proponents of the vernacular. But my point was that the most significant contributions of architecture to society included not only built works, but also concepts and ideas. I also argued that in architecture, one can design by starting with a concept (a theoretical assumption, a typological configuration, an ideological belief, and so on) and then develop the design to adjust the concept to a specific context (site, geography, sociocultural climate, etc.). I called this "contextualizing a concept." Alternatively, one can start by responding to a context (site, geography, sociocultural climate) and develop the scheme into a concept (typology, abstract configuration, etc.). I called this "conceptualizing a context."

I soon realized that sometimes decisions need to be made when there are several justified architectural concepts and programmatic, social, or environmental contextual approaches, in order to resolve the numerous constraints that architecture entails. The criteria for such decisions could be expanded to pragmatic issues: How much does it cost? How long does it take? But such pragmatic criteria seemed to belong to the realm of "context." There had to be something else. How do you combine a concept (an abstraction) and a context (an immediate and tangible reality) in one single move? Could there also be unexpected, possibly intuitive correlations between concepts and contexts?

Why "Poetics"?
At the end of a lecture called "Conceptualizing Content" at the Architectural Association in London, Colin Fournier, a close friend and partner in the early days of designing the Parc de La Villette, asked the following question from the audience:

"Bernard, you give the appearance of absolute logic as you articulate the reciprocal influence of concepts and contexts over one another. You have been very careful in every project to show how it emerged out of what you used to call *"la force de l'évidence."* But I have witnessed you when you work. Aren't there moments when decisions are made that do not quite proceed from such an objective, strategic approach? What about what you haven't mentioned—the unexplainable moves? There must be unexplainable moves…things that you cannot explicate in terms of constraints that are measurable and understandable."

Was there a "hidden discourse behind [my] discourse," as Colin suggested? I remember telling him that I would respond in my next lecture at the AA. Of course, I didn't—it took me several years to articulate a proper response, one that occurred to me only as I was preparing this last *Event-Cities* volume and trying to express the special connection that these projects have in common. Reiterating arguments I had developed in past volumes didn't seem accurate. After all, there are architectural intuitions—unexpected emergences—that exceed or even transcend the ruthless logic of a rational working method.

I thought back to 1978, when I was asked by the editors of the British magazine *AD (Architectural Design)* to write a text for a special issue on Surrealism. The magazine issue was particularly important because it included thoughtful contributors like Rem Koolhaas and the architectural historians Dalibor Vesely and Kenneth Frampton. In my essay I wrote about Marcel Duchamp, Georges Bataille, Frederick Kiesler, and Antonin Artaud, discussing their potential for an architecture that had hardly ever existed, an unbuilt and hidden history. While Constructivism and Expressionism in the arts had strongly influenced architecture, Surrealism never had much of an effect, perhaps because its protagonists' works were too close to a literal poetic discourse made of words and painterly images. Lautréamont's famous dictate— "as beautiful as the chance encounter of a sewing machine and an umbrella on a dissecting table"—had rarely found architectural equivalents.

Poetic Devices

It occurred to me that the common denominator among the projects presented in this and other *Event-Cities* volumes was a sort of strange poiesis or, more precisely, the use of poetic devices both consciously and unconsciously. The hovering roof at Le Fresnoy; the floating gallery beam of the Musée Cantonal des Beaux-Arts in Lausanne, Switzerland; the multiple cones of the Binhai Science Museum in Tianjin, China; the folding envelopes for a watchmaking headquarters in Geneva, Switzerland; the seemingly levitating, tilted glass gallery in Gröningen, The Netherlands; the perched glass enclosure of the Parthenon Gallery in the Acropolis Museum in Athens; all those circular projects, have been accompanied over many years by strict and fairly rational explanations. However, something invariably escaped the orderly process of thought.

So what about Colin's question? What about the "unexplainable moves"? What about the irrational encounters of "umbrellas" and "sewing machines"—elements that defy logic and reason?

My architectural projects mostly started with strategic moves. The first was often the "Knight's Move" from chess (one step sideways, two steps forward). For example, preserving existing buildings intended for demolition and inventing a roof hovering over them (Le Fresnoy); reconceptualizing the initial program into a concept of superimposed points, lines, and surfaces (the Parc de la Villette); or successfully advising a university client to change sites (the Athletics Center at the University of Cincinnati, Ohio). Another move was the *case vide* or "empty slot," a rational process I also used at La Villette. In this method, I would ask members of my office to study design alternatives, together with possible transformations or permutations ("options" or "variants"). The process was reminiscent of Oulipo and Raymond Roussel's writing strategies. (It also provided a competition tactic: What can we do that no other competitor will do?)

These rational games simultaneously extended my early theoretical explorations of the relationships among space, event, and movement; conceptualized contexts; and the "words" and "works" of architecture. An early theoretical project, *The Manhattan Transcripts* (1976-81), explored the interactions among programs, the city, and the movement of bodies in space. Altogether, such moves collectively made up a set of ideas and operations that generated a piece of architecture, yet none involved a specific method, technique, or style. Putting together this final *Event-Cities* made me realize that these exercises in the making of architecture had developed a strange coherence. I began to call it a "poetics" (*une poétique*).

Whose Poetics?
To step back a bit: Nothing in *Event-Cities 5* is intended as a poem. I do not believe that architecture is poetry or the "frozen music" that Goethe famously referred to. However, several projects use methods and devices that can be seen as part of an individual examination of making, a singular or specific study of how architecture comes to be. This notion requires the detour of explanation through analogy.

The poet writes poems. A critic may analyze the poems and write commentary that has its own literary quality and may even use poetic devices; it then becomes a work of literature on its own. For example, when the 20th-century critic Roland Barthes wrote *S/Z*, analyzing a short story by the 19th-century writer Honoré de Balzac, the resulting work was more than a theoretical investigation and critical exegesis. *S/Z* tells us about Balzac, but it also tells us about Barthes and his exploration of literary concepts from the perspective of a lover of language and the "writerly" text. Barthes' text is a discourse on literature and the poetics of writing, developed with the knowing intimacy of a great *amateur* of the craft. Similarly, the architect Claude-Nicolas Ledoux, born in 1736, built for two-thirds of his adult life, then wrote about it for the last third. (The French Revolution of 1789 prevented Ledoux from building.) The written part of Ledoux's work extends the argument of the built part and enriches it by generating new unbuilt architectural ideas which, when illustrated, produced drawings that are almost indistinguishable from the earlier built work. What these examples have in common is that they are simultaneously creation and commentary, invention and critique, practice and poiesis.

The term "poetics" has considerable history in architecture. Think of *The Poetics of Space* (1958), by the brilliant "philosopher of the imagination" Gaston Bachelard, with its emphasis on the primitive archetypes of "house," "cellar," "attic," and "nest." Or Maurice Merleau-Ponty's *Phenomenology of Perception* (1945), which had an enduring influence on a particular group of architects, architectural writers, and theorists drawn to its focus on spatial ambiance and the privileging of inner, sensory experience. Anthony Antoniades' *Poetics of Architecture: Theory of Design* (1992) argued in favor of the making of architecture through the lens of esthetics, emphasizing imagination, fantasy, and creativity. And Kenneth Frampton's *Studies in Tectonic Culture* (2001), subtitled "The Poetics of Construction," is a masterful reminder that structure and construction are as significant in architecture as space or abstract form. The list goes on, including Juhani Pallasmaa and Christian Norberg-Schulz, among others.

Genealogies

Still, my own genealogy lay elsewhere, in 20th-century French artistic, literary, and philosophical figures who used the term "poetics" to address the foundations and boundaries of their disciplines. Starting with the early Georges Bataille and Maurice Blanchot and moving from the Surrealists to the Situationists to the Poststructuralists, my cultural universe included Henri Lefebvre, Michel Foucault, Roland Barthes, Gilles Deleuze, and Jacques Derrida, to cite just a few. Their particular readings, which crossed the frontiers of literary, urban, historical, and social thought, were rarely shared by my phenomenologically inclined architectural colleagues.

I turned to Derrida when asking some of the questions that inform this final volume. At once a rigorous analyst of language and a closet architect, fascinated with the inherence of architectural metaphors in the discipline of philosophy, Derrida, who died in 2004, was a valued interlocutor and one of the "allies" in different fields who enriched my architectural thought. If the core concepts of the Parc de la Villette (1982-1998) were developed independently, their elaboration drew on his influence and our discussions. For example, Derrida's notion of the "event" as "invention," from the Latin *invenire* (to discover or find), informs the concept of the *folies* as points of intensity, much as the theory of deconstruction underlies the decentered plan and project of the park. Hence it was hardly unexpected that, when thinking through the unexplainable aspects of my work, I turned to a little-known, elliptical essay by Derrida, "Che cos'è la poesia?" (1988).

In answering the question "What thing is poetry," Derrida describes the poem, poetic or, as he prefers it, "poematic" as a singular thing, a kind of constructed situation, "the advent of an event," which requires us to "disable memory, disarm culture, know how to forget knowledge, set fire to the library of poetics." The poem requires us to "renounce knowledge...without ever forgetting it" and to proceed with "learned ignorance" of the rules, norms, and constraints that make up the "library" of a discipline. Are these Colin Fournier's "unexplainable moves," the decisions taken when logic and objective strategy fail, decisions that cannot be explicated in terms of "measurable and understandable constraints"? Derrida is clear that amid this uncertainty or lack of certitude, decisions must be made, and that such poetic decision-making is itself an ethical act. In a famous interview from 2004 with the newspaper *L'Humanité*, Derrida argued that the very moment of "not knowing" defines ethical responsibility.[1]

---

[1] Derrida's text "Che cos'è la poesia?" first appeared in the Italian journal *Poesia* in its November 1988 issue. The version cited here is from the translation by Peggy Kamuf in *A Derrida Reader: Between the Blinds*, edited with notes by Peggy Kamuf. New York: Columbia University Press, 1991, 221-37. For Derrida's approach to poetics and ethical responsibility, see Jacques Derrida, *Poétique et politique du témoignage*. Paris: Editions de l'Herne, 2005. The interview with *L'Humanité* appeared on Jan. 18, 2004 as "Derrida, penseur de l'événement."

On Cities
Developing a project discourse over more than four decades inevitably raises questions and entails course corrections. It is also an exercise in humility. In 40 years, the attitudes of architects, urban designers, and landscape architects, as well as local citizens and politicians, toward cities have evolved considerably. Urban conditions have changed, and with them social and ethical responsibilities. The world is a different and more uncertain place than it was when I first addressed cities as generators of "events" leading to new and stimulating social conditions.

Hence the question: Has the very idea of "event-cities" been transformed by nearly half a century of intense human activity? What is the difference between a city that celebrates a culture of congestion—where buildings act as generators of intense excitement and heterogeneous activities—and a tranquil city, with its avenues and squares turned into an "urban forest" designed to soak up the carbon generated by decades of overcrowding? Are the pulsating "Global Cities" celebrated in the second half of the 20th century to be replaced by a pedestrian 15-minute lifestyle connecting home and office, as opposed to transcontinental links and lifestyles bridging London and Tokyo, or New York and São Paulo? Is the alternative to stay local? Should "bioregionalism" replace "globalism"? Did the COVID-19 pandemic of 2020 generate a paradoxical trend: increased teleconferencing that facilitates global exchanges while allowing us to stay at home, permanently in place?

History may tell us that a major turning point took place on September 11, 2001, when two remarkable inventions of the 20th century collided: an exceptional mass transport medium (the airplane) and an exceptional symbol of urban development (the skyscraper). Considering the violence of their encounter, and aside from political issues and human loss at the time, the reciprocal glamour of airplanes and towers never quite recovered. Even as air tourism and skyscrapers continued to expand, the latter higher and higher, their cultural validity was increasingly questioned, along with their intense carbon content. The discourse has changed, along with the nature of the debates. Climate awareness, new technologies, and of course social networks in culture and politics have opened entirely new areas of action and interaction for the responsible and innovative architect.

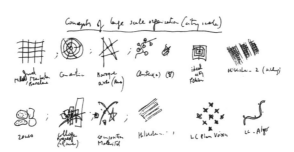

Inventing the Impossible

Let me therefore return to poetics, ethics, decision-making, and invention. In the first quarter of the 21st century, arguments about design and climate science have often focused on technological issues: decarbonization, thermal insulation, energy conservation, natural or passive ventilation, thermal bridges, heat wells, and so on. Ninety percent involve important technologies but minimally affect our modes of living, working, relating to one another, or the visual and spatial interrelationship of architecture with its close environment.

Leaving aside some politicians' denial of Planet Earth's circumstances, most solutions embraced by regulators and major construction companies are solely technological. Yet our ethical responsibilities may also require spatial and programmatic creativity. It may well be a matter of inventing new typologies and proposing new modes of living, as translated architecturally.

Think of the typological differences between houses in a hot, dry North African climate with horizontal living patterns around a central patio versus English brownstones with their vertical living around a narrow central stair: climate differences explain the distinctions (as well as the logic of property values). What strikes me is how few major architectural concepts have emerged in the decades since climate issues have moved to the forefront. Whether one agrees or not with the inventions, 1920s concepts such as the house lifted on *pilotis* or the *Ville Radieuse* were novel concepts that in large part resulted from the effect of the Great Influenza epidemic in 1918. More recently, when industrial spaces became widely available in the 1970s during the New York City recession, new living habits were invented combining living, working, sleeping, cooking, and bathing, often in a single open loft space. At different times and scales, these were new concepts—in social, programmatic, architectural, and urban terms.

What will be the new poetics and ethics of architecture in the cities of tomorrow?

Bernard Tschumi
January 2024

EVENT-CITIES 5

The projects in *Event-Cities 5* explore some of the imaginative dimensions of architecture. While the first four volumes in the series addressed the rationality of architectural concepts, including the development and use of abstract devices as generators of architectural schemes, *Event-Cities 5* explores whether rationality occasionally reaches the inexplicable and the poetic.

Part A pursues circular configurations as autonomous entities that simultaneously establish dialogues with their context, whether geographic, historical, or programmatic.

Part B1 explores how the superposition of disparate components, like in the Surrealist game of Exquisite Corpse, occasionally produces bizarre wholes that retain the differences of their parts.

Part B2: Architecture can be indifferent to or conflictual with its context. It can also exaggerate its specificity by engaging in a conversation with a site and its past.

Part C looks at analogies as a means of interaction with context through similarity or likeness. This approach develops an intelligible image for a building through visual or conceptual resemblance to, or representation of, a specific program, culture, or history.

Part D: An urbanist poetics? No matter their size, and for better or worse, most buildings perform critical roles in the overall fabric of cities. When it comes to large projects, splitting a singular scheme into a series of discrete but related parts generates an urban environment that may be more attuned to the specifics of the context.

Part E: Occasionally an architect is asked to design an extension, programmatic modification, or simple technical updates to a project they constructed several years earlier. How does an author respond to their existing building (sometimes already protected by landmark status) without negating its architectural singularity?

Part F: Books and exhibitions conceived by architects on their own work are important. In the selected examples, each of these exhibitions, developed in tandem with books, aims to foreground architectural thinking.

As with other *Event-Cities* volumes, the drawings and images reflect various stages of the design process—all are intended to emphasize concepts, notations, and strategies. Several of the accompanying texts are partly excerpted or adapted from sources including competition documents, press materials, and presentations.

Prologue

Advertisements for Architecture, 1976–78
There is no way to perform architecture in a book. Words and drawings can only produce paper space, not the experience of real space. By definition, paper space is imaginary: it is an image.

Several early theoretical texts were illustrated with *Advertisements for Architecture*, a series of postcard-sized juxtapositions of words and images. Each was a manifesto of sorts, confronting the dissociation between the immediacy of spatial experience and the analytical definition of theoretical concepts. The function of the *Advertisements*—reproduced again and again, as opposed to the single architectural work—was to trigger desire for something beyond the page itself. When removed from their customary endorsement of commodity values, advertisements are the ultimate magazine form, even if used ironically. The logic of the *Advertisements for Architecture* asks, because there are advertisements for architectural "products," why not advertisements for the production (and reproduction) of architecture?

Sensuality has been known to overcome even the most rational of buildings.

Architecture is the ultimate erotic act. Carry it to excess and it will reveal both the traces of reason and the sensual experience of space. Simultaneously.

Look at it this way:

The game of architecture is an intricate play with rules that you may break or accept. These rules, like so many knots that cannot be untied, have the erotic significance of bondage: the more numerous and sophisticated the restraints, the greater the pleasure.

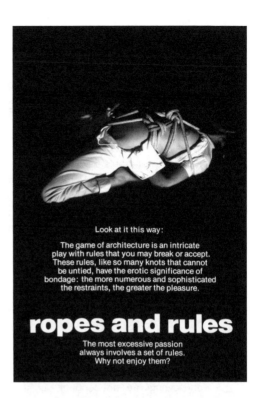

ropes and rules

The most excessive passion always involves a set of rules. Why not enjoy them?

To really appreciate architecture, you may even need to commit a murder.

Architecture is defined by the actions it witnesses as much as by the enclosure of its walls. Murder in the Street differs from Murder in the Cathedral in the same way as love in the street differs from the Street of Love. Radically.

If you want to follow architecture's first rule, break it.

Transgression.
An exquisitely perverse act that never lasts.
And like a caress is almost impossible to resist.
TRANSGRESSION

The Manhattan Transcripts, 1976–81

Architecture is not simply about space and form, but also about event, action, and what happens in space. *The Manhattan Transcripts* differ from most architectural drawings insofar as they are neither real projects nor mere fantasies. Developed in the late '70s, they proposed to transcribe an architectural interpretation of reality.

Plans, sections, and diagrams outline spaces and indicate the movements of the different protagonists intruding into the architectural "stage set." A special mode of tripartite notation underscores the relationship between space, movement, and event. Photographs show the actions; plans reveal the changing architectural manifestations; and diagrams indicate the movements of the different protagonists. The *Transcripts'* explicit purpose is to transcribe things normally removed from conventional architectural representation, namely the complex relationship between spaces and their use, between the set and the script, between "type" and "program," between objects and events.

The dominant theme of the *Transcripts* is a set of disjunctions among use, form, and social values; the non-coincidence between meaning and being, movement and space, man and object was the starting condition of the work. Yet the inevitable confrontation of these terms produces effects of far-ranging consequence. The *Transcripts* aim to offer a different reading of architecture in which space, movement, and events are independent, yet stand in a new relation to one another, so that the conventional components of architecture are broken down and rebuilt along different axes.

The Manhattan Transcripts were first exhibited in solo exhibitions in New York at Artists Space (1978), P.S.1 (1980, group), and Max Protetch Gallery (1981), as well as in London at the Architectural Association (1979), and published in 1981/1994.

Installation view of *Architectural Manifestos*, Artists Space, New York, 1978

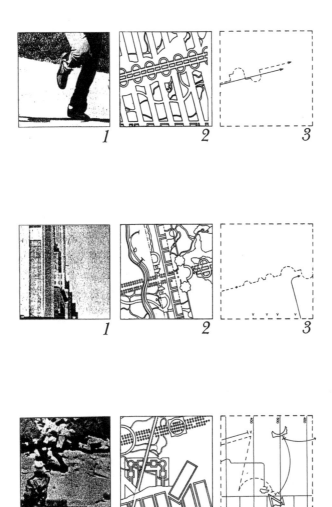

The Manhattan Transcripts (The Park), 1976–77

20th-Century Follies, 1979–82

Abstract Constructions

Between 1979 and 1982, in parallel with theoretical drawings and essays, several low-budget "site-specific installations" were conceived in the context of ephemeral art installations in mostly urban settings. They explored spatially and tested materially some of the concepts developed concurrently on paper.

The abstract "follies" were built over a three-year period in New York, Middelburg, and London as site-specific installations. A city-plan version of follies was developed for Documenta Urbana in Kassel. In New York, the "Broadway Follies" located a series of abstract constructions at irregular intervals to constitute an architectural sequence along the over 30-mile length of Broadway, extending more than the length of Manhattan.

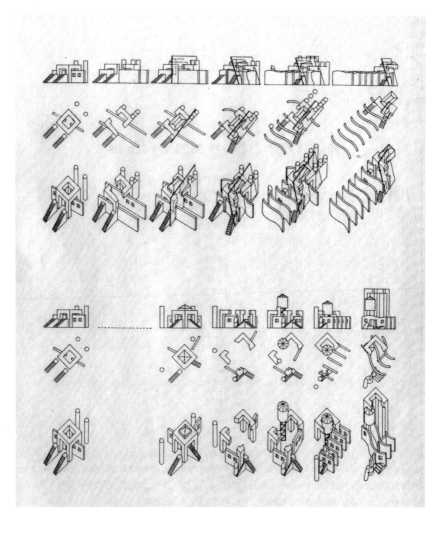

NEW YORK

31

20th-Century Follies: Staircase for Scarface, Castle Clinton, New York, 1979
Black painted plywood, fiberglass mannequins

NEW YORK
33

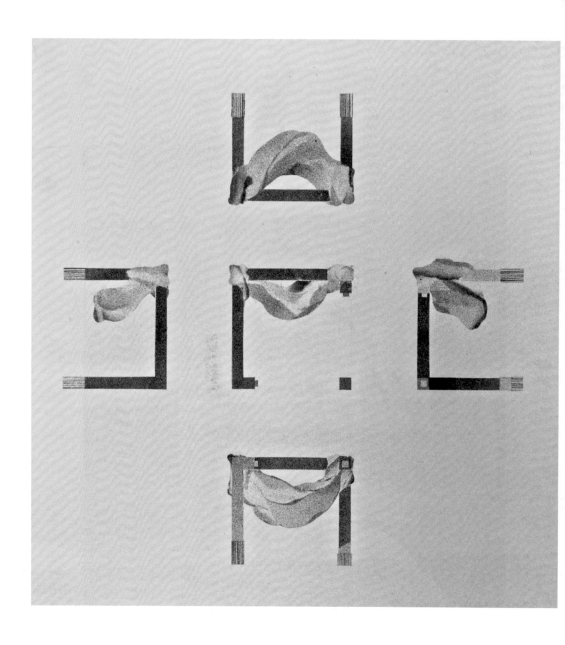

20th-Century Follies: Dag Hammarskjold Plaza, New York, 1980
Black painted plywood, white fabric

NEW YORK

35

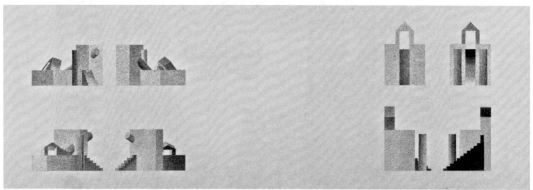

20th-Century Follies: Middelburg, The Netherlands, 1980
Plywood, black felt

MIDDELBURG

37

20th-Century Follies: Wave Hill, New York, 1982
Painted perforated steel uprights, galvanized sheet metal ductwork, fabric

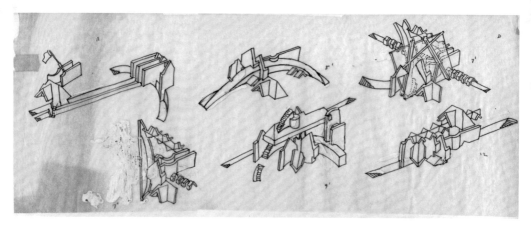
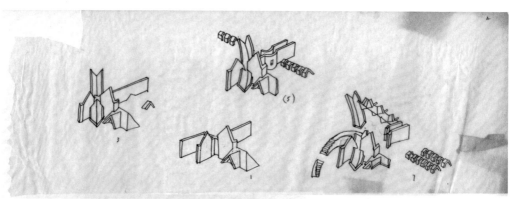
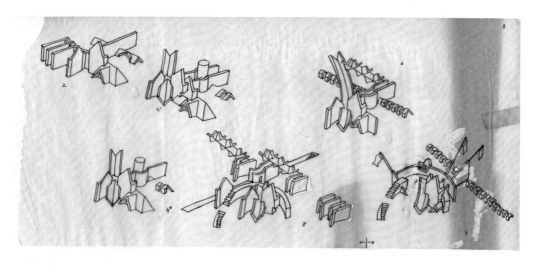

20th-Century Follies: Kassel Deconstructions, Documenta Urbana, 1982

KASSEL

41

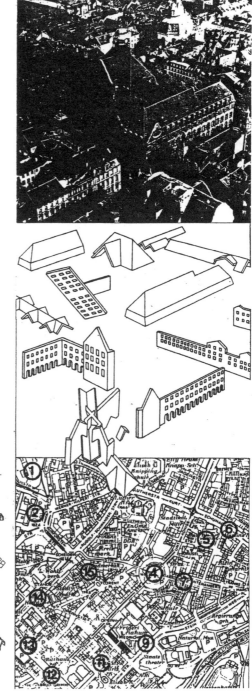

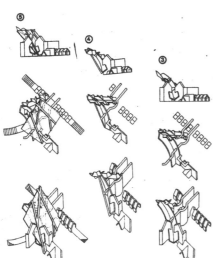

The names "folly," "Follies," or "20th-Century Follies" were given to suggest a touch of derision, a poetics of the absurd, since most of these experimental constructions were meant to be urban, and far from a "mock-Gothic ruin built in a large garden or park" (*The Oxford Dictionary of Phrase and Fable*). The *folie*, with its French spelling, used for the Parc de la Villette (1982-98) (see *Event-Cities 2*), referred specifically to the word's double meaning of "madness" and "unreason."

List of folly and *folie* projects (see opposite):

Architectural Association, London, England, 1979

Castle Clinton, New York City, USA, 1979

Dag Hammarskjold Plaza, New York City, USA, 1980

Wave Hill, New York City, USA, 1982 (A)

Middelburg, The Netherlands, 1980 (B)

Broadway Follies, New York City, USA, 1981 (C) (unrealized)

Documenta Urbana, Kassel, Germany, 1982 (D) (unrealized)

Parc de la Villette, Paris, France, 1982-83 (E)

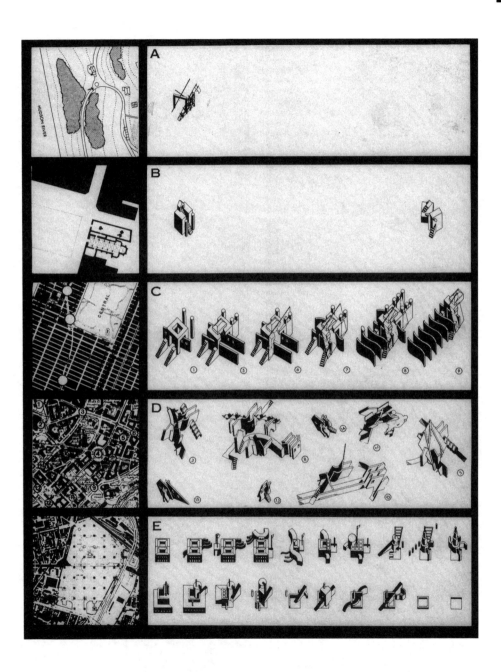

From folly to *folies*: Spatial concepts tested over the years become clearer and more coherent in the 1982-83 competition for the Parc de la Villette.

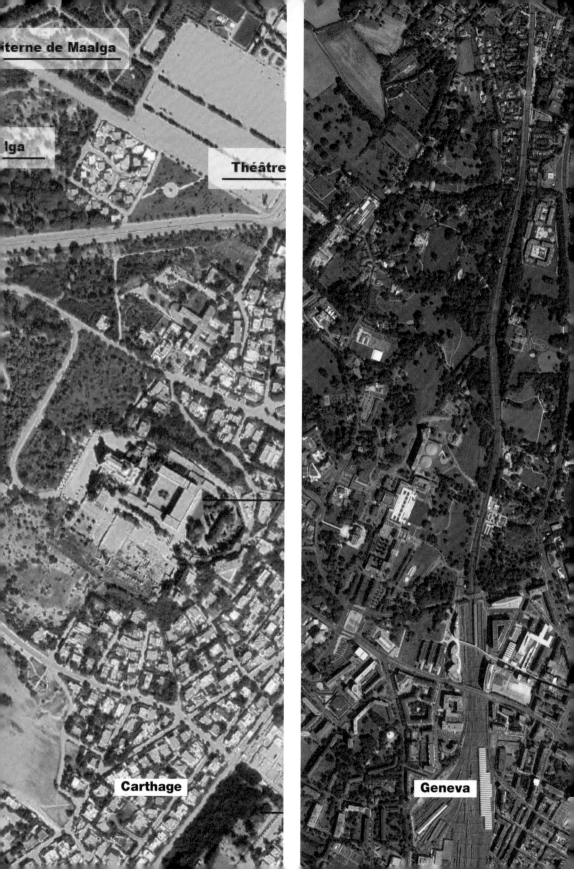

CARTHAGE NATIONAL MUSEUM, CARTHAGE (2022)

MUSEOPARC, ALESIA (2015)

WORLD HEALTH MUSEUM, GENEVA (2018)

FINANCE CULTURE CENTER, SHENZHEN (2020)

LE ROSEY CENTER FOR SCIENCE & ENTREPRENEURSHIP, ROLLE (2017-25)

A. *Circular Autonomy and Dialogue*

In architecture, circles are simultaneously conceptual abstractions and material volumes. They are utterly rational and yet irrational at the same time. The circle's ratio between enclosed surface and outer envelope is among the most economical and energy efficient in architecture, yet the circle is sometimes deemed wasteful in a crowded urban context.

Part A explores circular configurations as autonomous entities that simultaneously establish dialogues with their context, whether social or environmental. They are a way to maximize the flexibility of internal layouts and the orientation of buildings to their external sites. Circles and cylindrical volumes also allow the treatment of tectonic materials as continuous surfaces, avoiding compositional approaches to the design of facades.

Carthage, Carthage National Museum, 2022

With Hugh Dutton Associés and Michel Desvigne Paysagiste

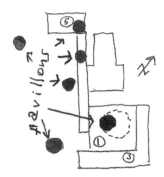

Gardens and Crowns

Four concepts (architectural, ecological, environmental, and structural) inform a museum celebrating an ancient civilization.

CARTHAGE
51

Aerial view

Rings hovering over the archeological landscape (with trees on top)

Carthage, the capital of the Carthaginian Empire in the last millennium BC, is located near Tunisia's capital city, Tunis. Carthage fell to the Roman Empire in the second century BC. Exceptional archaeological ruins are still visible in the remains of the historical city.

The Architectural Concept

Required is the revitalization of an existing museum surrounded by archaeological ruins. The site contains several millennia of different cultures. This multiplicity requires avoiding the cliché of a single building that would exacerbate the Christian 19th-century part of the site through a "classical" composition directly extending the old "Cathedral." Such centrality would contradict the Punic and Roman history of Carthage, especially by adding an additional level onto existing buildings whose scale would challenge the archaeology of the site and its history. The symbol of Carthage cannot be a single overpowering, ostentatious volume.

Instead, the scheme proposes the addition of circular structures that hover carefully over the existing ruins, accommodating a variety of activities including reception, restaurants, a library, an auditorium, and exhibition spaces.

The Ecological Concept

The existing site is vast and sometimes unwelcoming. Consequently, our intention is to animate it and give it an identity representing the multiplicity of civilizations in Carthage. The project proposes to turn the site into a "garden of gardens," with three museum pavilions that seem to levitate above the ruins. The existing historical buildings will be revitalized. Near the ruins, shading pods are designed to punctuate the successive stages of a promenade in discovery of the site. These shading pods will house benches and visual information explaining the features and history of the nearby ruins.

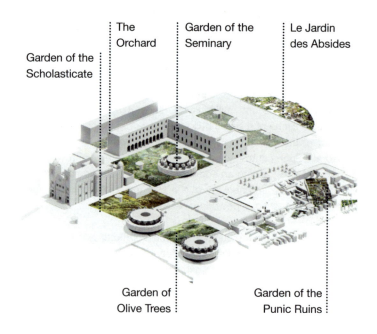

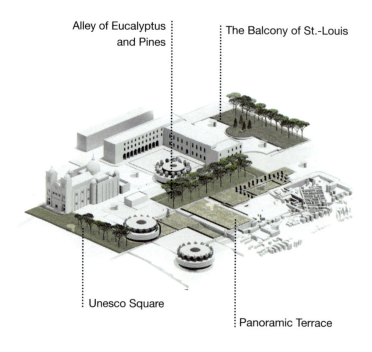

A series of gardens and terraces

CARTHAGE 55

Alley of Eucalyptus and Pines

Panoramic Terrace

Garden of the Seminary

Garden of the Scholasticate

Garden of Olive Trees

Garden of the Punic Ruins

The Environmental Concept
The construction system optimizes energy consumption through ecological design. The ground floor is made of simple, rough materials that are thick enough for good thermal inertia. All large openings are located in shady areas to avoid excessive solar gain.

The roof is a light, ventilated double fabric to maximize interior comfort. It is stretched over an outer structure that serves as a sunscreen. The fabric is a material with a low rate of transmission and absorbency. It has an ETFE lens oculus, offering zenithal light filtered by fabric at the level of the roof stiffeners.

The pavilions read more like transitional landscape elements than permanent constructions. The landscaping suggests a levitating support level that is lightened by the canvas covering and facade. The glass facade is shaded and made less visible through reflection. The building periphery is planted with trees and grass, camouflaging the presence of the building. Visitors can contemplate the entire site from the landscaped terraces.

The trees along the circular terraces protect the facades from solar radiation and minimize the impact of the building from the outside. The floor is set back and seems to disappear. A set of stretched fabric claustra keeps the walls and the edges of the slab cool, preventing them from overheating.

The Structural Concept
Pavilion structure: The circular pavilions containing all programmatic elements in the landscaped section of the project belong to the same family of structural typologies. They are circular, with a radial structural frame system comprising a light cover in luminous architectural fabric stretched over floating rings.

The three large programmatic pavilions (Reception, Temporary Exhibitions, and Cultural Center) consist of a radial structure:
- The ground floor is made from low-carbon concrete and supported on eight posts, inscribing a circle on the periphery and forming a self-stabilizing table. This location is optimal for supporting the circumferential planters of the upper floor on a grid of radial beams. The slab is ribbed on the central part in the continuity of the radial beams. They decrease toward the center in order to optimize weight.
- The second level has a light radial metal structure covered with fabric.

CARTHAGE

57

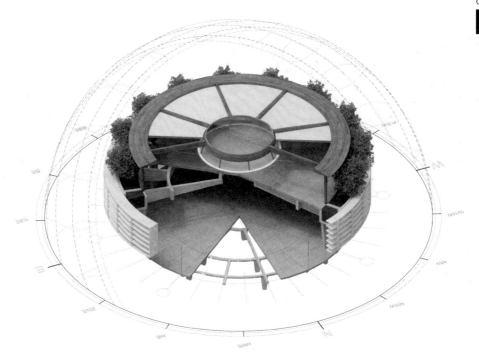

Structural diagram and sectional perspective of entrance pavilion

Alésia, MuséoParc, 2002–12; 2015

2002: Original scheme: an Interpretive Center and a Museum
2012: Completion of the Center; the Museum remains unrealized.
2015: Updated program for the Museum

ALÉSIA

61

Dual Panoramic Fortification

The project marks an archaeological site in central France and commemorates the history of the battle between Julius Caesar and the Gauls in 52 B.C. The new museum recreates battlements and earthworks and provides interpretation for the area.

INTERPRETIVE CENTER

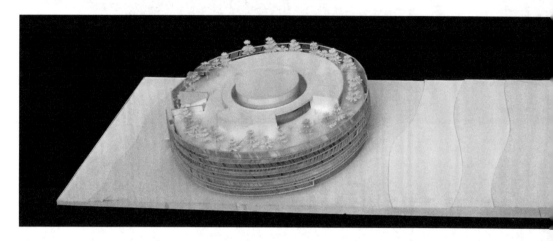

The overall scheme consists of two separate but related structures (see *Event-Cities 4*). One building is a museum located at the position of the Gallic installations during the siege, at the top of the hill above the town. The second building is an interpretive center located at the Roman position in the fields below. The museum is built of stones, similar in look to the town buildings but using contemporary technology. It is buried partially into the hill so that, from above, it appears as an extension of the landscape. The interpretive center is sheathed in wood, much as the Roman fortifications would have been at the time of the siege. The roof of the building is a garden planted with trees and grass, camouflaging the presence of the building when seen from the town above. A keen awareness of the surrounding landscape as it pertains to the historic battle is integral to the visitors' experience.

MUSEUM

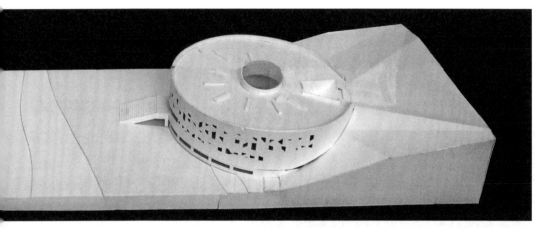

Diagrammatic model: The Intrepetive Center (left) and Museum (right) are one kilometer apart.

The original project is made of non-identical twins—two buildings with a simple cylindrical shape. Of the two, the interpretive center has been built, while the museum awaits realization. The envelopes adapt to their surroundings through materials, de-emphasizing the form of the buildings. By pairing the structures, integrating the buildings with the landscape, and using a simple round typology, the buildings defer to the battle site while fostering respect through their muted visual presence. The strategies of giving maximum presence to historical events and sensitively inserting the buildings into their natural environment respond to the ambition of the project and reflect the modesty demanded by archaeologists. To be both visible and invisible is the paradox and challenge of the project.

Approaching the Museum (from above)

ALÉSIA
75

Approaching the Museum (from below)

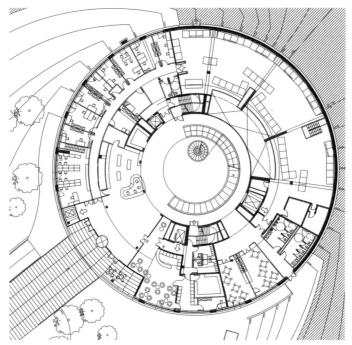

Level 1: entrance, offices, education area, and collection storage

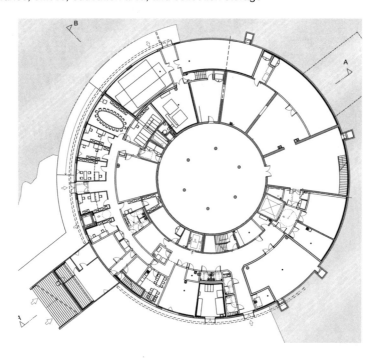

Level 0: offices, storage, and mechanical systems

ALÉSIA

77

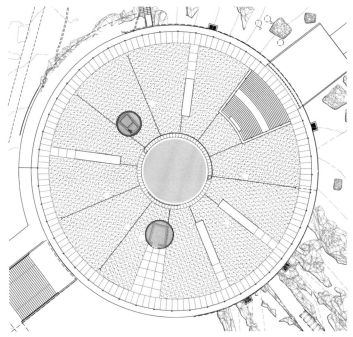

Roof level: terrace overlooking the ruins

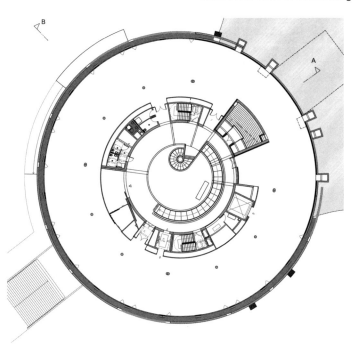

Level 2: main gallery

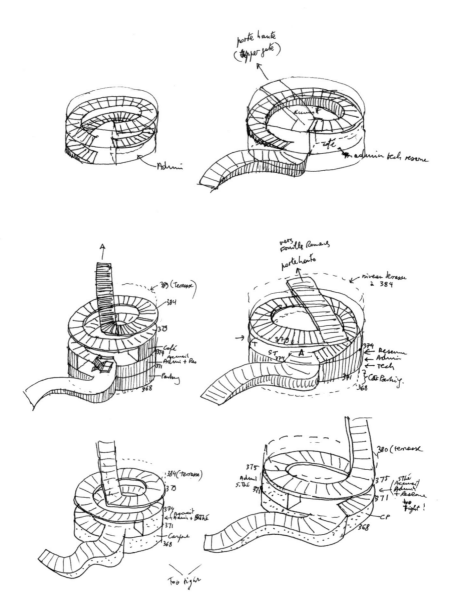

Movement vector spiral: preliminary sketches

Interior views (atrium)

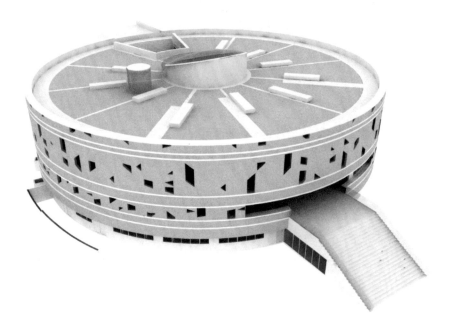

Overall volume

ALÉSIA

81

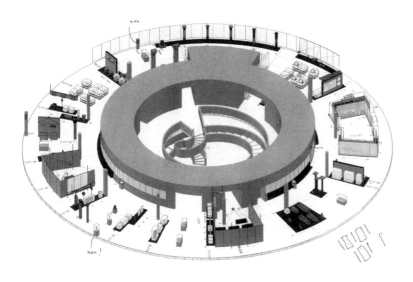

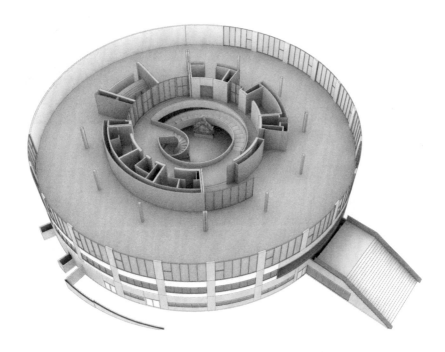

Exhibition galleries level

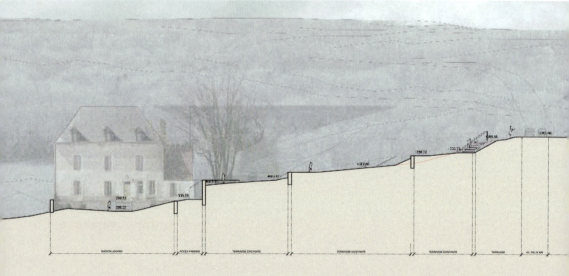

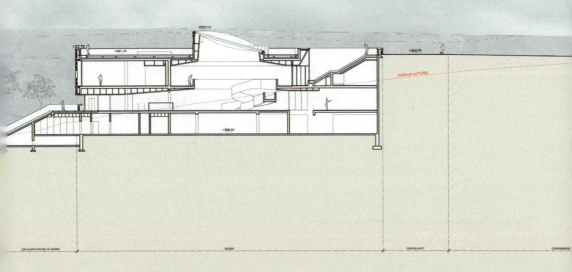

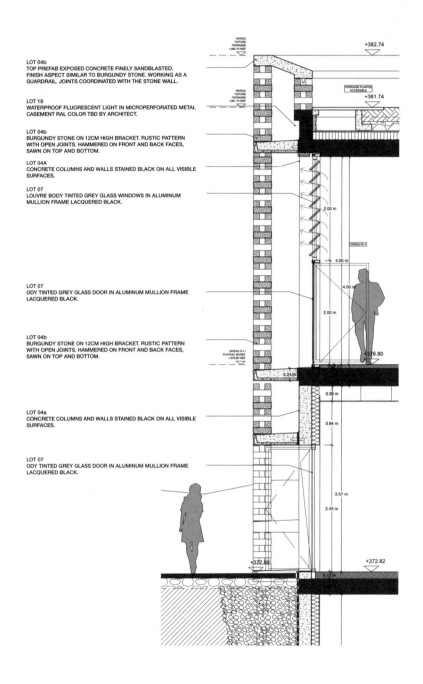

Section showing independent stone envelope

ALÉSIA
85

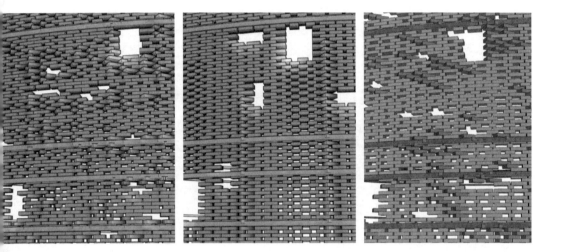

Studies of stone configurations in preparation for a full-scale prototype (following page)

Geneva, World Health Museum, 2018

GENEVA

Compositions

"The World Health Museum will tell the stories about individuals and global health of the past, present, and future so that people can experience, appreciate, understand, and become empowered to improve their health and health determinants."

(Excerpt from the 2018 draft working paper, "Health for All: A Museum for All")

World Health Organization Headquarters: The 1959 competition-winning scheme by Jean Tschumi (1904-62) was built posthumously and inaugurated in 1966.

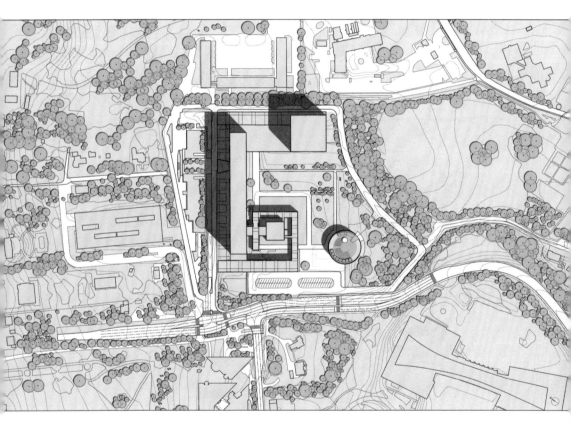

Five major elements and a garden define the WHO's 21st-century master plan:
- the 150-meter-long, nine-story Main Building;
- the 16 by 22 by 22-meter white cube of the Executive Board Room, surrounded by
- a six-meter-high, two-story rectangular spiral;
- the existing garden with a hill, which acts as an ordering device for the site;
- the eight-story cubic Extension, located on the eastern edge of the site; and
- the proposed two-story circular Museum, which will be a new addition to the site.

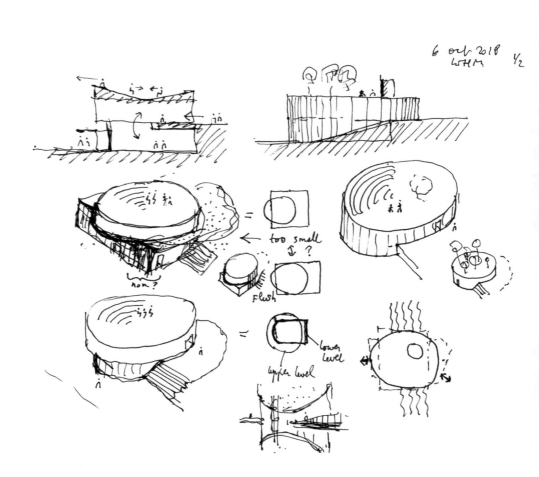

GENEVA
93

View of the Museum with the Main Building in the background

VERSION 1A: Garden above square box

VERSION 4: Museum as landscape

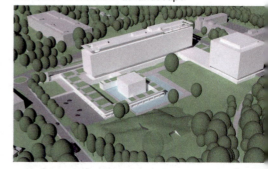

VERSION 4C: Garden above drum

VERSION 4D: Amphitheater above drum

"Compositional" Strategy

The 4,000-square-meter size of the proposed Museum and its service of a projected 300,000 visitors per year suggest a three-level construction, with primary access on the intermediate or ground level. The architectural intent is to design a building no taller than 10 to 12 meters so as not to dominate the nearby 16-meter-tall white cube of the Executive Board Room. For the future Museum, a variety of volumes with different geometries were tested before settling on a round building, partly embedded in the nearby hill located at the south edge of the site. The exact placement of the cylindrical element is situated on axis at the end of the original garden spiral to provide both direct and symbolic access to the Main Building.

The Museum's diameter is approximately 42 meters; it is placed at a 42-meter distance from the two-story original wing with the aim of achieving a cohesive ordering of the various architectural volumes on the site.

This distancing move allows an engagement with the nearby hill, originally made from earth removed to accommodate the foundations of the Main Building during its construction. Covered by vegetation, the hill provides a remarkable symbol of nature on the site and an opportunity for the new building to establish a direct dialogue with its topography. A landscaped terrace on the Museum roof turns it into an outdoor meeting place as well as part of the hill.

PLAN: LEVEL 0
FLOOR PLATE: APPROX. 1,333 M²

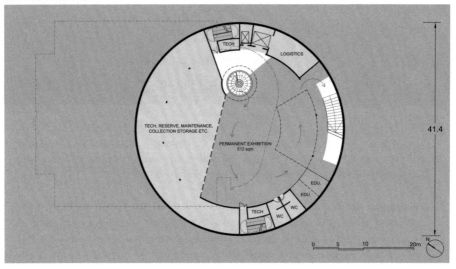

PLAN: LEVEL -1
FLOOR PLATE: APPROX. 1,333 M²

PLAN: ROOF

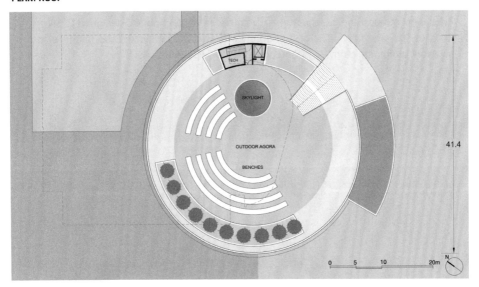

PLAN: LEVEL +1
FLOOR PLATE: APPROX. 1,333 M²

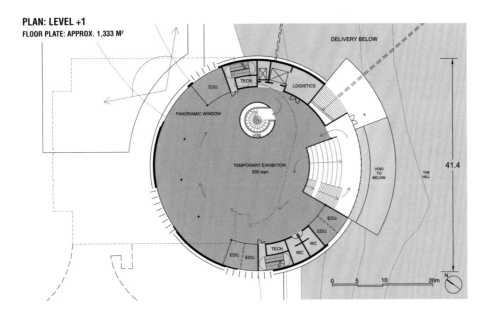

Envelope

A glass surface that is smooth but has depth acts as the outer envelope—a translucent white glass screen with no visible support, placed in front of a partially opaque, textured concrete wall sheltering the interior spaces and galleries. The Museum entrance and its fenestration are made from glass panels designed to pivot to allow full apertures. The textured concrete wall subtly evokes the image of a network or epidemiology, signaling aspects of WHO operations.

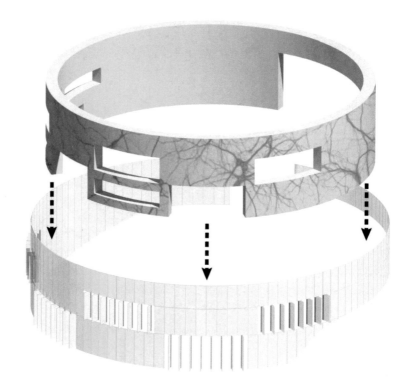

INNER ENVELOPE
(CONCRETE)

OUTER ENVELOPE
(GLASS)

GENEVA
99

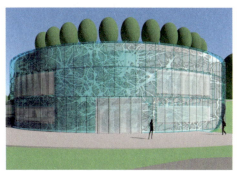

Envelope concept studies

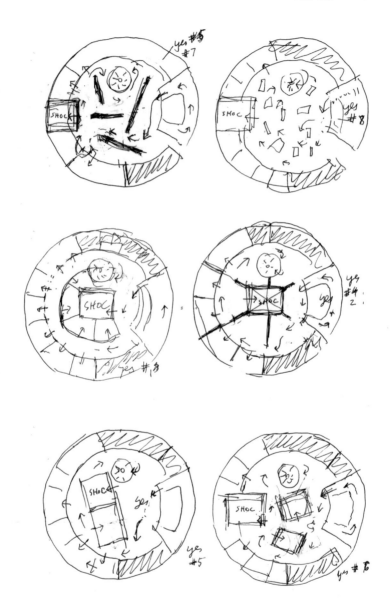

"Architectural" parts are carefully distinguished from those that are "informational" or "curatorial." For example, movement vectors or movement areas (entrance, staircases, walkways, stepped agora) and all main walls are considered architectural.

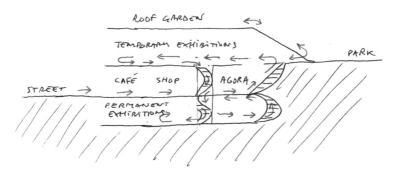

Perspective view from the upper level of the Museum

A quiet dialogue—respectful but not imitative—is established with the other buildings.

Left: Main Building (1960). Center: Extension (2015). Right: Museum (2018)

Shenzhen, Finance Culture Center, 2020

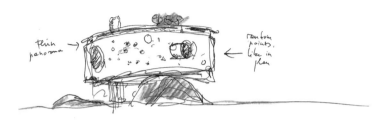

Chance Encounters over Nature

A new type of facility is planned for Shenzhen: A Finance Cultural Center (FCC), combining a museum, a trading platform, and a large multifunctional auditorium. The FCC aims to provide a place of history, creativity, and exchange.

Early diagrams:
The internal organization of the building is simultaneously about concept and experience. Three interior spaces combine to produce varied environments—a diagonal for finance, a horizontal for culture, and a vertical for the future.

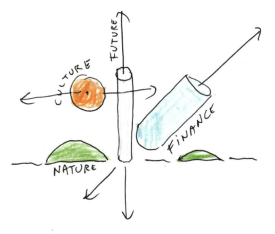

A hill park is formed on top of the large, buried auditorium. Lifting the main volume off the ground provides a strong urban presence while opening to the adjacent park. The circular geometry relates to all parts of the surroundings. The cylinder is supported and punctured by the three programmatic tubes.

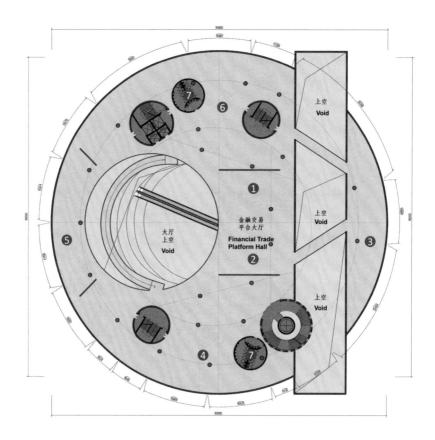

Level 5: Financial Trade Platform

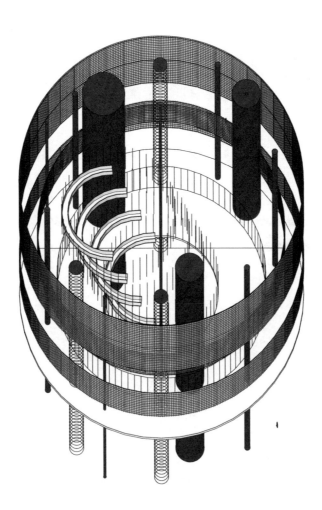

Axonometric diagram

The FCC's envelope is patterned with abstractions of the digits 0 and 1, alluding to the digitalization of culture and finance. The multiple configurations of modules with integrated LED lighting animate the exterior and create a dynamic expression.

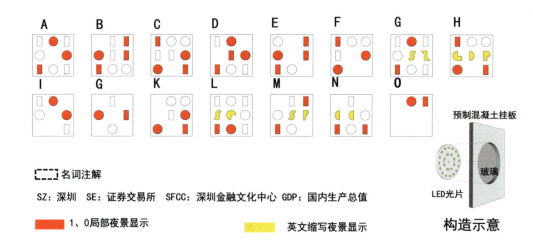

Module pattern

South elevation

Module configuration on envelope

East elevation

Sectional model

Rolle, Center for Science and Entrepreneurship, 2017–25

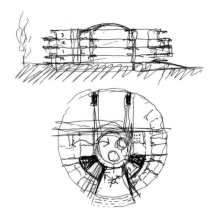

Twin Circles

A few years after Bernard Tschumi Architects completed a concert hall for the Institut Le Rosey, the client needed an adjacent second building. While the previous building was "introverted," oriented inwards, the new one aims to be "extroverted."

Context

The historical architecture of Le Rosey, with its small buildings topped with imposing sloping roofs, had already entered the 21st century with the landing of Bernard Tschumi Architects' "flying saucer," as the locals called Carnal Hall. (See *Event-Cities 4*.) This philharmonic concert hall for the Lake Geneva region, with an artistic and music studies center for the students of Le Rosey, brought new modernity to the august institution.

The dome-shaped, all-steel building was designed to meet the artistic needs of the Rosey community. In contrast, the ambition of the new building is about science. The architectural question became the following: How to establish a dialogue without one or the other building suffering, so that the whole became greater than the sum of its parts? The new building is called the Center for Science and Entrepreneurship (CSE).

Location

With Carnal Hall completing the historic axis of the campus, the new CSE building was necessarily off-center in relation to it. This allowed the creation of a dramatic diagonal opening connecting the historic axis to the new Center.

Taking advantage of site topography, the entrance to the CSE is marked by a monumental but gentle staircase leading to a large rectangular opening forming a portico, all topped by a hanging garden.

Volumes

The CSE is circular, of the same diameter (about 75 meters) and height (about 18 meters) as Carnal Hall, but with five levels to the other's two major levels. (At the top of the dome, the CSE is 22 meters high.)

Its flat dome shape, with a restrained metal envelope reflected in the light, gives the original Carnal Hall a deliberately "soft" appearance. On the other hand, the CSE risked appearing much more massive, not only compared to Carnal Hall, but also to the low-rise historical buildings of the school.

The last level of the new building is set back, while the upper- and lower-ground floors are integrated with the sloped topography. The added presence of planters on the circular exterior walkways affords changing seasonal colors.

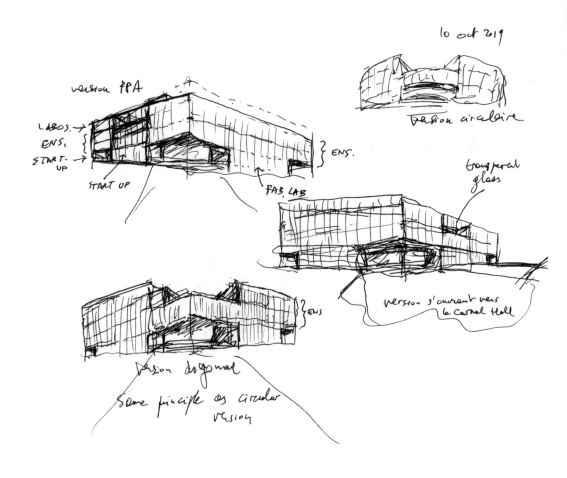

Initial diagrams: A rectangular volume with a central atrium and a main entry at 45°

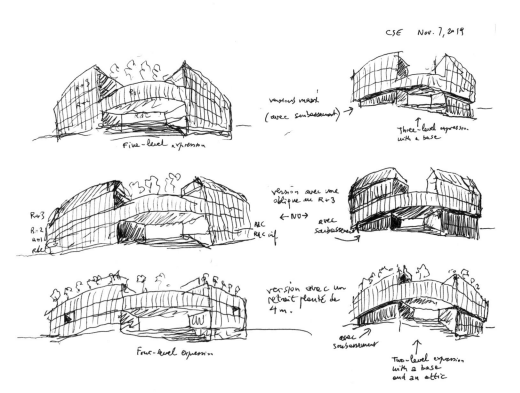

Final concept diagrams: A circular volume with a central atrium and a main entry on axis

R+3
Labs

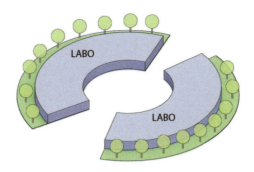

R+1
R+2
Classrooms

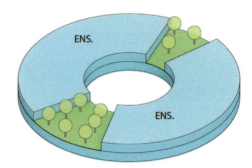

RDC SUP.
Start-Ups

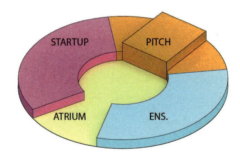

RDC INF.
FabLab

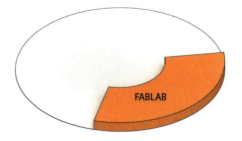

SPRING

SUMMER

AUTUMN

WINTER

An evolving seasonal filter on the exterior

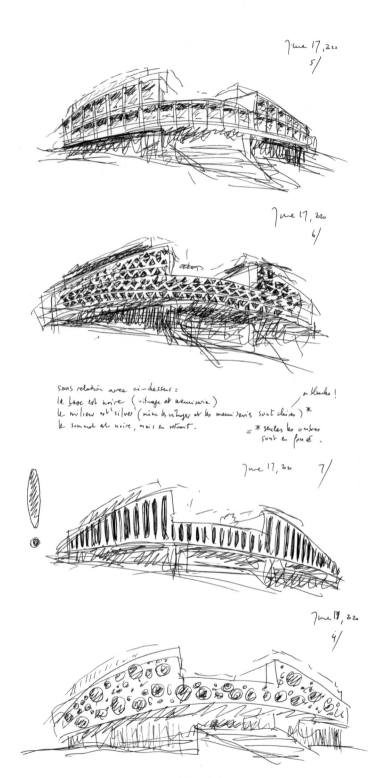

Early diagrams exploring options for the materiality of the envelope

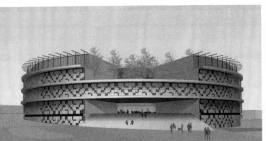
OPTION 28 | STAINLESS STEEL (SOUTH/NORTH) + FINS (EAST/WEST)

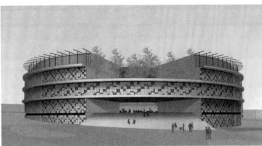
OPTION 29 | STAINLESS STEEL (SOUTH/NORTH) + FINS (EAST/WEST)

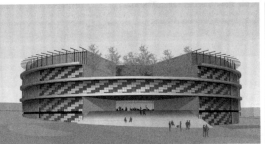
OPTION 30 | STAINLESS STEEL (SOUTH/NORTH) + FINS (EAST/WEST)

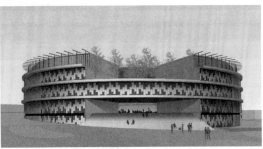
OPTION 31 | STAINLESS STEEL (SOUTH/NORTH) + FINS (EAST/WEST)

OPTION 32 | STAINLESS STEEL (60/120) RANDOM

OPTION 33 | STAINLESS STEEL 120

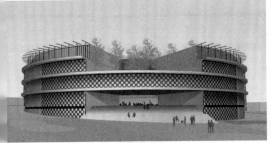
OPTION 25 | STAINLESS STEEL 50x50 (SOUTH/NORTH) + FINS (EAST/WEST)

OPTION 26 | STAINLESS STEEL 75x75 (SOUTH/NORTH) + FINS (EAST/WEST)

Testing envelope strategies with multiple opening options (solids, voids, patterns)

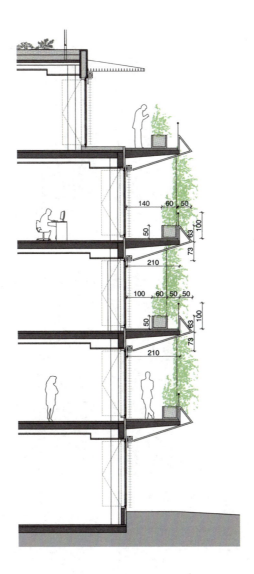

The green walkways (balconies)

The Rosey campus extends over a splendid park surrounded by trees. The CSE project proposes green walkways on its periphery, allowing classrooms to open outward during fine weather. Open for individual students or small groups, the green walkways include native plant species that change shape and color with the seasons, creating a dynamic building that reflects the continuous seasonal transformation of its surroundings.

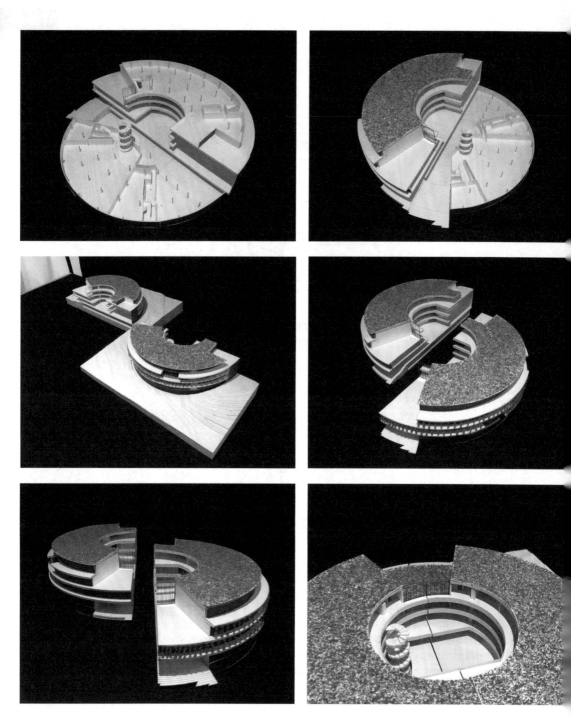

Study model

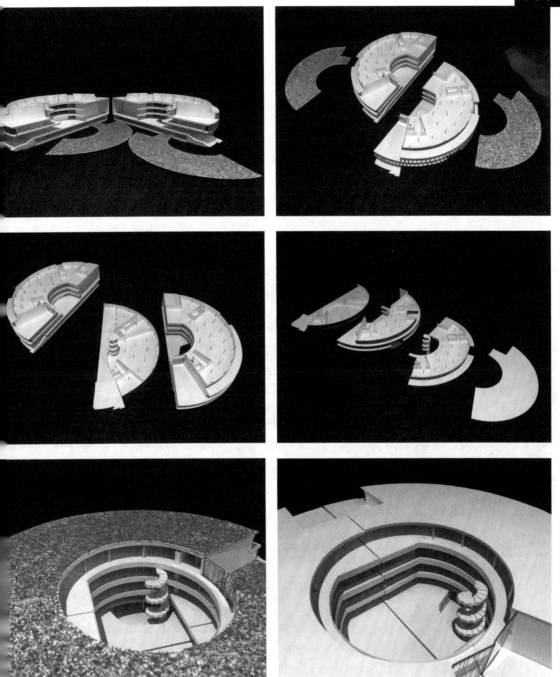

Perspective view of envelope, exterior walkways, and main entrance

ROLLE
135

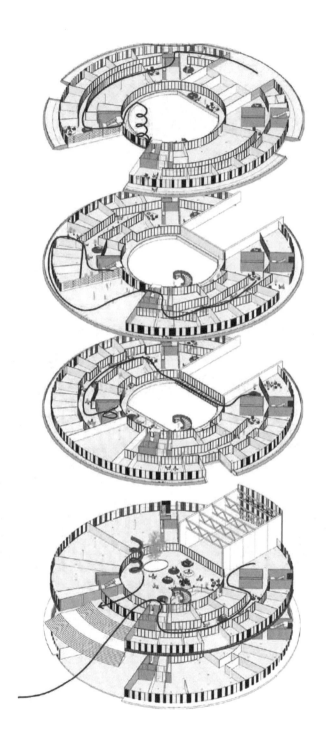

ROLLE
137

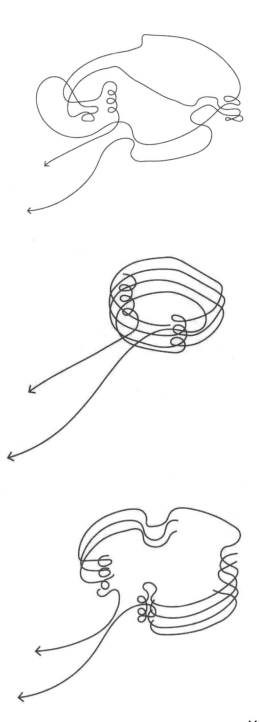

Multiple movement vectors

The central level of the atrium offers space for temporary science installations, a slide in a double-helix configuration, and an exotic tree.

On the upper floors, designed as two semi-arcs, the two levels of classrooms and one level of laboratories are accessible through circular walkways opening onto the atrium and acting as spontaneous workplaces.

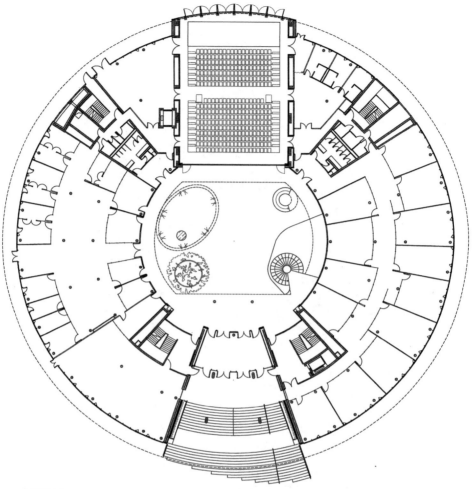

Level +1

Interior

Upon entering the CSE: A large circular atrium bathed in natural light acts as the center of gravity for the building, showcasing the varied activities of the Center.

Opposite the entrance, the Pitch Room, a rectangular room with multiple possible configurations, is a space for presentations and theatrical performances. The Pitch Room opens toward both the atrium and the landscape at the corner of the site. On the left is the Start-Up (an incubator for new ideas). On the right, in front of the classrooms, a large spiral staircase leads down to the FabLab (a maker's space), whose window can be seen below. Upwards, the staircase leads to classrooms and laboratories, as well as green spaces, on the top levels.

ROLLE
141

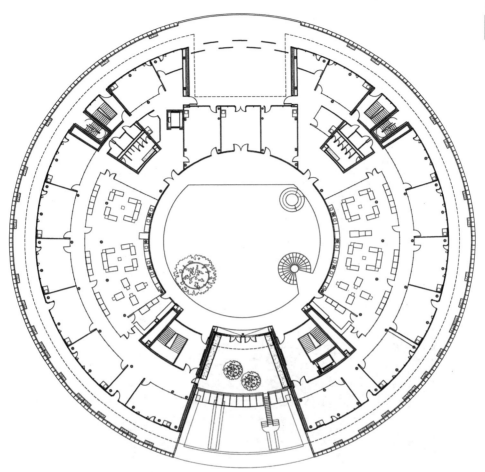

Level +4

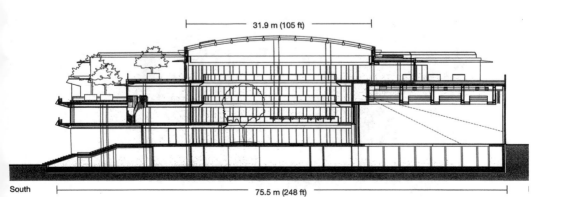

31.9 m (105 ft)

South   75.5 m (248 ft)

FLEXIBILITY STRATEGIES

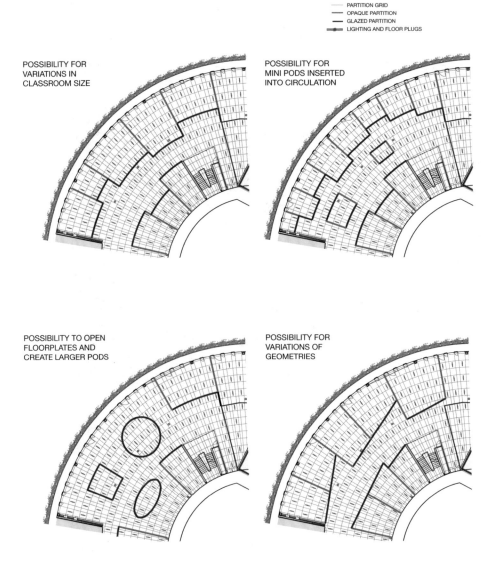

Classroom spaces are designed to be flexible, with wide circulation areas allowing small groups to meet. Mini-gardens and outdoor walkways with planters on each floor encourage students and teachers to invent new ways to learn and teach. On the first level, a teachers' lounge in a central and strategic position encourages a direct dialogue between teachers and students.

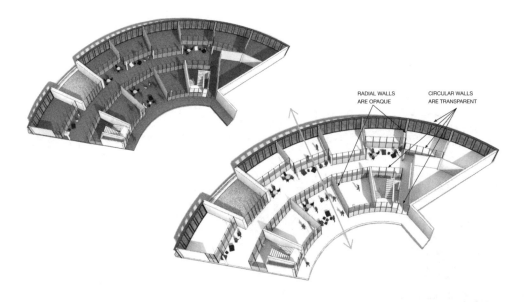

Circular hallways with study areas and glazed classrooms

The Center for Science and Entrepreneurship (CSE)

ROLLE
147

The Le Rosey Concert Hall (Carnal Hall)

View from the north

ROLLE
151

PRESIDENTIAL HOTEL,
DOHA (2013)

TOUR HONORIA,
MONACO (2016)

ARCELORMITTAL
HEADQUARTERS,
LUXEMBOURG (2017)

B1. Abstract Superpositions (Concepts)

Like the Surrealist game of Exquisite Corpse, the superposition of disparate components occasionally produces bizarre wholes that retain the differences of their parts. A base-middle-top tripartite organization is used to respond to programmatic elements and site requirements and to generate interstitial conditions and unexpected adjacencies where the different volumes meet (contextualizing a concept).

Doha, Presidential Hotel, 2013

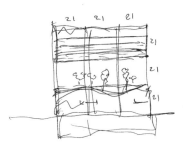

Suspended Volumes

Sometimes the site and program are highly generic. The answer is a simple cube, articulated into a "classic" tripartite configuration, capable of multiple expressions and interpretations. Both context and concept remain intentionally abstract, resulting in a dreamlike quality.

The Presidential Hotel in Doha proposes a type of hotel made of three differentiated parts: the more public areas (restaurants, conference rooms, cafés, etc.), the more private ones (rooms and suites), and an "in-between" space that can accommodate a variety of moods and ambiances.

The hotel stands at a prominent location on its Khalifa Avenue site at an important urban crossroads. It aims to provide an image for the city in a slightly surreal way. It has a base, a middle, and a top, but with unusual effects.

Base: On entering the lobby, a large glass dome appears, offering views into the in-between space above to give a sense of the events happening in the hotel on any given day. Gilded elevator shafts emphasize verticality and lead the eye to the exclusive world above. Materials are chosen to give the lobby a rarefied feel.

Middle: The in-between space functions as a suspended oasis. Shaded by the hovering volume of the suites above, the 54 x 54-meter undulating landscape of trees and fountains accommodates private parties, string quartets, or light shows. An ovoid lounge is suspended on the side for meetings and conferences of up to 50 people.

Top: On the upper part, guest rooms and suites are arranged around a central court on three floors. Large suites all have individual patios. Here, the emphasis is on privacy, quiet, and rest. Guests have dramatic views of the city. The separation from other hotel activities offers an escape for business or vacation travelers.

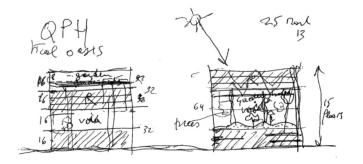

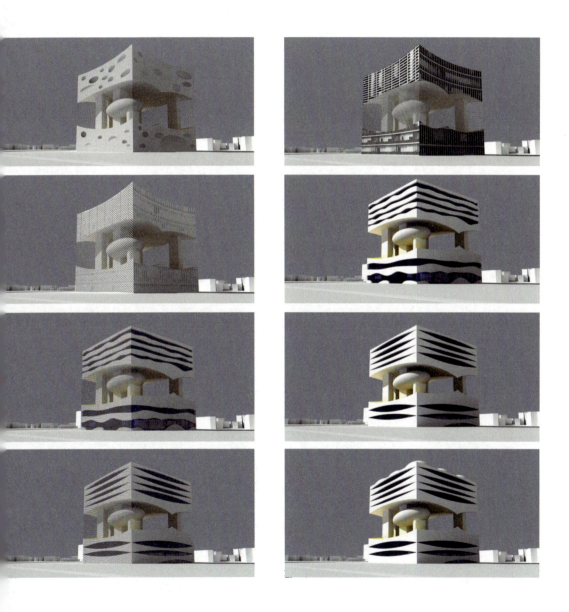

Testing multiple variations

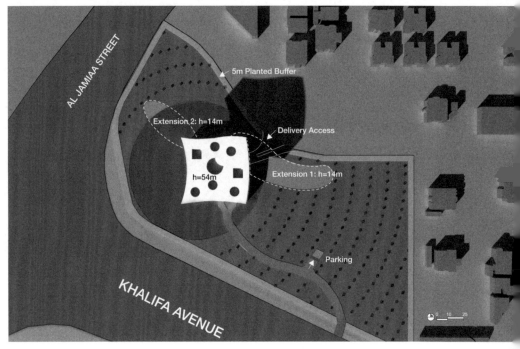

Highly differentiated programs articulated around a suspended void

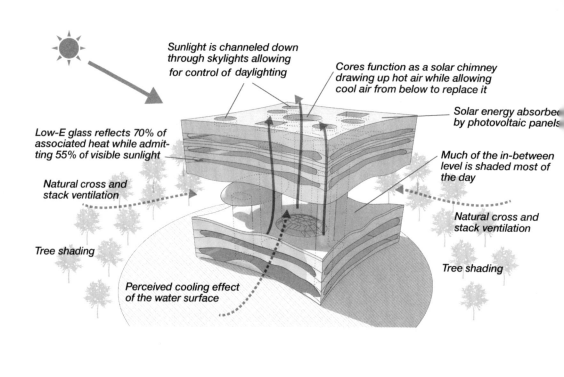

Monaco, Tour Honoria, 2016

MONACO
165

Tripartite Articulations

How to provide an identity to a tower in the city center of Monaco? How to maintain contact with the historical scale of the city, its legendary hills, and its exceptional waterfront? How to give the tower a unique character while addressing functional and economic requirements?

Concept   Colors

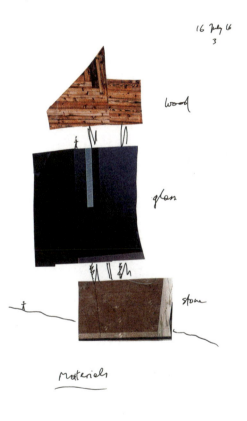

Characterized by its three distinct volumes and two articulated spaces, the Monaco Tower aims to contribute to the dynamism of the Principality of Monaco as well as the history of its architecture. Monaco is a city of extremes. Between its rugged topography and its picturesque landscape, the city has been built up to take advantage of its surroundings and economic realities.

In this context, a 21st-century tower is proposed for the city, its inhabitants, its visitors, and its image. The result is not a simple vertical structure. Two platforms or "Skydecks" provide an extension of the city, acting as public spaces high up in the air. At the base of the tower, the podium welcomes visitors into a large vertical hall that leads to a suspended garden (accessible through a public elevator) on the first Skydeck. On the second Skydeck, a restaurant offers a 360-degree panoramic terrace with remarkable city views. Bordering the two Skydecks, three volumes provide spaces for offices, social housing with loggias, and finally, large residences with panoramic views at the top.

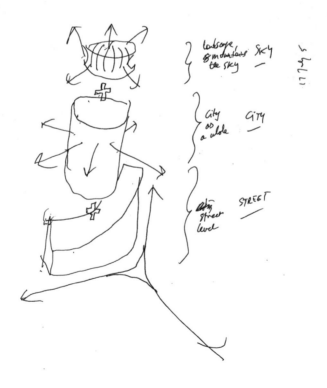

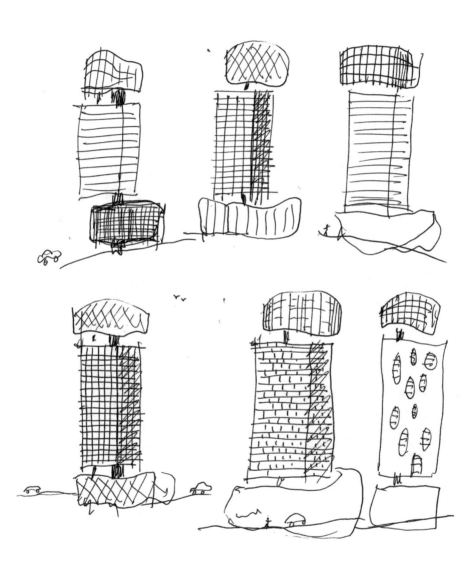

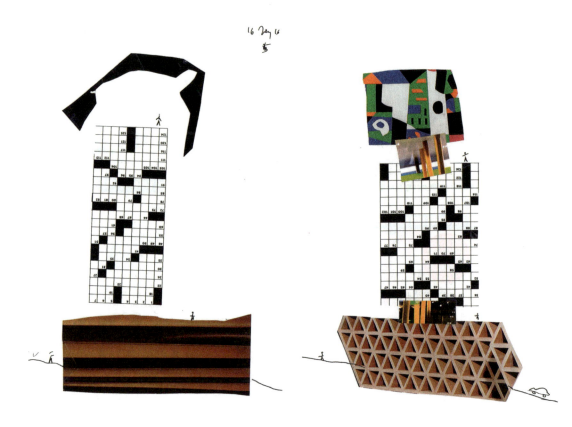

MONACO
171

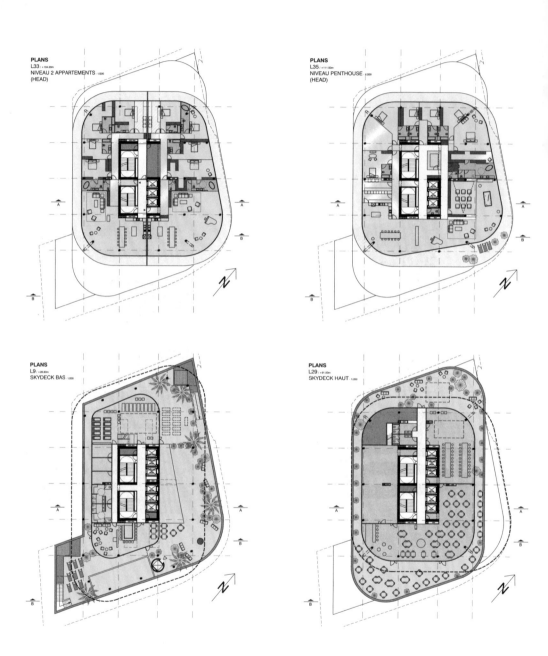

Plans of tower Head (above) and Skydecks (below)

MONACO
173

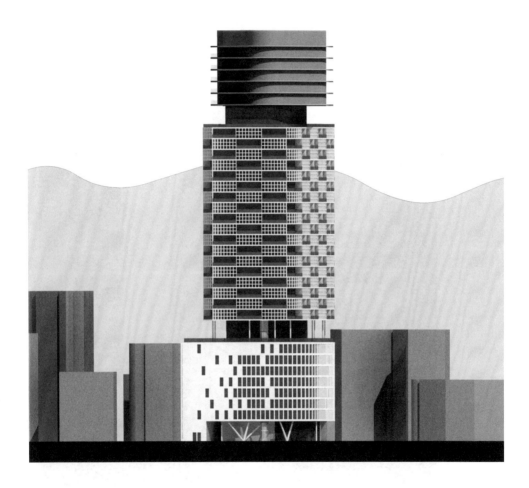

Southeast elevation

Luxembourg, ArcelorMittal Headquarters, 2017

LUXEMBOURG
177

Autonomous Parts

A multinational steel company based in Luxembourg requires a headquarters building. Its program differentiates three parts: conference halls, rental offices, and main offices for the sponsor. The architectural intent is to conceive a building that expresses its functions through its volume and silhouette, while vitalizing the subdued, bureaucratic surroundings of the city's office sector.

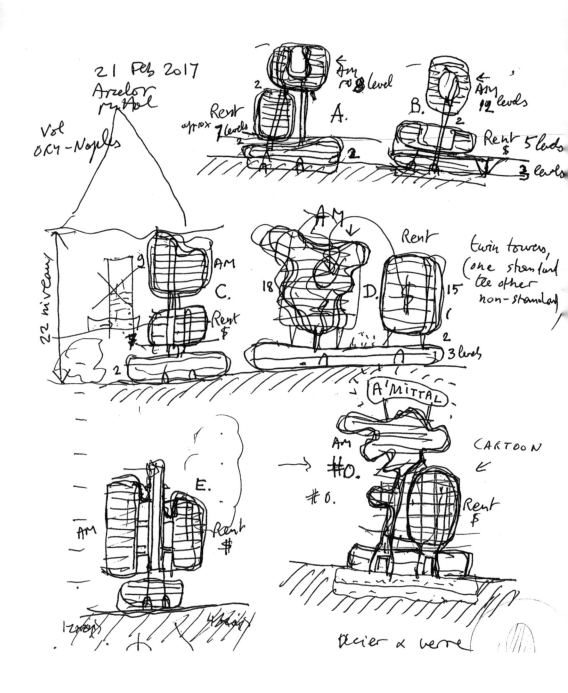

Early massing strategies for the three main programmatic components

LUXEMBOURG
179

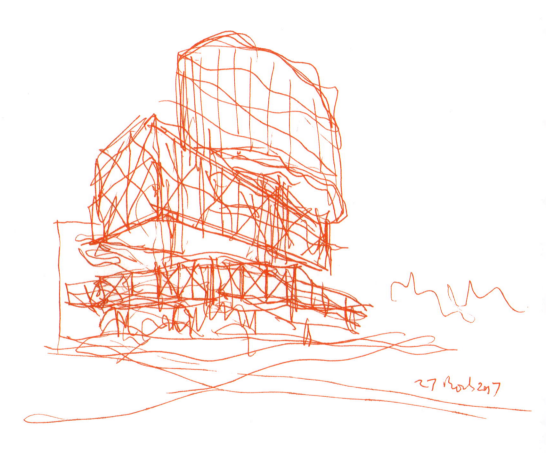

Differentiating three distinct programs using steel construction as a common denominator

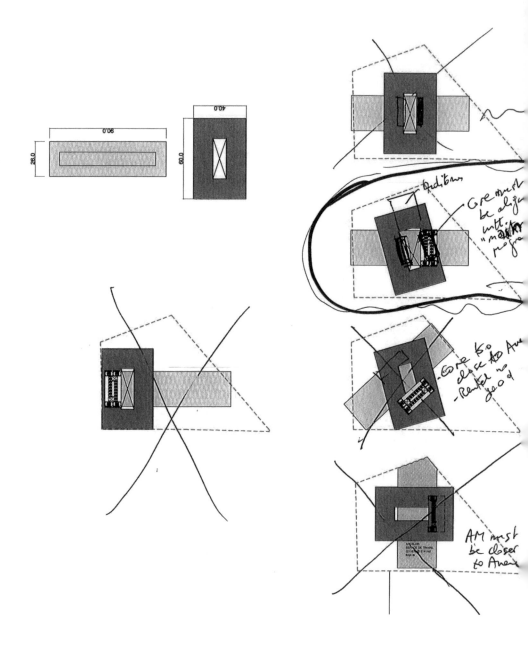

Testing various core configurations and site orientations

LUXEMBOURG
181

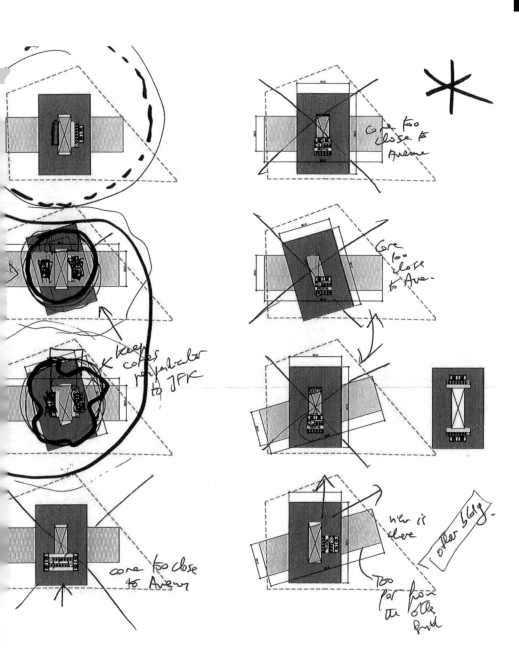

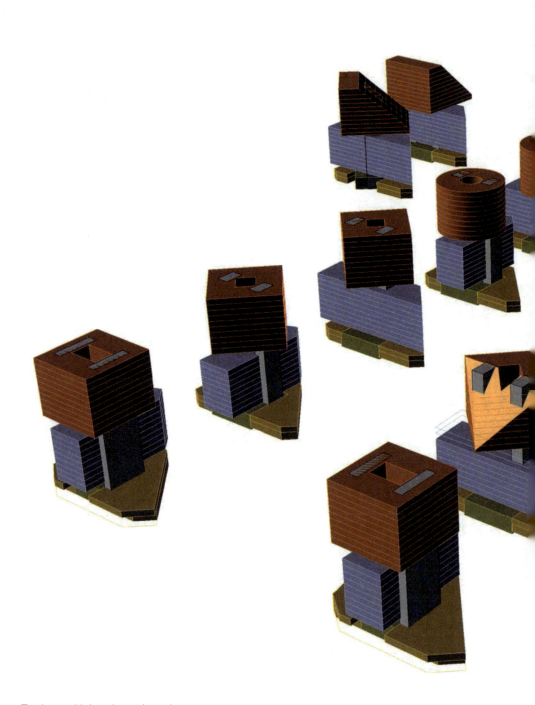
Testing multiple volumetric options

LUXEMBOURG

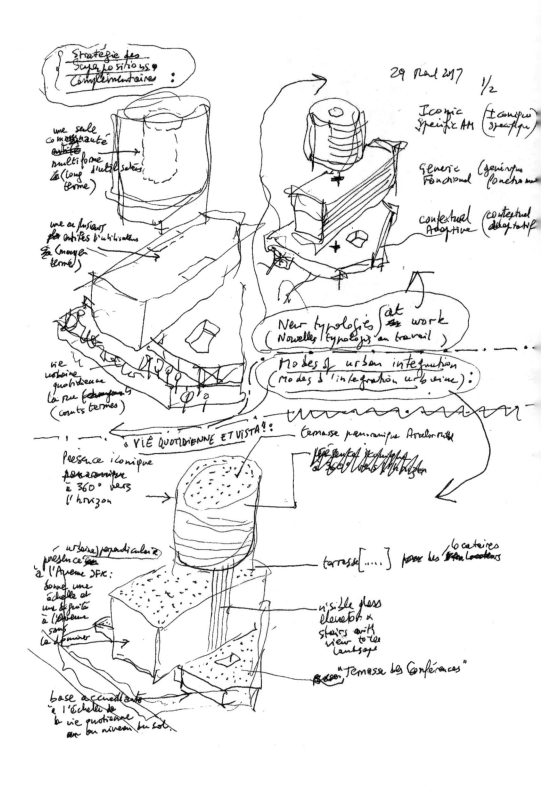

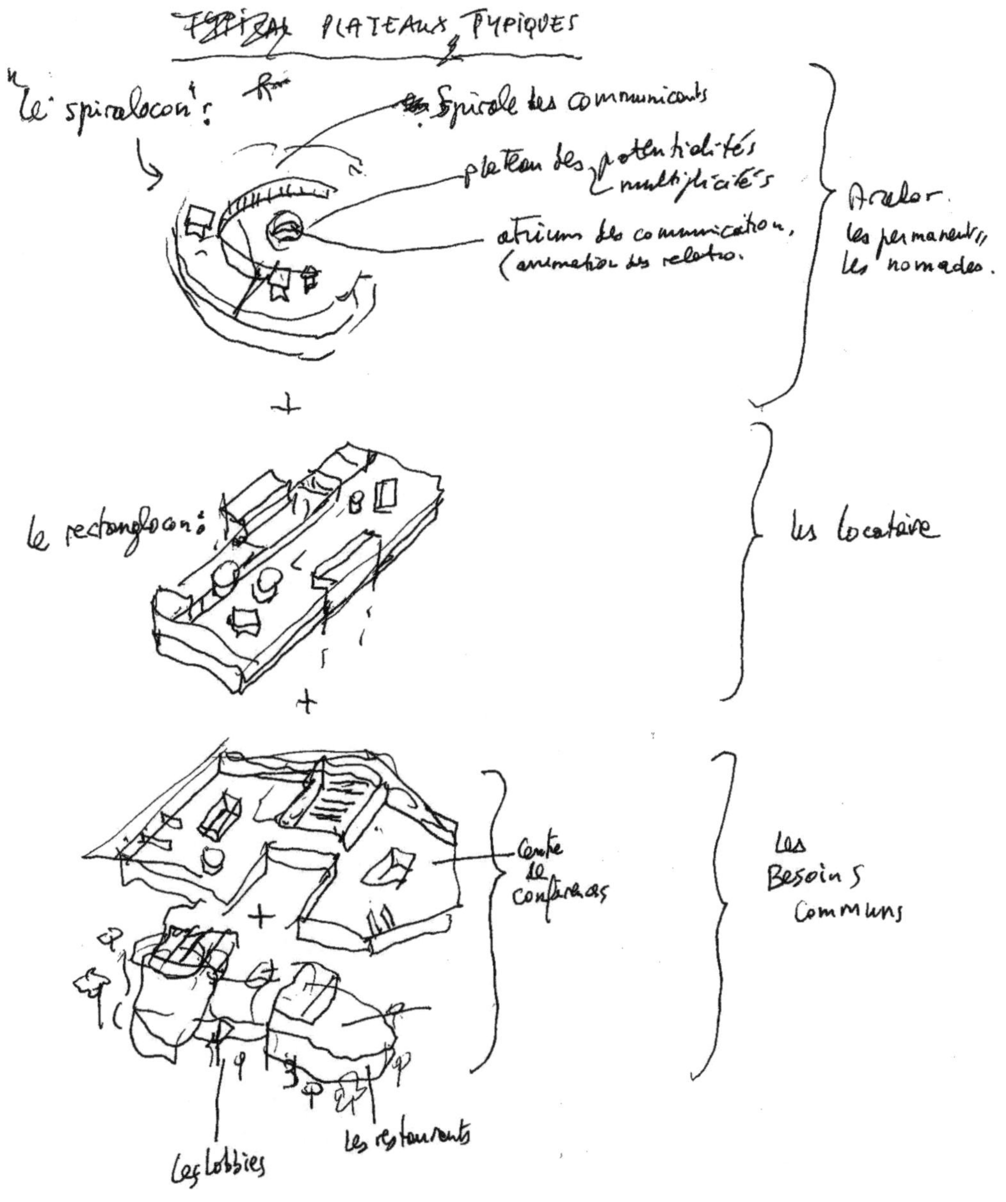

PLATEAUX TYPIQUES

"le spiralocon" — Spirale des communicants
— plateau des potentialités / multiplicités
— atrium des communication (animation des relations.

} Ateler.
les permanents,
les nomades.

le rectangloconi

} les locataire

Centre de conférences

} Les Besoins Communs

Les lobbies   Les restaurants

Diagrams clarifying the concepts

The urban and architectural argument
Taking advantage of programmatic requirements demanding a strict separation between the steel company and the rental offices, the 100-meter tower is composed of three distinct parts in a vertical sequence of volumes articulated by garden terraces. The lower volume is public, containing a conference center and restaurants; the middle volume is intended for rental offices, while the top volume is reserved for the head offices of the steel company.

The "base" is urban, responding to the site geometry by relating to the scale of pedestrian spaces. It includes lobbies and shared spaces such as restaurants and the conference center. Located on the roof of the conference center is a suspended garden specifically intended for conference-center users.

The "middle" offers office spaces for sale or rent, accommodating flexible work patterns. Above the rectangular volume is a garden terrace intended for renters.

The "top" provides a contemporary mixture of lifestyle and invention. Concern for well-being, flexible use, and potential reconfiguration and evolution of program are required. With those aims in mind, a new type of space acts simultaneously as a free horizontal plate and a four-percent ramp allowing for communication among the different departments. Each level (3,000 square meters, including cores) is composed of two parts—the horizontal floor plate (1,200 square meters) and the light-graded ramp with its accompanying levels. Both allow multiple configurations—closed offices, open spaces, meeting spaces, and isolation booths. The principle of the "stepped ramp" is at once simple and innovative. It allows flexibility of use and continuity from one level to the next.

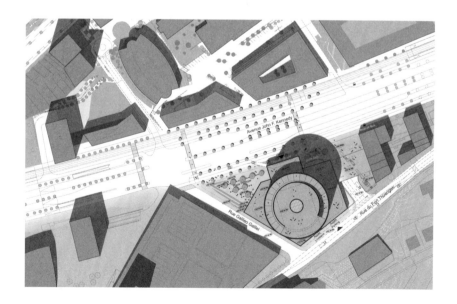

LUXEMBOURG
187

The structural engineering argument

The building is conceived as a communication tool, providing a symbol of advanced steel construction in the 21st century. The tower relies solely on the two steel-braced frame cores surrounding the stairs and elevators to resist vertical and lateral loads and to provide overall stability.

Each floating volume provides a network of full-height trusses at the lowest level that cantilever from the core. These trusses provide an initial work platform during construction and are integrated into the final structural system. The layout of the bracing patterns has been set to minimize the need for temporary erection scaffolding during construction.

The upper cylindrical volume similarly utilizes perimeter truss framing that is supported off the central cores through a multi-level outrigger truss to reach from cores to perimeter.

The rectangular volume is divided into an efficient, flexible structural grid of approximately 9 x 5-meter column bays, with the central line of columns transferred to the perimeter trusses at the lowest bar level.

The double-core principle—one dedicated to the main company, the other to rental spaces—has numerous advantages, including added structural stability. All three masses cantilever off the two braced-frame cores utilizing full-height steel-truss framing along the facade. The cantilevered masses are approximately balanced about the cores, thereby minimizing any overturning moment on the cores due to gravity load while still maintaining the excitement of relatively long overhanging structures.

LUXEMBOURG
189

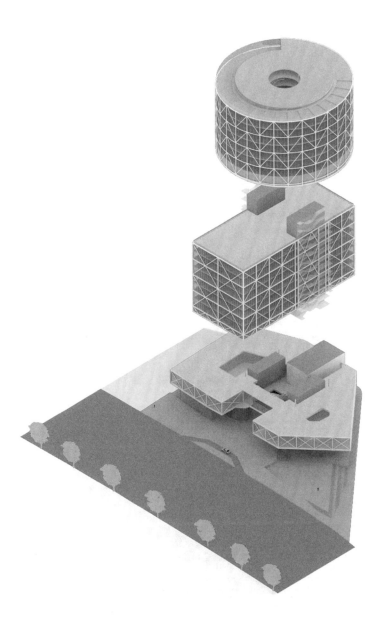

Exploded axonometric diagram

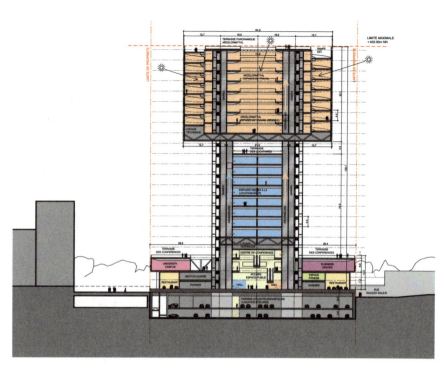

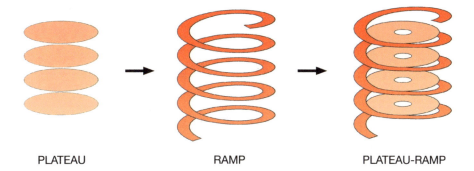

PLATEAU   RAMP   PLATEAU-RAMP

The top volume

Ascending or descending the spiral occurs on the periphery on one-third of the floor-plate. Along the facade, large flat landings (each approximately 40 square meters) allow for offices and open spaces to be distributed. The ramp and the flat landings coincide every five meters. The flexible plan allows the maximum amount of space to communicate, expand, or adapt according to the needs of different teams.

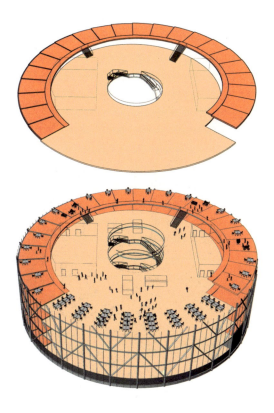

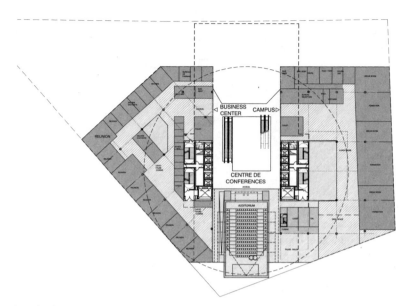

Base: Level +1

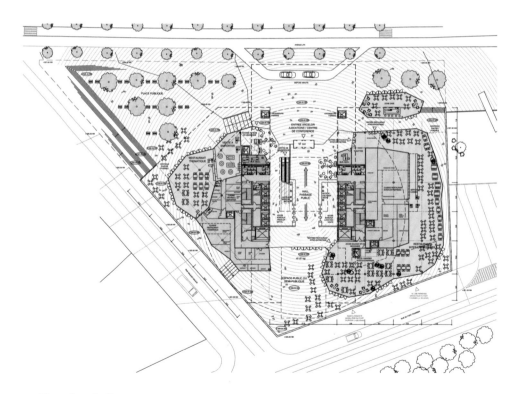

Base: Level +0

LUXEMBOURG
193

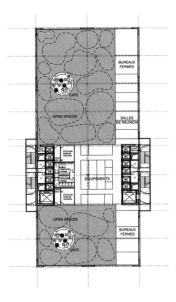

Middle volume: Configuration 1

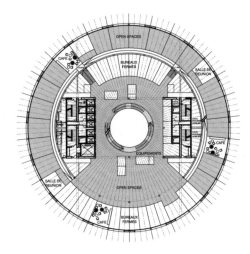

Top volume: Configuration 1

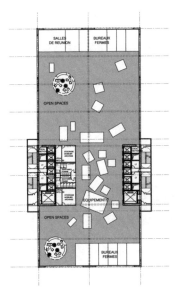

Middle volume: Configuration 2

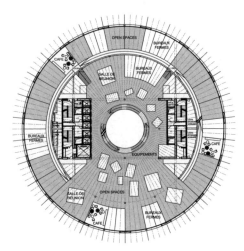

Top volume: Configuration 2

LUXEMBOURG
195

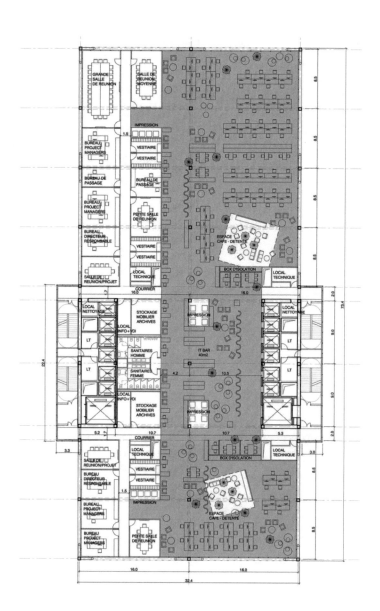

Middle volume

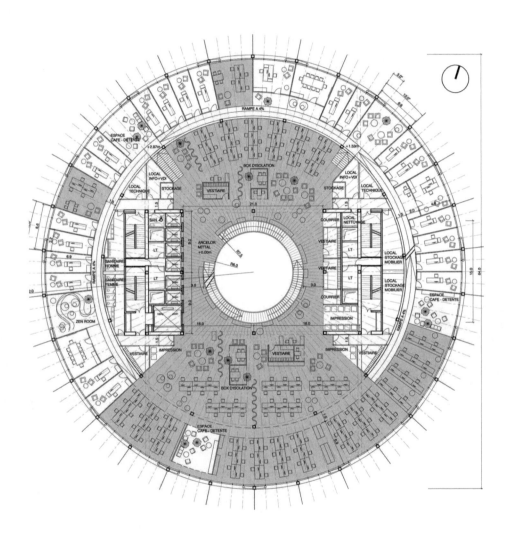

Top volume

Close-up view from the avenue

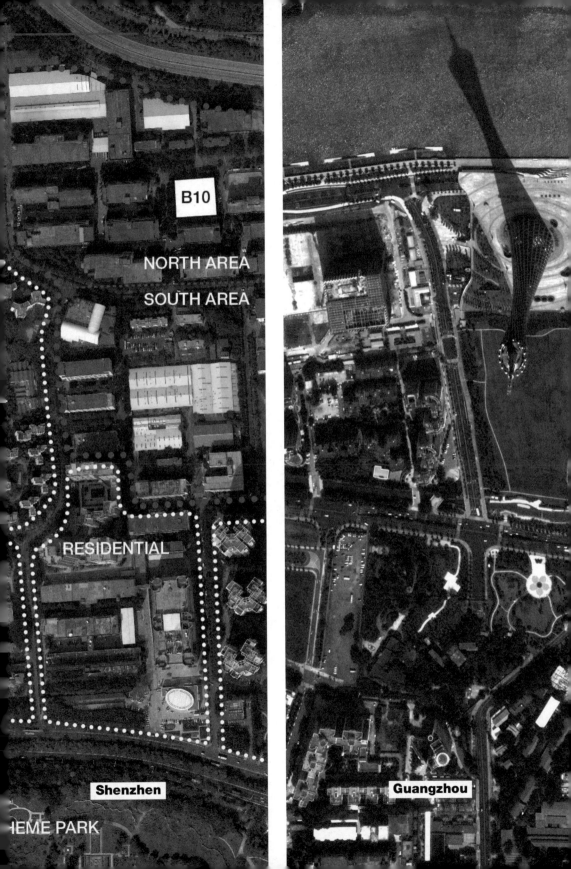

YINXU RUINS MUSEUM, ANYANG (2019)

MUSEE CANTONAL DES BEAUX-ARTS, LAUSANNE (2010)

OCT-LOFT MASTER PLAN, SHENZHEN (2011)

GUANGZHOU MUSEUM, GUANGZHOU (2014)

B2. Site-Specific Superpositions (Contexts)

Superpositions may be a way to address the relationship between the old and the new. While architecture can be indifferent to or conflictual with its context, it can also reinforce a context by exaggerating its specificity. Each of the projects presented in Part B2 takes an existing site characteristic as an opportunity to engage in an ongoing conversation with the past and possibilities of a place by focusing, amplifying, or even exacerbating a given site condition (conceptualizing a context).

Anyang, Yinxu Ruins Museum, 2019

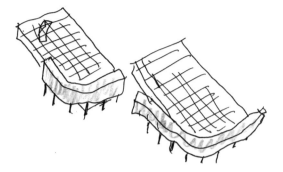

The River and the Ruins

How to give a specific identity to an archaeological museum without resorting to solemn historicism or symbolic whimsy? How to combine the strict functional requirements of a research institution with the poetic origins of one of the world's oldest civilizations?

The Huan River is one of the most important parts of the Yinxu archaeological site in China. This project for the Yinxu Museum celebrates the river and the remarkable Shang Dynasty ruins founded along it by mediating the landscape with the river on the west and the existing city blocks on the east. The ancient excavations are visible across the river.

The proposed Yinxu Museum is a new type of institution for conservation and display, designed for both researchers and the public at large. It is also a museum that aims to provide a bridge for a district with a rich past and a promising future. Based on the conviction that archaeology should not be anchored in nostalgia and pastiche, this museum design celebrates the archaeological history of China in Yinxu through a contemporary and singular symbol.

ANYANG
207

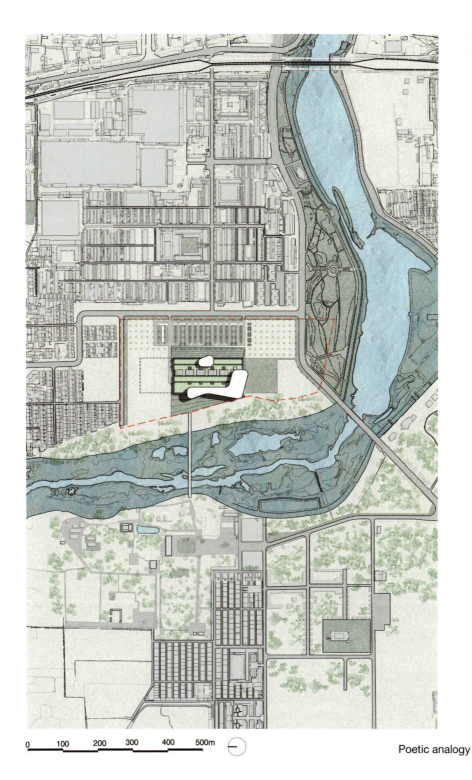

Poetic analogy

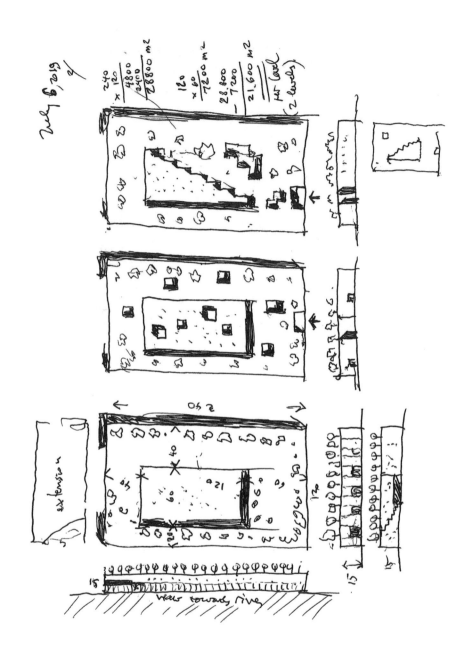

A simple rectangle is partly sunk into the ground as an archaeological gesture; various configurations are tested for the interior open courtyard and roof garden.

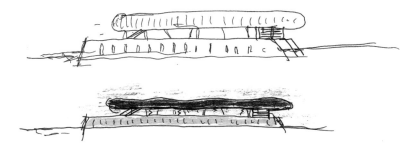

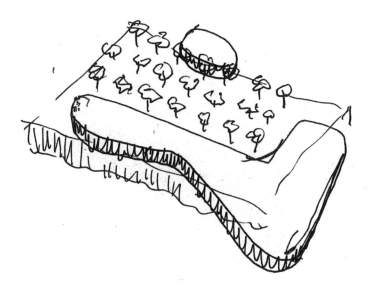

The Museum is made of three parts: the River Gallery, the Suspended Garden, and the Excavation Base. It is oriented to the west to allow contemplation of both the river and the ruins. The front of the museum displays its in-between Garden and the floating River Gallery, along with the excavated concrete Base containing the Conservation Department.

Chance encounters: Perspective view of the entrance

The River Gallery hovers over the research departments of the Museum.

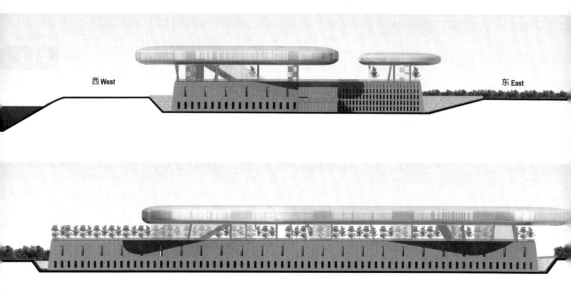

The Excavation Base is a monolithic concrete volume with thin vertical windows.

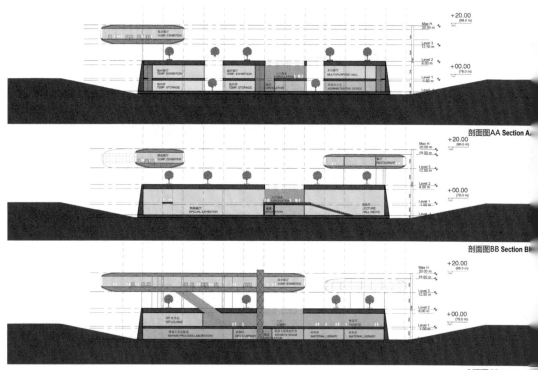

The program suggests three major levels for the Museum.

ANYANG

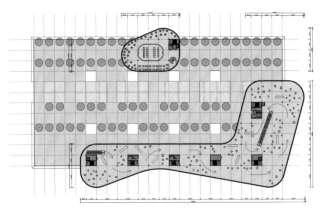

Level +3

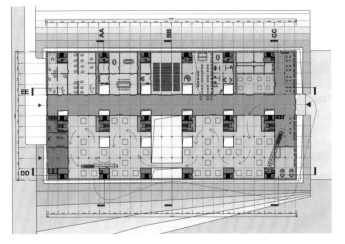

Level +1

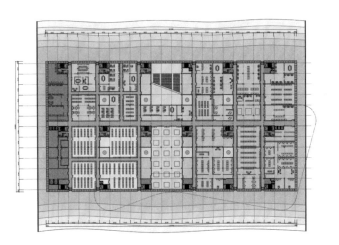

Level -1

The importance of the city and the river is expressed through three elements: the Excavation Base, the Suspended Garden, and the River Gallery.

The main entrance, located on the upper ground floor, opens onto a large passageway containing shops, café, and auditorium. The lower gallery displays large archaeological artifacts. The renowned Chariots Exhibition is designed as a sunken excavation pit, evoking the workplace of archaeologists. Within the Excavation Base and well-lit by the interior courts is the Research Department.

Upstairs, the River Gallery opens a panoramic view toward the river and the ruins.

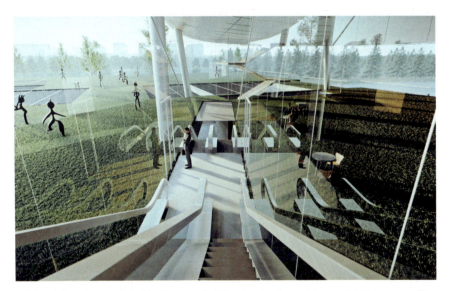
The visitor descends to the Suspended Garden for the outdoor exhibition areas. The in-between landscape is a common space for public use.

Lausanne, Musée Cantonal des Beaux-Arts, 2010

LAUSANNE
217

Hovering Vista

A new Musée des Beaux-Arts is planned alongside Lausanne's main railway station square. This scheme for an invited architectural competition proposes an electronic, floating gallery beam but preserves an early 20th-century wooden industrial structure located at the center of the site.

LAUSANNE
219

Rather than demolishing the old train hall, our proposal preserves and celebrates the beauty of the raw wood industrial structure.

The existing train depot from 1911

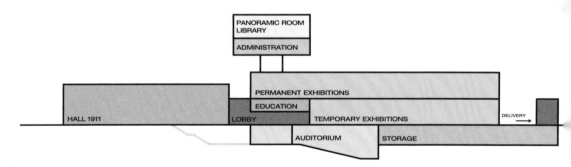

The original hall now acts as an open-air setting that is covered so it can host multiple artistic events, including music festivals. Its vocation is to be a key element of the new Museum building.

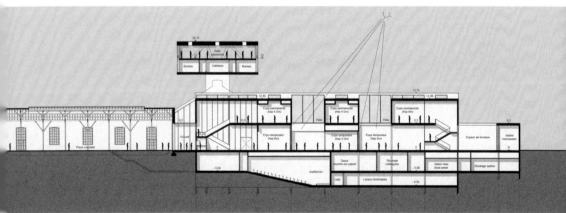

Section looking south

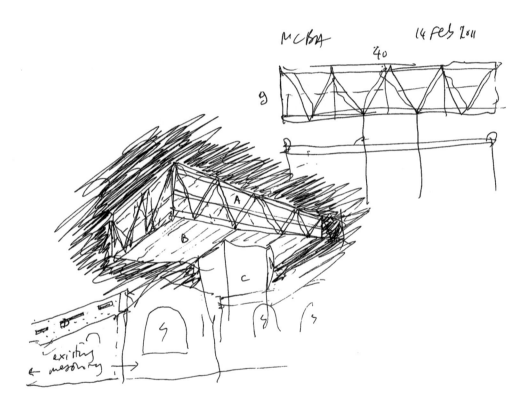

The combination of the levitating electronic slab and the historical wood structure generates a surreal complement to Lausanne, a surreal city on its own, characterized by multiple bridges hovering over a central valley.

View from the floating panoramic gallery (the Slab) toward Lake Geneva and the Alps, revealing an unsuspected landscape

R+1 Plan (+6.50 m)

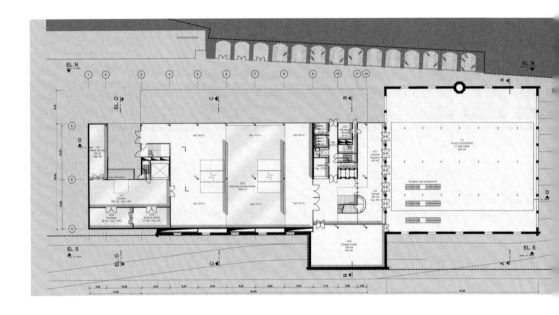

RDC Plan (± 0 m)

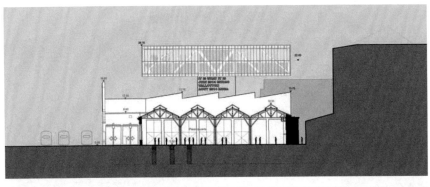
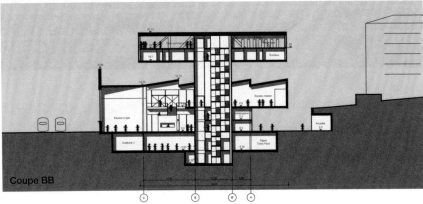

Sections looking west

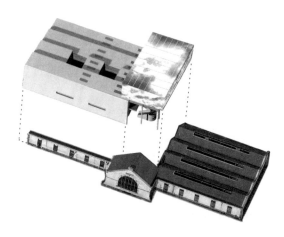

Axonometric diagram of the old and new

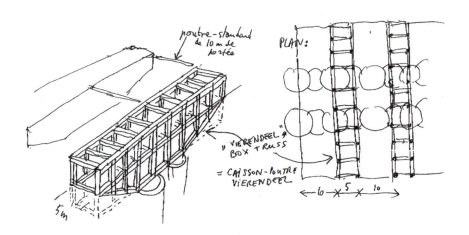

Precedent: Competition entry for Ponte Parodi, Genoa (2001)
For an immense abandoned grain silo, a simple intervention proposes to transform radically both the port's use and image. A light and transparent glass box lies on top of the concrete silo and is the contemporary container for new activities in the city.

GENOA
227

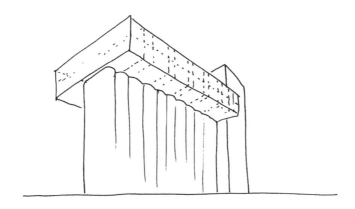

The glass box is "transprogrammed" with commercial, cultural, residential, and/or athletic facilities, all housed in the same container with panoramic city views.

Shenzhen, OCT-LOFT Master Plan, 2011

SHENZHEN
229

Insertion/Densification

How to complement recent architectural history by addressing both past and future?

Hovering Structures: References

El Lissitzky's Horizontal Skyscraper (ca. 1924)

Arata Isozaki's City in the Air (ca. 1962)

Simple children's games provide unexpected lessons, as exemplified by the vertical sticks that collect and hold different horizontal rings.

The project's brainstorming phase explored ideas inspired by nature, like mushrooms, which grow a large canopy from a slender support.

Context

Expanding new construction on the outskirts of towns may waste valuable resources. One of today's challenges is how to densify so as to stimulate invention and progress while preserving the historic character of existing city neighborhoods.

Preservation

In a unique planning strategy, an obsolete industrial area of the Chinese city of Shenzhen was to be preserved and transformed rather than demolished. The prerequisites of the project were not only to retain the existing buildings but also to provide strategies for their adaptive reuse. A 50,000-square-foot (5,000-square-meter), three-story factory building was designated as the first transformable facility, with its size to be doubled and turned into a museum. The proposed uses for the surrounding area included culture, education, and entertainment, with additional high-density housing and office buildings to be located in the immediate vicinity.

Proposal

New buildings suspended above older ones have long been a staple of utopian dreams. Today, it is finally possible to construct those utopias, as recent precedents have demonstrated. However, what is still needed is a productive concept—a way to make individual component objects as well as a coherent whole. Nature, for example, knows how to grow wide structures on narrow and crowded ground. Imagine a city inspired by mushrooms! To further such investigations about the insertion of abstract concept-forms into preexisting contexts, this project uses circular configurations superposed over the old rectilinear buildings located below them. The circles are notional placeholders: They could be replaced by squares, triangles, or any other configuration without altering the nature of the concept.

SHENZHEN

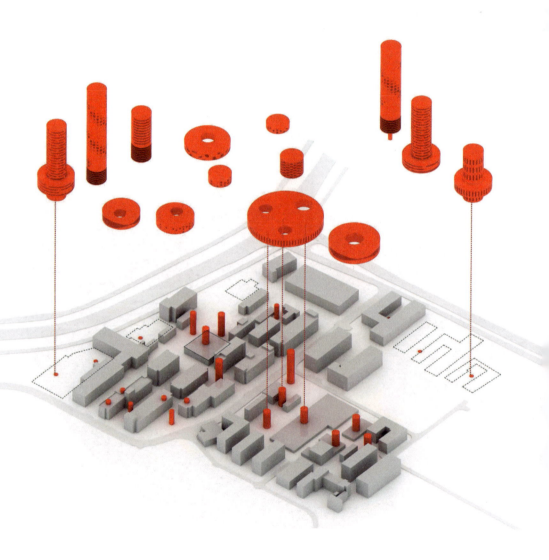
Exploded axonometric

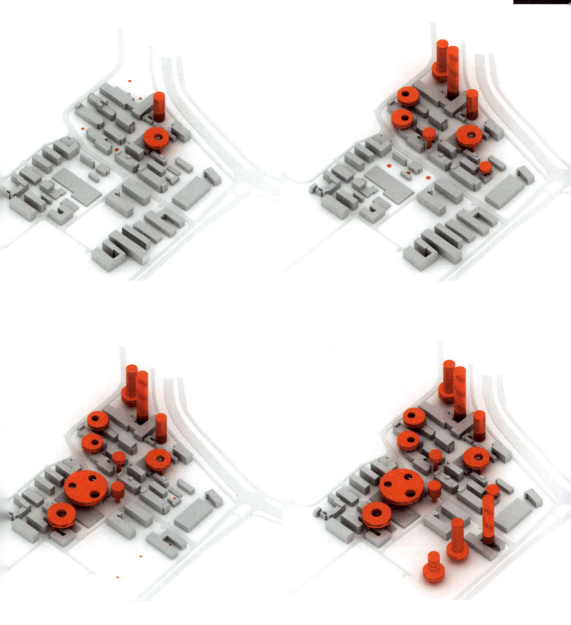

Phased densification

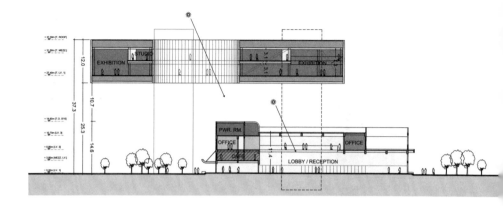
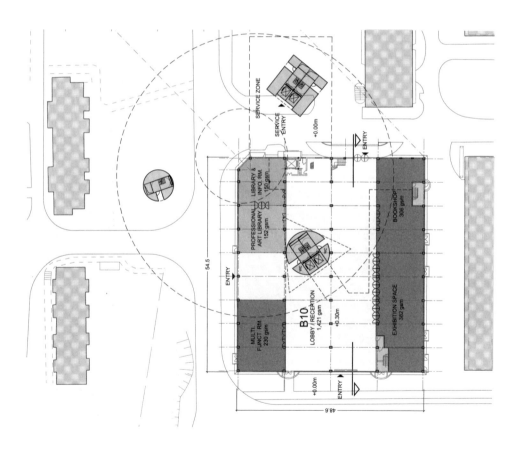

Circular extension above existing rectangular volume

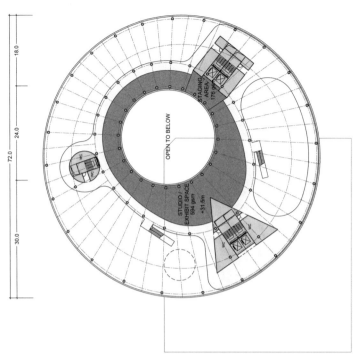
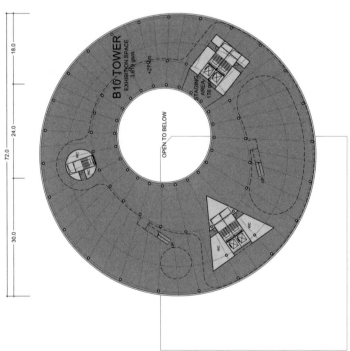

Circular extension: Level +1 and Mezzanine

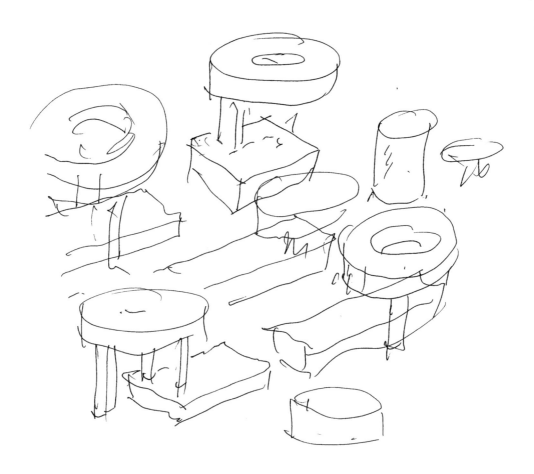

As neighborhoods transform, the strategic use of spaces above the existing urban fabric allows for new contemporary structures to coexist with and address both past and future.

Circular museum hovering over existing rectangular building

Guangzhou, Guangzhou Museum, 2014

GUANGZHOU
241

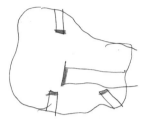

Directed Dialogue

How to arrive at an architectural concept directly derived from a specific local condition without resorting to superficial anecdotes? How to identify contextual characteristics that can be turned into architectural concepts?

Old Guangzhou - shaped openings, red incisions

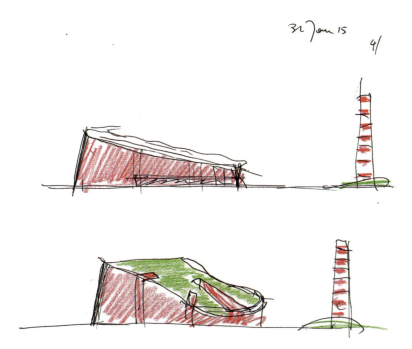

31 Jan 15 4/

Red

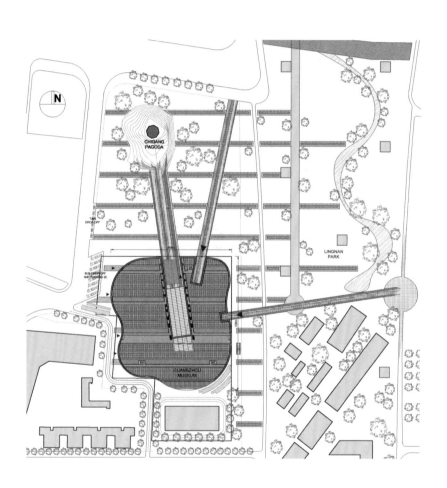

Presentation to the competition jury
Architecture can start with a program (functionalism) or a site (contextualism) or a style or ideology (classicism, modernism, postmodernism, regionalism, etc.). The Guangzhou Museum focuses on eight ideas or concepts.

- First Concept (defining)

The site has several existing constraints. Their resolution makes the outline of the Museum resemble the outline of the outer walls of the old city of Guangzhou.

- Second Concept (directing)

The Guangzhou Museum is a Museum of the City. One of Guangzhou's most prized and sacred constructions, the Chigang Pagoda, is located immediately north of the site. The Museum and the Pagoda are made to engage in a tight dialogue so that the two buildings can be read together as a pair. Large indentations are cut into the mass of the Museum, with one pointing toward the Pagoda. A second cut-out looks toward Canton Tower and a third toward the future Cultural District. By showing three directions, the Museum is like a Chinese Compass, pointing to the past, the present, and the future. This concept generates the Museum's architecture.

- Third Concept (framing)

The main indentation (looking toward the Pagoda) is the central atrium of the Museum. This atrium frames the Pagoda to the north. Slightly to the right, it frames Canton Tower. To the east, it opens onto the new cultural district.

- Fourth Concept (moving)

A canal or small river connects the fountain water inside the main atrium to the Pagoda. This "cascading" effect is intended to act like perpetual motion, giving life to the still artifacts. The main movement vectors are located around the cascade.

- Fifth concept (articulating)

The galleries are articulated by means of parallel service walls containing energy, ducts, structure, fire stairs, etc., providing great flexibility.

- Sixth Concept (enclosing)

The wall surrounding the Museum is made with rich chromatic and textural variations, thanks to a concrete treatment that resembles sandstone. This wall also offers irregularly placed openings to bring in light wherever needed.

- Seventh Concept (filtering)

The Museum roof provides an accessible, suspended landscape that insulates and filters daylight for the galleries.

- Eighth Concept (extending)

The striated configuration of the roof landscape expands to the park surrounding the building, integrating the Museum with the City, as opposed to an isolated object.

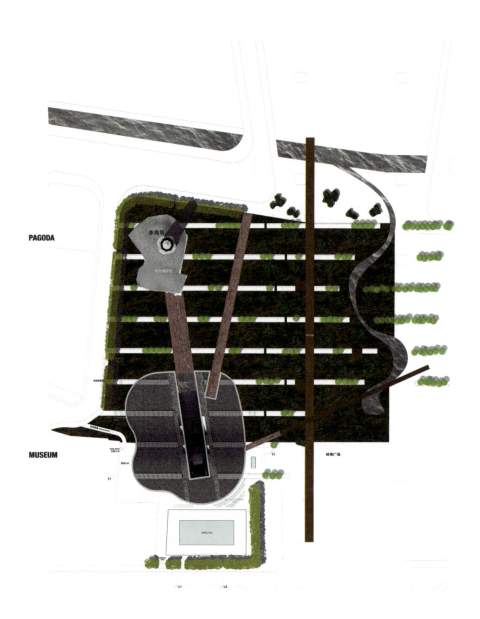

Site plan with canals, parallel gardens, and the three indented cuts pointing toward the Chigang Pagoda, Canton Tower, and future Cultural District

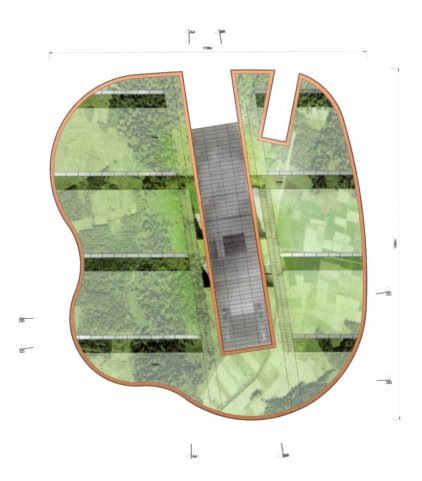

Plan of stepped roof garden with bands of clerestory windows

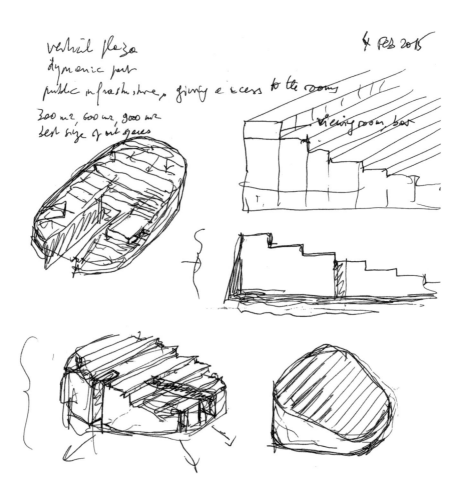

Early massing diagrams

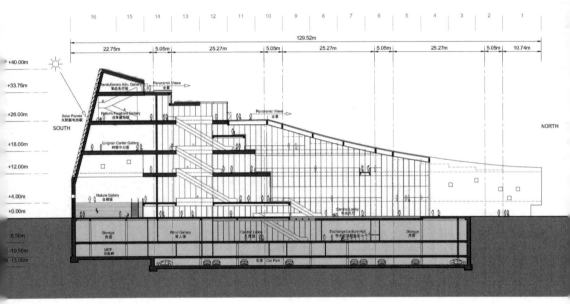

North-south section

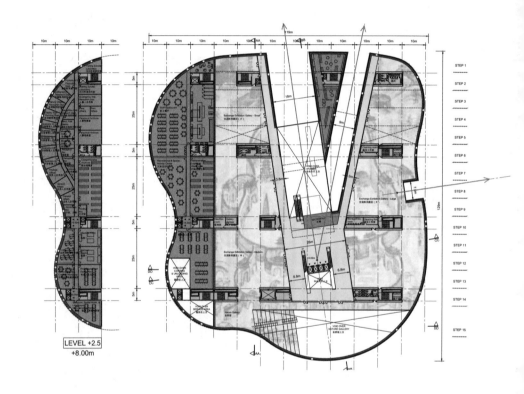

Intermediate stepped level (Level 2)

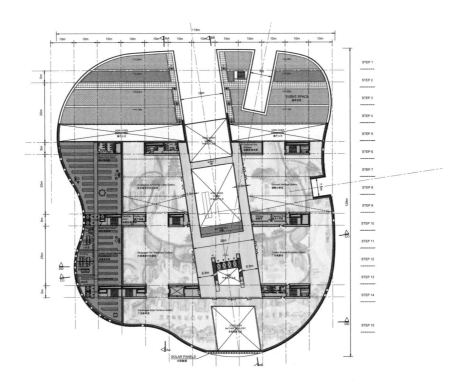

Top stepped level (Level 3)

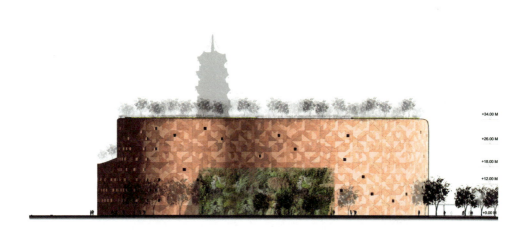

Stage 1 Elevations

Stage 2: The addition of 3,000 square meters of solar panels covering the south facade

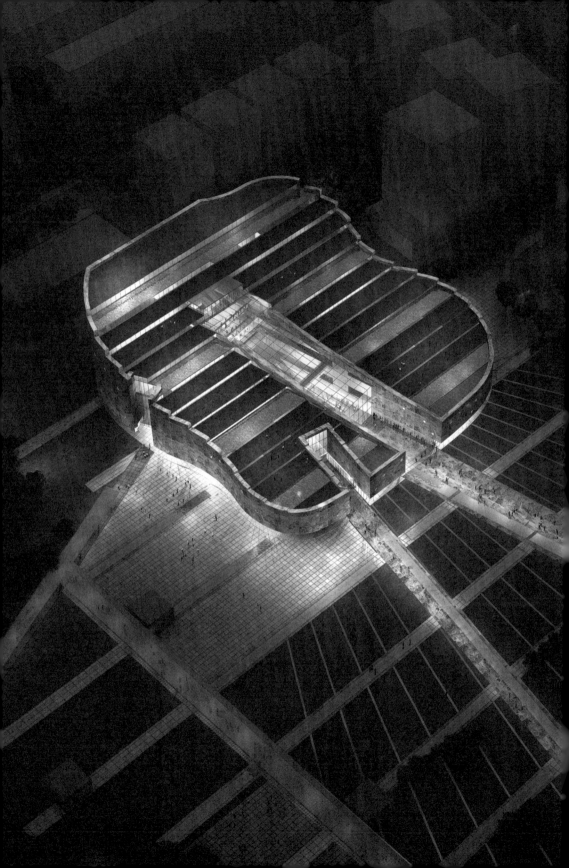

View toward the Pagoda from the main indentation

Perspective view of the main entrance

Geneva

Grottammare

CITE MUSICALE, ILE SEGUIN, PARIS (2012)

BINHAI SCIENCE MUSEUM, TIANJIN (2013-19)

CARAN D'ACHE HEADQUARTERS, GENEVA (2021)

A.N.I.M.A. CULTURAL CENTER, GROTTAMMARE (2012-14)

C. Analogical Reference

Analogies act here as a way of interacting with context through similarity or likeness. This approach develops an intelligible image for a building through visual or conceptual resemblance to, or representation of, a specific program, culture, or history. Not a duck or a decorated shed, but rather a latent correlation. Analogies can be visual and metaphorical, spontaneous and systematic.

Paris, Cité Musicale, Ile Seguin, 2012

PARIS
265

Ship, Lantern, Passage, Garden

Competition model in its violin case

"…gold ingots…their cylindrical form with two rounded ends…"

—Raymond Roussel, *Impressions d'Afrique*, VIII

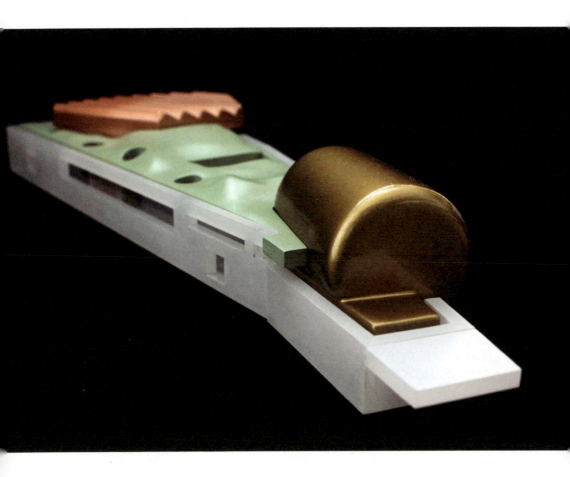

In *Impressions d'Afrique* (1910), the French writer Raymond Roussel tests self-imposed constraints the way architects exacerbate programmatic demands. Over 100 years later, this competition project pays homage to Roussel, who influenced a number of Surrealist authors and artists, among other thinkers.

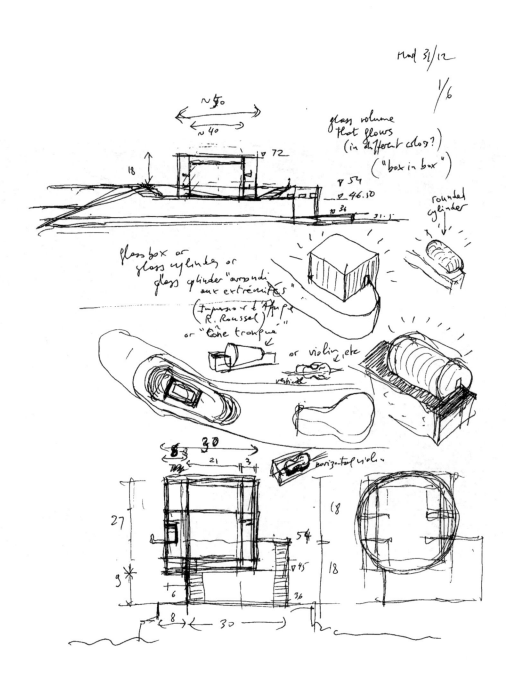

Initial diagrams

PARIS
269

2 April 12
Given
Subway to Cee

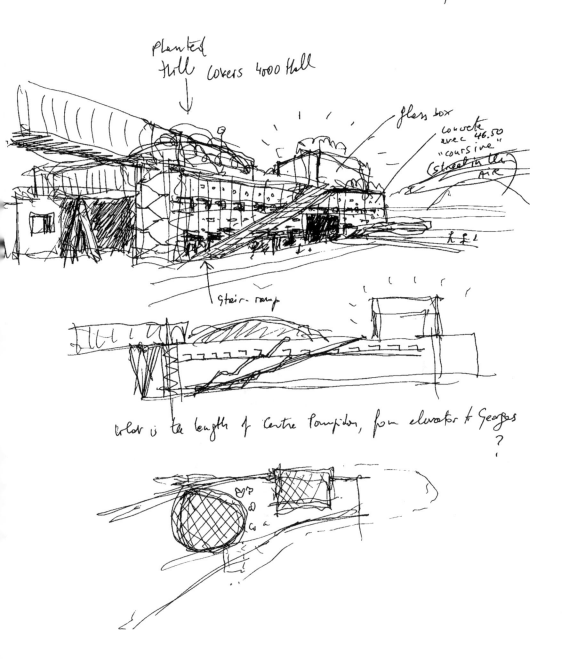

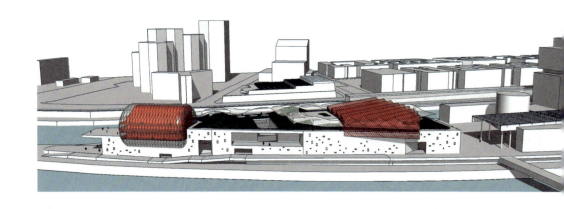
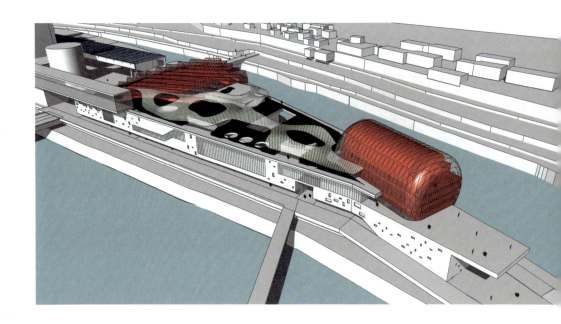

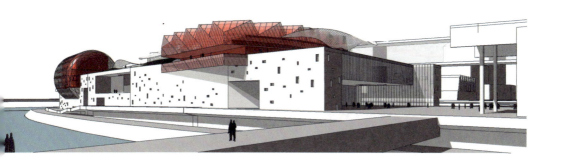
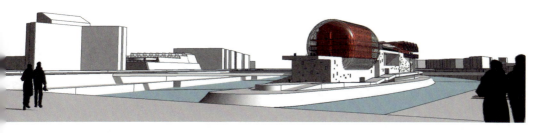

A formerly industrial island on the Seine just outside of Paris, the Ile Seguin once housed the Renault automobile factory but was abandoned for several decades. It became the frequent subject of urban and architectural revitalization attempts, most of which remain unrealized.

This architectural project rearranges the program into several specific themes: the ship's hull, the musical street, the magic lantern, and the hanging garden. Each theme acts as a potential hub of activity in a musical sequence that is accessible both before and after concerts and at all times of day.

The concert halls are entered from a single main outdoor plaza through a vast overhanging portico, channeling visitors into the large interior hall. From there, visitors can access the two main concert halls, a 6,000-seat facility primarily for entertainment-oriented musical productions, and the smaller halls. The facilities are connected by the "Rue Musicale," conceived as a musical score in three dimensions, in which visitors can walk amid displays and exhibitions. Escalators lead visitors to the hanging garden on the roof, with its trails and promenades, as well as to an amphitheater shaded by pleated glass with photovoltaic panels.

The Philharmonic Hall is shaped like a large glass cylinder which sits at the bow of the ship like a beacon. It provides an image for the district and is easily seen from an existing major bridge across the river. From inside, the Philharmonic Hall provides breathtaking views of the city and the surrounding river during day and at night.

Note: The architectural competition for the Cité Musicale was a public-private partnership (PPP) competition between the three largest French construction companies, who each invited two separate architects to compete independently against one another with their respective proposals. While committed not to divulge confidential design information, each construction company provided technical support to the two competing architects. Unexpected but possibly coincidental project similarities were the result of this unusual competition format.

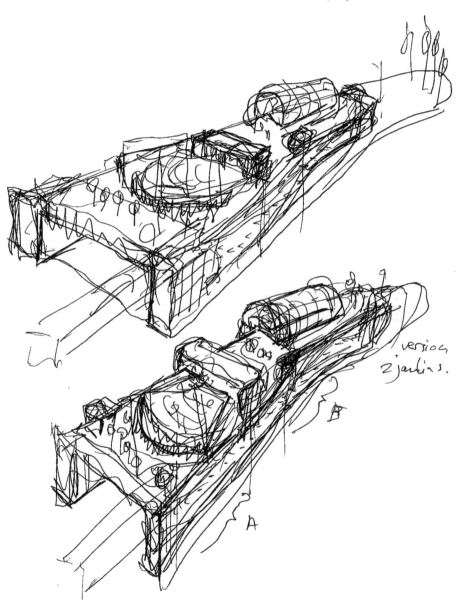

Early notations

SOUTHWEST

Façade côté Sèvres

NORTHEAST

Façade côté Boulogne

Elevations and longitudinal section

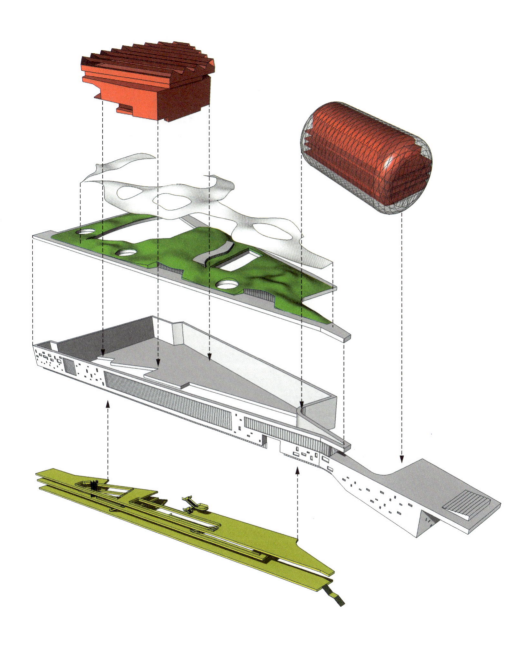

Exploded axonometric diagram

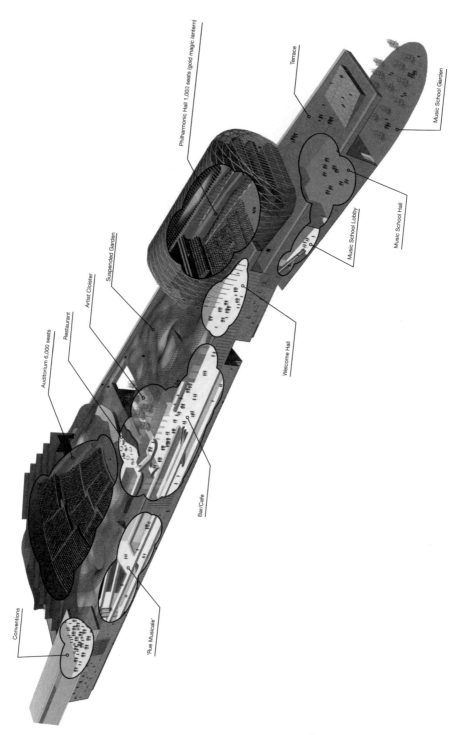

Programmatic distribution

Hanging garden

Main entrance

Philharmonic Hall

The "Rue Musicale"

*Tianjin, Binhai Science Museum,
(master plan 2010) 2013–19*

TIANJIN
281

Industrial Cones

How does one develop a contemporary spatial envelope related to an industrial past?

BINHAI 18 Jan 11
SILHOUTTE (CONCEPT):

← 150 → ↕ 30

Museum of Industry

The Master Plan

The Tianjin Binhai area is a rapidly evolving part of China that is representative of both old and new industries. Bernard Tschumi Architects was first invited to design a master plan with several museums, including a Museum of Industry, to address this dialogue, while establishing a cultural center that could become a focal point for the district. How does one create a new symbol for culture in the region, allowing for individual architectural expression within a distinctive framework?

Arranging multiple parts of a common set is standard in most cultures, including in China. This project starts by testing and comparing analogies: a tray of pots suggested a group of distinct objects on a podium; masks implied envelopes independent of their content, etc.

Multiple Individual Expressions (Pots) with a Common Denominator (Tray)

Individual Expressions with a Theme (Masks)

Taking the major pieces of the program and laying them out on the site in different configurations raised the question: How could each cultural building be given equal architectural weight in the master plan? The answer was a cultural district in a park divided into four equal quadrants, which frame the distinctive buildings inside them. These structures surround a plaza located in the middle of the park.

The four architectural object-buildings in the park correspond to the hollow courtyards of the commercial zone, establishing a solid and void relationship between the two major parts of the required program.

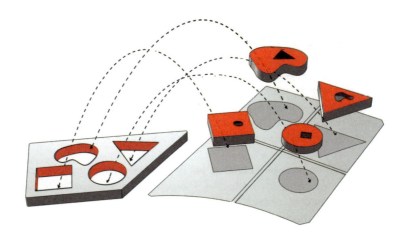
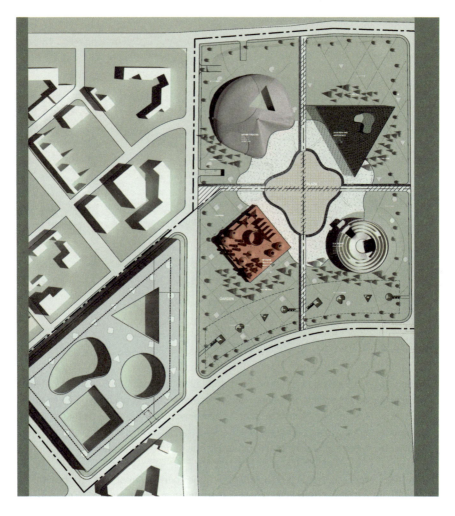

TIANJIN
287

This master plan proposes that individual architects work freely within their own sites, and each building is read with equal value in a collective configuration. Aside from the footprint, there were no rules or directives given to the future designers of the district. The strategy is less about what the architecture looks like, but rather about how each individual piece relates to the others. The strategy then pits the buildings against one another in friendly competition, pushing each to extremes. Circle, square, triangle, and free-form are shown here to emphasize the recommended differences between the four buildings, both in shape and in material.

Four volumes extracted from an adjacent continuous solid become four freestanding architectural objects. The relationship develops a dialogue with the nearby district.

The Preliminary Conceptual Scheme
A first preliminary concept was designed for a hypothetical site from the 2010 master plan. Although our low-rise square scheme had been selected, the new priorities of local planners required a taller, rectangular configuration. The clarity of the original concept allowed for a smooth transition and refinement when faced with a new site and adjusted program.

The Science Museum Final Concept
The Binhai Science Museum, a 33,000-square-meter (355,200-square-foot) structure, was completed in 2019. Designed in 2013 and 2014, the Museum showcases artifacts from Tianjin's industrial past through contemporary technology, including spectacular rockets for space research. The project is part of the city's Binhai Cultural Center and contains facilities for cultural events and exhibitions as well as offices, restaurants, and retail spaces.

The Science Museum is designed to articulate the rich industrial history of the area, which is the site of high-volume manufacturing and research. A series of large-scale cones defines major rooms throughout the Museum. The central cone connects all three levels of the Museum. A spiraling ramp ascends to the top level, offering an unusual spatial experience of the modern vertical city by reinterpreting an ancient industrial typology. The central cone is almost double the height of the interior of the Guggenheim Museum in New York.

The cones provide even natural light to gallery spaces and reduce the energy loads required for artificial lighting. Their tapered forms also concentrate warm air, which can then be channeled out of the building in summer or back into the galleries in winter. Glazing surfaces are minimized except when desired for program.

The perforated copper-colored facade gives a unified presence to the building, despite its large size and disparate programmatic elements. The metal panels help reduce heat gain.

The roof is accessible to visitors and acts as a promenade, with striking views over the surrounding city.

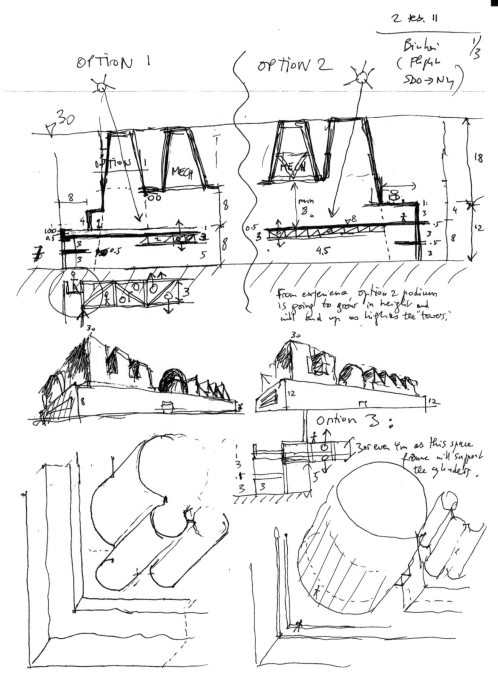

Analogy is both spontaneous and systematic.

Roofscape from the preliminary conceptual scheme

TIANJIN

291

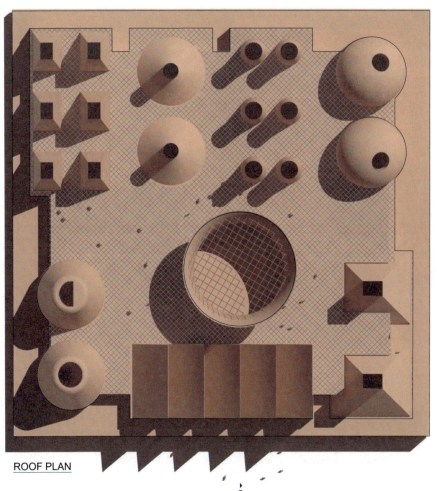

ROOF PLAN

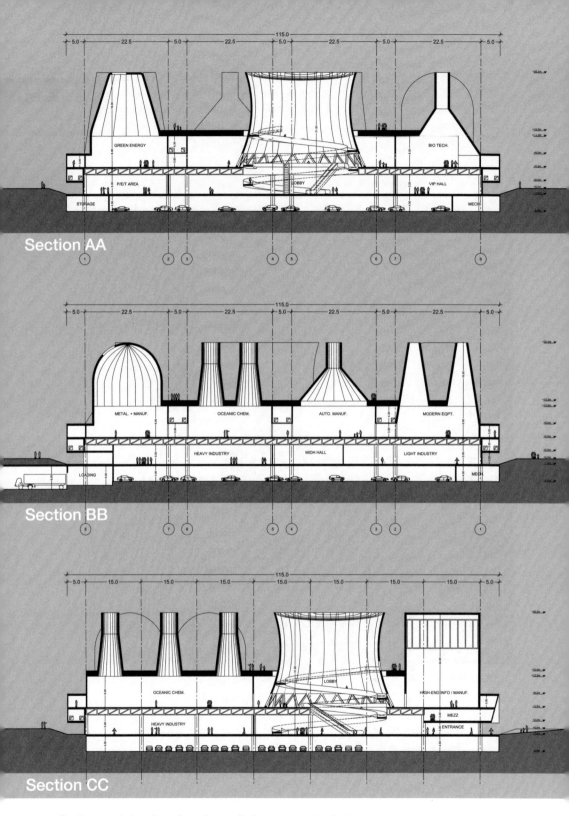

Sections and elevations from the preliminary conceptual scheme

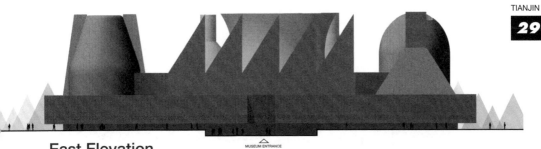

East Elevation

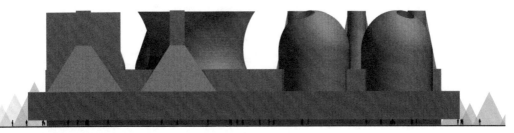

North Elevation

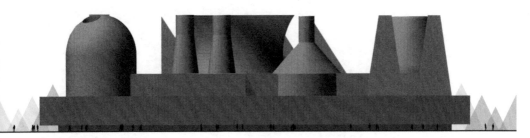

West Elevation

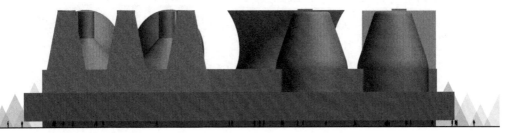

South Elevation

Perspective view from the preliminary conceptual scheme

TIANJIN
295

Interior views from the preliminary conceptual scheme

The Final Concept

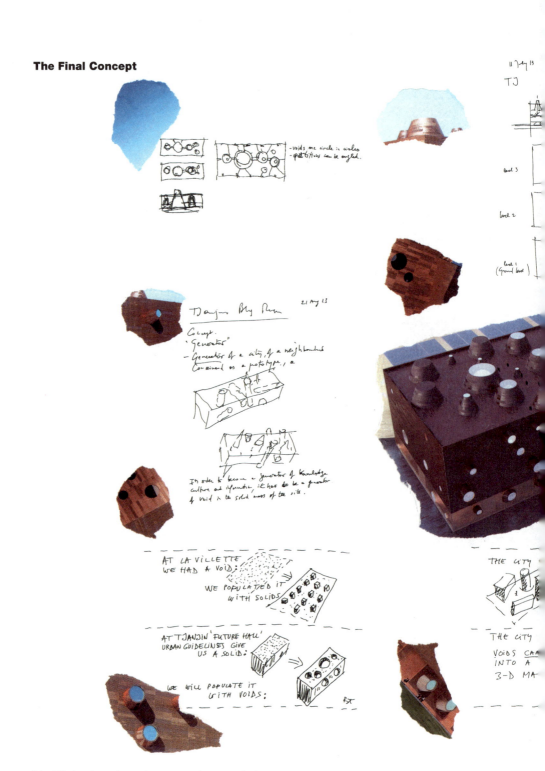

Modified volume based on new urban regulations.

A large central cone acts as a hinge connecting the building's site and programs.

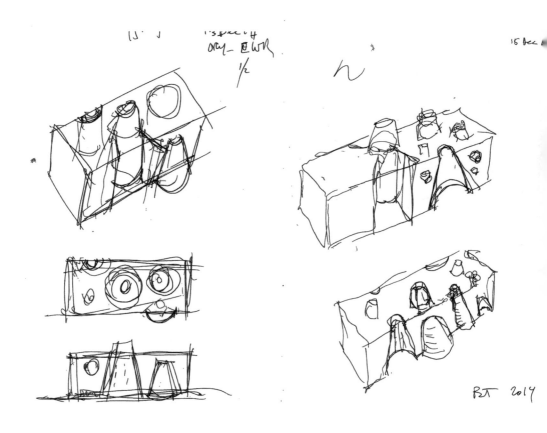

Diagrams, sketches, and notations: toward a final concept

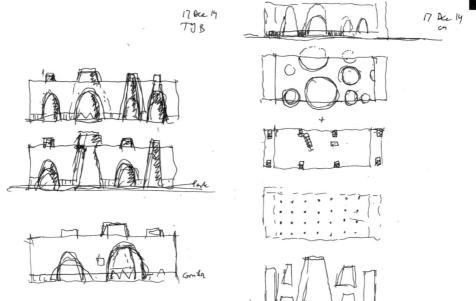
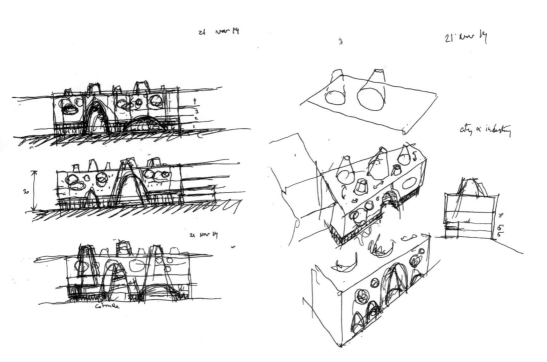

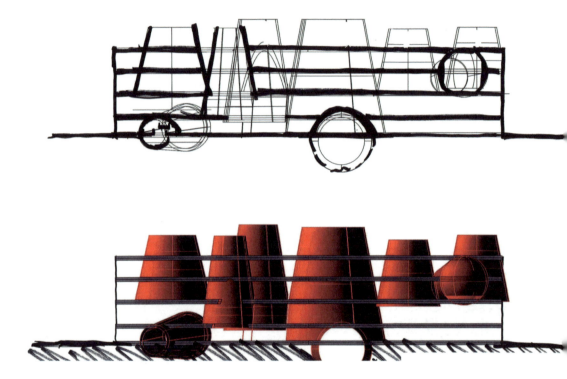

Analogy as a poetic image

TIANJIN
303

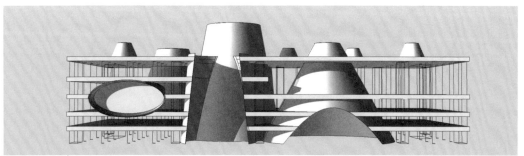
PASSAGE ELEVATION (NORTHWEST)

PARK ELEVATION (SOUTHEAST)

Hand-drawn ideas and revisions are adjusted at scale.

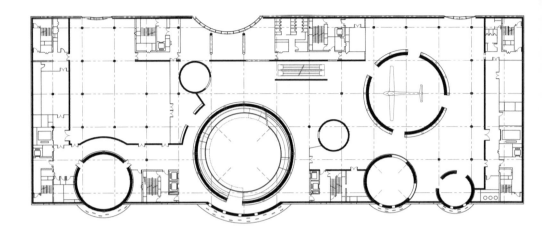
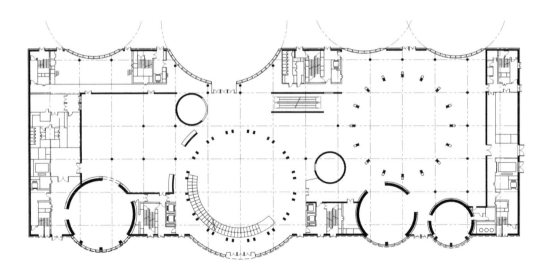

Main plan levels (upper level and ground level)

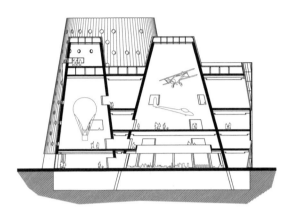

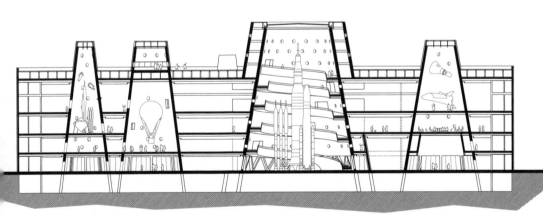

Main sections (transverse and longitudinal sections)

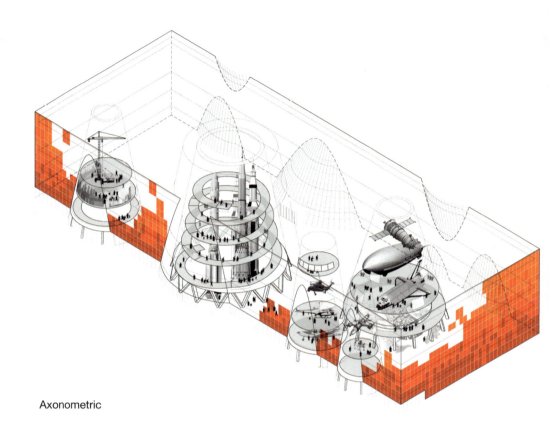

Axonometric

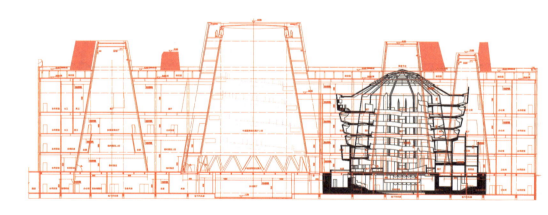

Section showing the Guggenheim Museum (New York) at the same scale

TIANJIN
307

Tests for the building envelope

PANELS ARE SPECIFIC TO EACH CONE - cones 01-02-03-04 have no similar panels

* panels are trapeze-shaped
* different colors correspond to same panel type (<u>per cone</u>)
* there is a 50mm gap between roof surface and the first roof panel

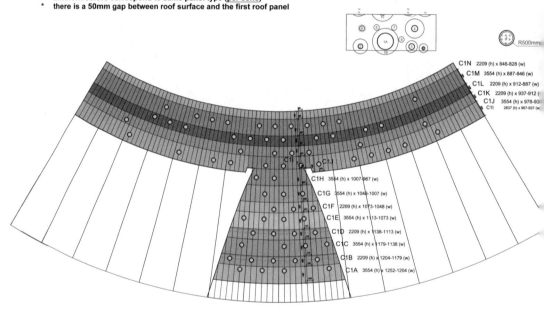

C1N	2209 (h) x 846-828 (w)
C1M	3554 (h) x 887-846 (w)
C1L	2209 (h) x 912-887 (w)
C1K	2209 (h) x 937-912 (w)
C1J	3554 (h) x 978-937
C1I	2637 (h) x 967-937 (w)
C1H	3554 (h) x 1007-967 (w)
C1G	3554 (h) x 1048-1007 (w)
C1F	2209 (h) x 1073-1048 (w)
C1E	3554 (h) x 1113-1073 (w)
C1D	2209 (h) x 1138-1113 (w)
C1C	3554 (h) x 1179-1138 (w)
C1B	2209 (h) x 1204-1179 (w)
C1A	3554 (h) x 1252-1204 (w)

R500mm

Panel principles and porthole locations for the building envelope

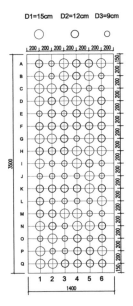
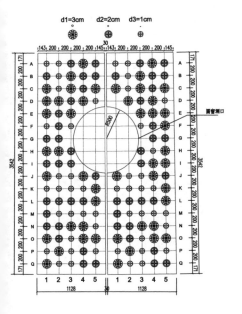
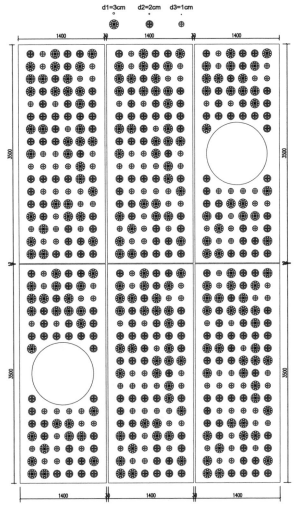

Perforations in the envelope panels allow air to circulate.

A small cone under construction

Steel structure for the main cone

Aerial photograph (view from the park)

A small cone before exhibitions are installed: study (left page) and realization (right page).

Geneva, Caran d'Ache Headquarters, 2021

Colored Pencil Allusions

A rigorous programmatic organization is complemented by a colorful envelope alluding to the identity of a major manufacturer of colored pencils.

GENEVA
327

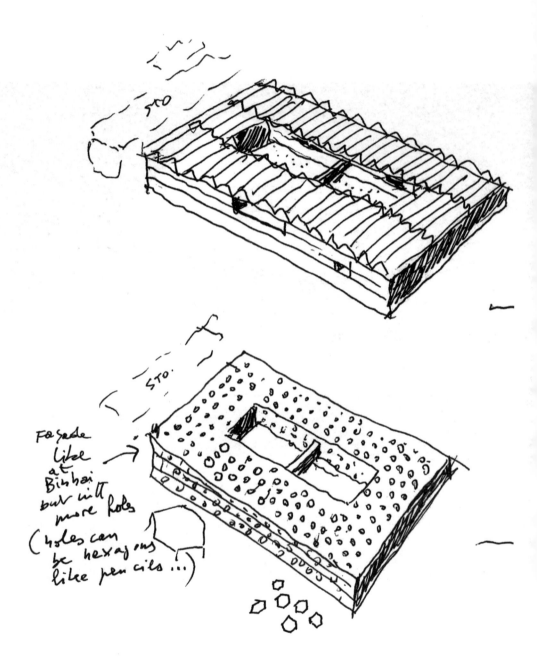

A leader in the manufacturing of color pencils, Caran d'Ache will be one of the first residents of a new district located in the outskirts of Geneva. The intent is to build a factory with excellent working conditions that also reflects the joyful image of the Caran d'Ache brand. The program of the building is neither complicated nor simple, due to the complex planning regulations of the site. This project's goal is to reinstate the dimension of pleasure through architecture.

Simultaneously minimalist and colorful, the factory is organized in three separate parts. The first is for production—the factory itself. A rectangular loop on two levels, suspended above ground in Phase I, provides both flexibility and natural light. Administration is located on the roof and easily accessible, encouraging interaction between "blue-collar" and "white-collar" workers. The second part is product arrival, departure, and storage, located at the northern entrance to the site. The third, a hexagonal volume, provides space for the Visitors Center, a place for learning about the history of Caran d'Ache and how its pencils are made. Each part has its own constructive and functional identity but belongs to the same family. The circulation is rational but encourages convivial encounters.

Three specific architectural concepts are proposed and combined:

What it does
The phasing constraints of the program are turned into an advantage: The suspended production volume allows the ground floor, which contains the patio and part of the car park, to remain unencumbered in Phase I. The construction of the second phase at this location does not affect the production facilities located above. This elegant phasing solution makes it possible to keep a large part of the site planted like a garden, while meeting the density requirements of local Eco Parc regulations.

What it looks like
The use of color is fundamental because Caran d'Ache's whole history celebrates the pleasure of color and creation. The color also opposes the frequently puritanical and historically color-averse nature of Swiss architecture. Finally, we feel that architecture should stimulate the pleasure of the senses. The building envelope is made of transparent glazing or opaque insulation, while the structure for Phase II is wood, which is five times lighter than concrete.

A signal for the pleasure of workers and visitors alike
The Visitors Center is made entirely of wood with a colored glass envelope. The Visitors Center is arranged on three main levels with a spectacular staircase-ramp and a panoramic lift. Its configuration is a hexagon, referring to the Caran d'Ache pencil, with a superimposed Swiss cross.

GENEVA
331

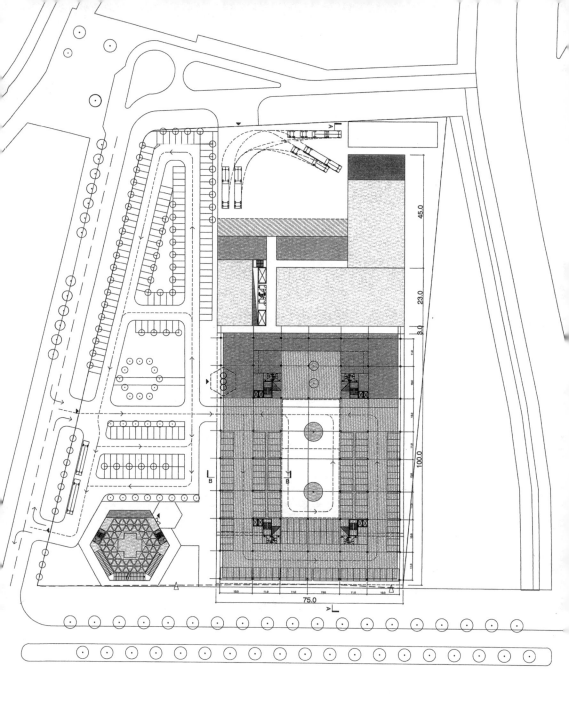

Ground floor plan, typical upper floor plan, and section

GENEVA
333

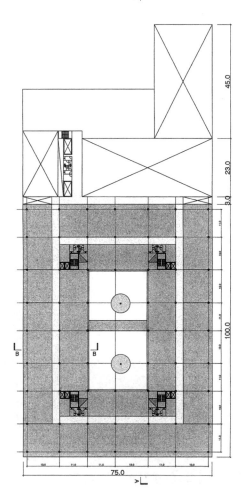

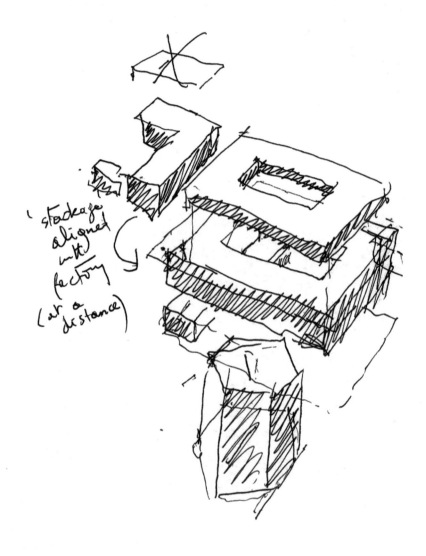

Exploded axonometric diagram

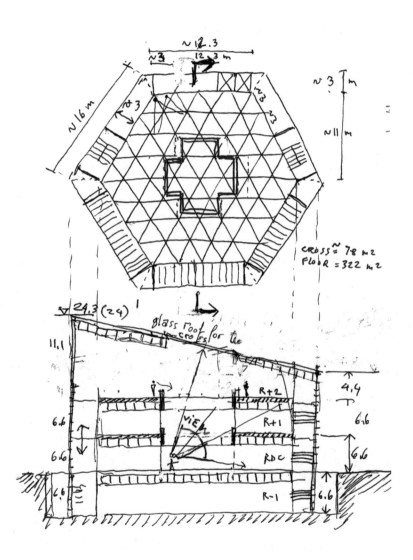

Visitors Center diagram

Grottammare,
A.N.I.M.A. Cultural Center, 2012–14

Courts and Facades

For an architect who often resists the idea of designing facades by rejecting their conventional clichés, the question becomes: How do you address such a "fundamental" architectural element?

THE SITE

THE URBAN AND HISTORICAL CONTEXT

Smaller volumes on a solid structure

Solid wall base made of small bricks

Multileveled circulation

Strong inside-outside transitions

Grottammare is located on the Adriatic Sea. This small Italian town and its nearby communities, together with a local foundation, decided to create a special facility, A.N.I.M.A., with a 1,500-seat multi-purpose auditorium (the Main Room), combined with a 250- to 400-seat meeting room, and educational, exhibition, and recreation spaces. Its location close by the sea and direct connection to a major highway suggested that A.N.I.M.A.—which stands for Art, Nature, Ideas, Music, Action—would become a major regional activator.

What it does
Rather than resorting to convoluted volumes to arrive at the predictable visual extravagance, this project's intent is to invent an architectural generator that stimulates culture and creativity for and in the region.

Interior organization of the spaces (the concept of the *cortile*) was socially and culturally important, but the outside image was equally significant. A simple square plan was devised with four equivalent but different facades and a fifth facade for the roof, each with its own vocabulary, so as to take into consideration sun protection, natural lighting, and ventilation while projecting a strong visual identity to the outside world.

The scheme's interior is like a small ideal city, with four internal courts and a Main Room, while the exterior explores contemporary sensibilities and culture. A.N.I.M.A. is an intellectual and social project rather than a formal one. It answers the following question: How can a building be simultaneously abstract and figurative, simple but not simplistic, economical without being cheap, while conveying a strong local identity and a global commitment?

What it looks like
Could a facade be designed without resorting to formal composition? Could it be neither abstract nor figurative, but almost "formless"? Raising these questions was both economic and cultural: At a time of economic crisis, indulging in formal geometries made from complex, voluminous curves did not seem a responsible option. The time of "Iconism" seemed finished, together with arbitrary sculptural shapes often made without consideration for context, content, or budget.

Similarly, the architectural conversation that emphasized the importance of an "autonomous" architecture, rooted in the constants of history, seemed obsolete in the face of dialogues with other disciplines, from literature to music to science. The work of Italian artists, including Vedova, Burri, Manzoni, Fontana, and even Fazzini, an artist born and active in Grottammare, was informative regarding specifically local conditions that were different from those in Shanghai, Dubai, or Mumbai.

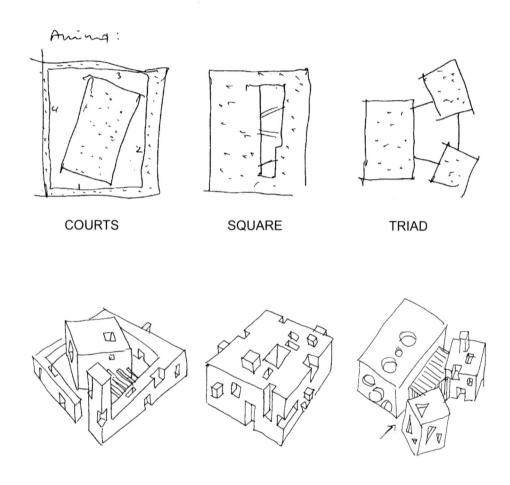

Several design concepts are developed concurrently, ultimately resulting in a combination of the "courts" and "square" strategies.

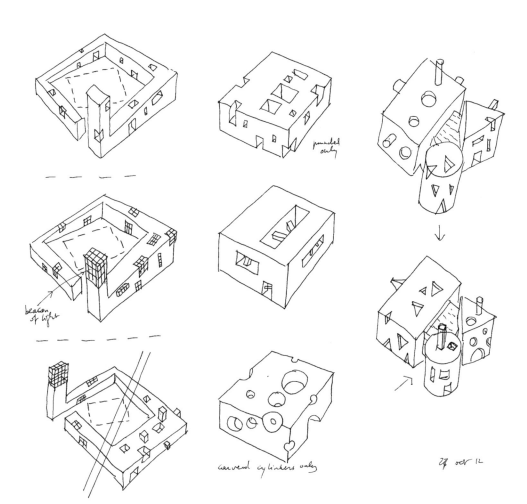

Iterative investigation as method:

Never start with a single idea. Work through a number of alternatives that can be called options, versions, or variants. They are often conceptually different, meaning that each will generate buildings which, in turn, will generate different uses and effects. These alternatives are often of equal value. However, architecture isn't about what things look like, it's about what they do. The individual alternatives each generate different events or effects.

1. COURTS

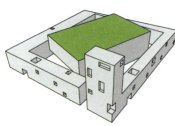
AERIAL VIEW FROM THE SOUTHEAST

GROUND VIEW FROM THE SOUTHEAST

2. SQUARE

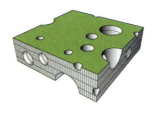

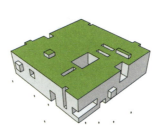

3. TRIAD

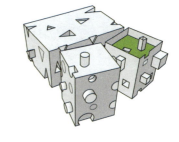

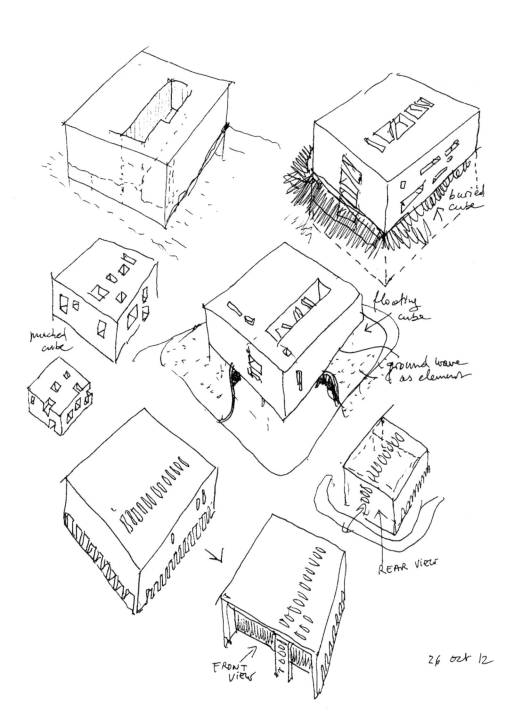

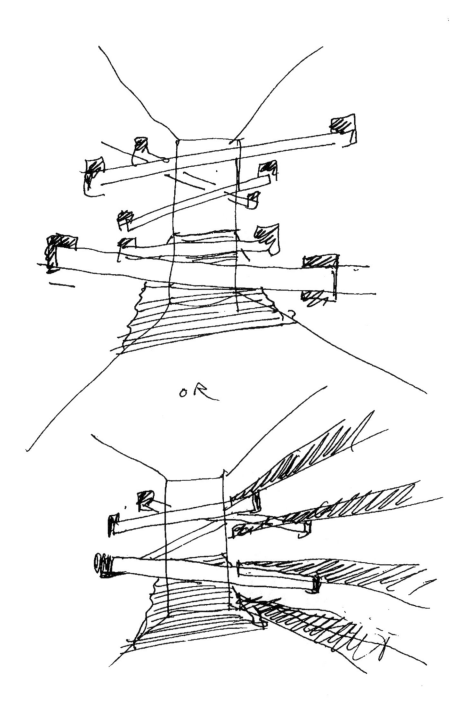

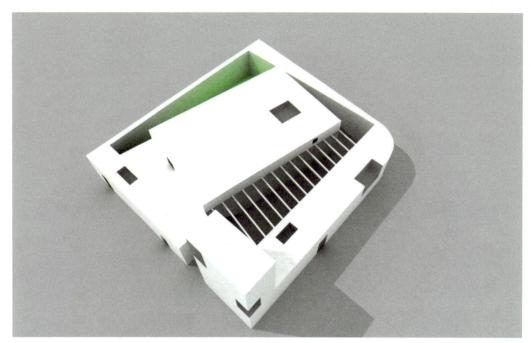

Courts: Views from southeast

GROTTAMMARE

351

Triad: Views from southeast

23 Dec 12
2

Main Room

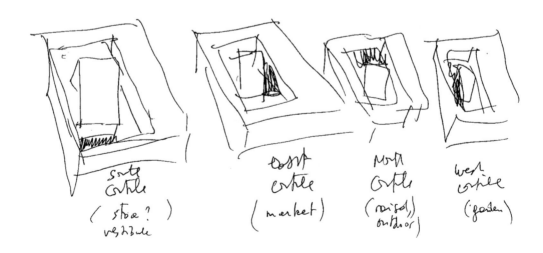

South Cortile (stoa?) vestibule

East Cortile (market)

North Cortile (raised, outdoor)

West Cortile (garden)

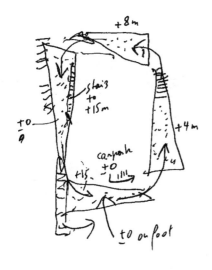

A.N.I.M.A.'s multiple *cortili* are experienced as a sequence or loop. The project is like a hill city, where each *cortile* is similar to a small town square located on a different level.

Arriving at final concepts

A.N.I.M.A. is designed around two ideas or concepts.

First, the building interior is to be read as a small town that generates unexpected events through its multiple plazas or *cortili*. Second, the building exterior is intended to be simple, with four vertical perimeter walls or *facciate* that investigate the concept of the facade rather than our more customary concept of the envelope.

On the inside, the plan is like an ideal square (72 by 72 meters) with the Main Room in the middle. Rotating the Main Room slightly generates a sequence of four trapezoidal courts that are places of social encounter and gathering. On the outside, the four facades of this ideal square are firmly anchored, with openings carved into each wall according to its orientation and use. At once abstract and figurative, A.N.I.M.A avoids conventional facade composition while nevertheless attaining a strong visual presence.

Together, the concepts of *cortile* (interior) and *facciata* (exterior) result in a building that is simultaneously simple and striking. The building pays homage to major contributions from Italian culture, in particular (on the front facade) to the local artist Pericle Fazzini.

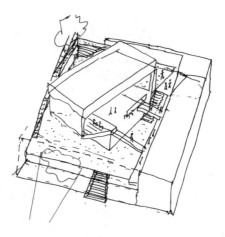

5 Jan 13

ELEVATIONS ANIMA
"Screen", "pattern" or "vernacular"?

"Screen": all voids are the same size & shape only the quantity of voids changes.
i.e. (line-grid)

"Pattern": all voids are the same shape but size may change gradually ("grasshopper")
(point-grid)

"Vernacular": all voids are different sizes and are located functionally, subjectively and at random.

+ "Fazzini" south screen elevation- regarding to local sculpture artist.

All the above is OK
Please test further.

Cortile: The building's interior concept

Generally, a *cortile* is an internal courtyard surrounded by an arcade, covered passageway, or terraces. This typology is associated with the Italian Renaissance, where it was developed at multiple scales.

For the A.N.I.M.A. project, the *cortile* concept transforms the building into an urban promenade or a compact city. As one walks from one town square to another, each courtyard reveals its own character.

All the *cortili* open onto the Main Room. The Main Room is a large, tall indoor space that can be used for many different types of activities—performances, fairs, etc. The first *cortile* is inside the building perimeter but acts as an exterior vestibule for the whole building. In the second *cortile* are meeting rooms and scientific spaces (i.e. cultural laboratories) spread across both the ground floor and the upper level. On the north side, behind the Main Room and resting on top of support spaces, the third *cortile* can host a variety of uses. As one continues around the Main Room, one climbs down to the fourth court or west *cortile*. Around it is a three-meter-high wall that protects visitors from the nearby highway. The four built sides of the A.N.I.M.A. Center act as a protective frame and a buffer between the adjacent areas and the Main Room.

South Cortile
Expo

East Cortile
Garden

North Cortile
Terrace

West Cortile
Market

Facciata: The building's exterior concept

Facades are a relatively recent Western invention. For thousands of years, the appearance of buildings' outer walls was generally dictated by the limitations of stone, brick, or wood construction. By separating the building's outer bearing wall from an applied surface treatment, the Renaissance allowed the development of formal composition and classical orders. In the 20th century, modern construction techniques and major cultural changes led to an abstract, modernist sensibility, while keeping the notions of formal composition inherited from the Renaissance. A particular postmodern reaction to modernist principles favored a return to premodern historicist connotations, as in the *Strada Novissima* exhibition at the 1980 Venice Biennale. However, postmodernism was short-lived, as many designers started replacing formal facades with envelopes, abandoning the distinction between vertical wall and horizontal roof.

From the outset, Bernard Tschumi Architects has investigated envelope materials that differ depending on the concept and context. For A.N.I.M.A., the intent was to address, once again, the question of the facade as a simple vertical plane, without the compositional techniques inherited over centuries.

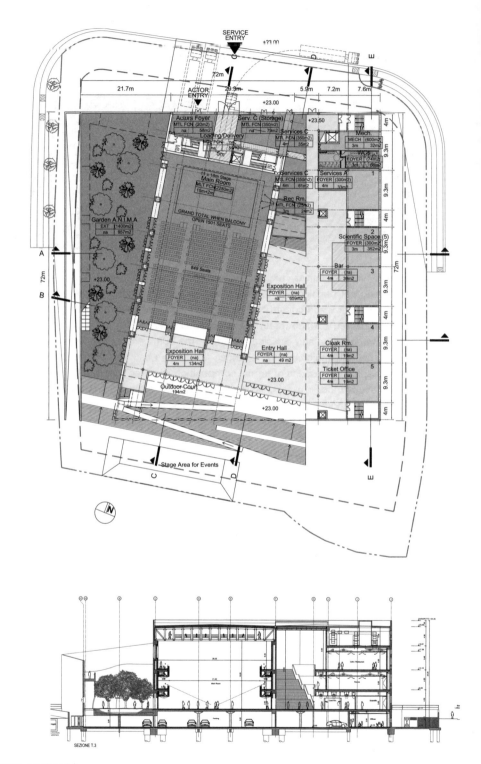

Transverse section AA

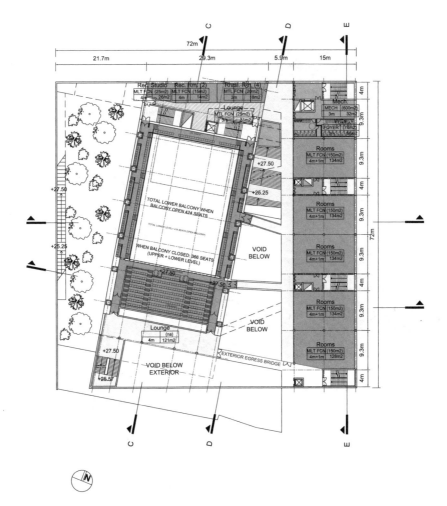

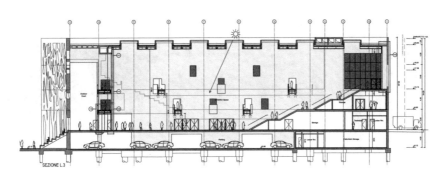

Section DD through the main courtyard

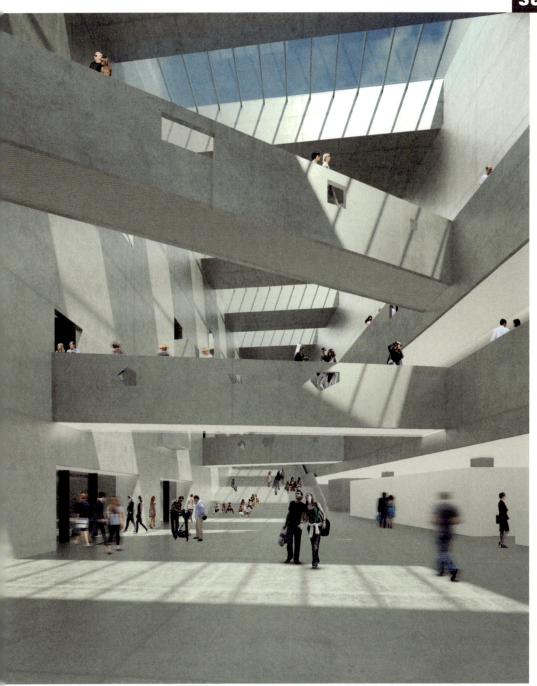

Views through the main courtyard

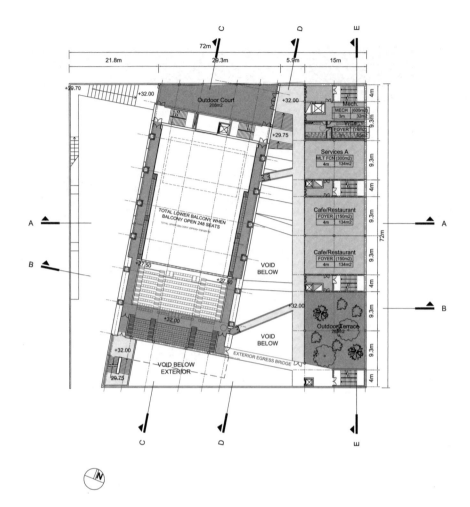

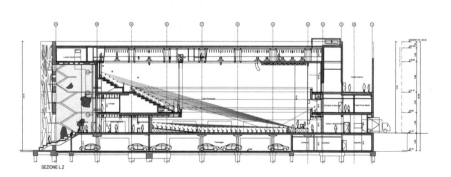

Longitudinal section CC through the Main Room

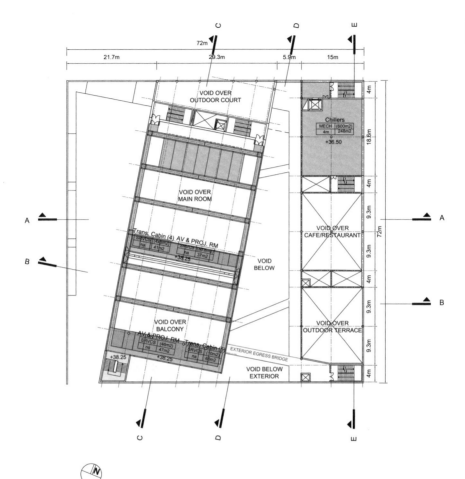

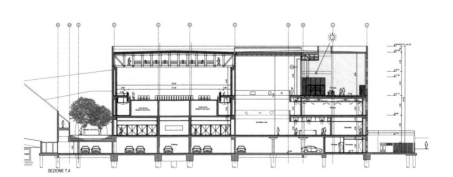

Transverse section BB through the balcony and main courtyard

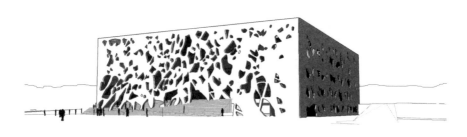

Facade studies: Each of the four sides is intended to be different from the others.

Facades=envelopes?

Strategies for the different facades: multiple configurations of solids and voids

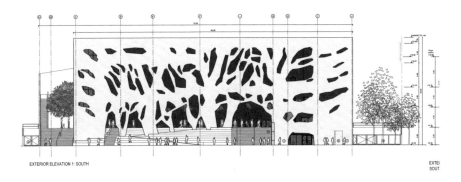

EXTERIOR ELEVATION 1: SOUTH

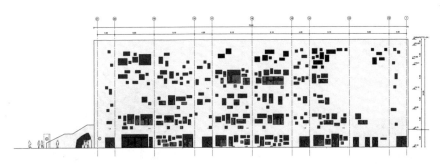

EXTERIOR ELEVATION 2: EAST

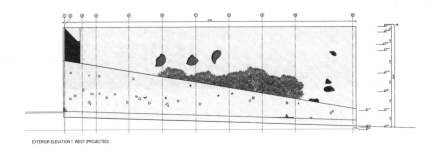

EXTERIOR ELEVATION 1: WEST (PROJECTED)

Four different *facciate* constitute the four exterior main walls of A.N.I.M.A., all using one primary material: white-colored concrete (poured in place, pre-cast, and/or moldable high-performance). Recessed openings accommodate entrances and windows.

East and north elevations

South and east elevations

Budapest

Paris-Saclay

XIANGMIHU AREA, SHENZHEN (2018)

100KM2 CITY, BEIJING (2018)

MUSEUM OF ETHNOGRAPHY, BUDAPEST (2016)

BIOLOGY-PHARMACY-CHEMISTRY CENTER, PARIS-SACLAY (2015-22)

D. Typological Urbanisms

An urbanist poetics? No matter their size, and for better or worse, most buildings perform critical roles in the overall fabric of cities. When it comes to large projects, splitting a singular scheme into a series of discrete but related parts generates an urban environment that may be more attuned to the specifics of the context.

Shenzhen, Xiangmihu Area, 2018

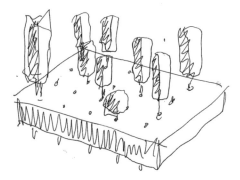

Singular Towers on Hanging Gardens

A master plan for a new financial district (4.9 square kilometers or 1.9 square miles) combines three urban archetypes: the tower, the garden, and the plinth.

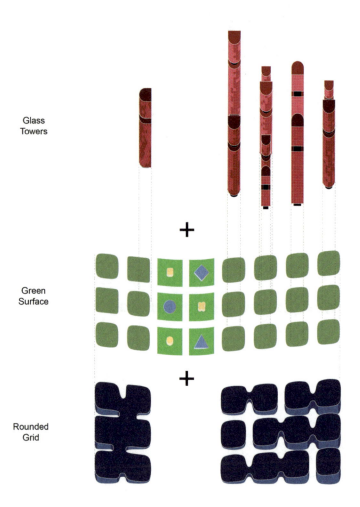

SHENZHEN
379

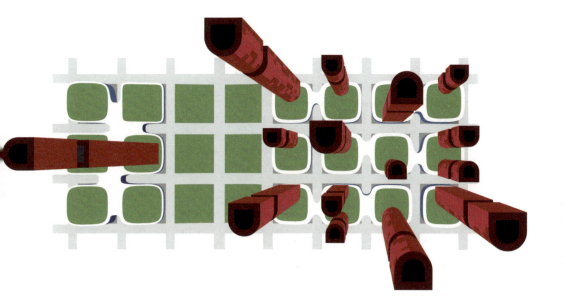

A rigorously organized set of towers atop a large, sloped podium of landscaped gardens

Architectural Urbanism

Embedded in a regular street grid, the project for Shenzhen's Xiangmihu district aims to introduce coherence and green space in a new neighborhood while tying together a diverse context. The collection of high-rise offices acts as a counterpoint to a conference and exhibition center as well as cultural and commercial programs located in the planted base or podium below.

The Base:
The Grid is like a game or strategy. The Grid can evolve according to varying programmatic needs or density requirements and is readily expandable. Its 120-meter by 120-meter size, similar to the famous urban grid in Barcelona, balances walkability with car access and provides appropriately sized blocks to support high-density towers. The Grid is not simply an abstract organizing system: It also physically materializes the existence of streets and street life. Gridded facades can accommodate advertisements and media screens to generate a dynamic 21st-century streetscape.

The Middle:
The podium roofs slope to create a green valley—a distinct identity for Shenzhen. Oblique gardens provide a superimposed city landscape that integrates natural elements in order to facilitate sustainable urban strategies. Each roof is a giant green park located over densely built urban programs. The podiums respond to the requirements of commercial offices and cultural facilities as well as the need for nature and its benefits in terms of social, recreational, and climate considerations.

The Top:
A special skyline has been conceived so as to become identifiable as one of Shenzhen's most unusual districts. This is not to say that the dimensions and form of these towers cannot change—in fact, quite the contrary. The tower and upper components of the towers are intended to be adaptable to programmatic requirements, market considerations, or visual criteria. The only stipulation is the recessed intermediate platform ("skydeck") between the lower and upper parts of each tower. The skydecks offer outdoor social spaces that are open to all occupants of a given tower.

Preliminary concept diagrams

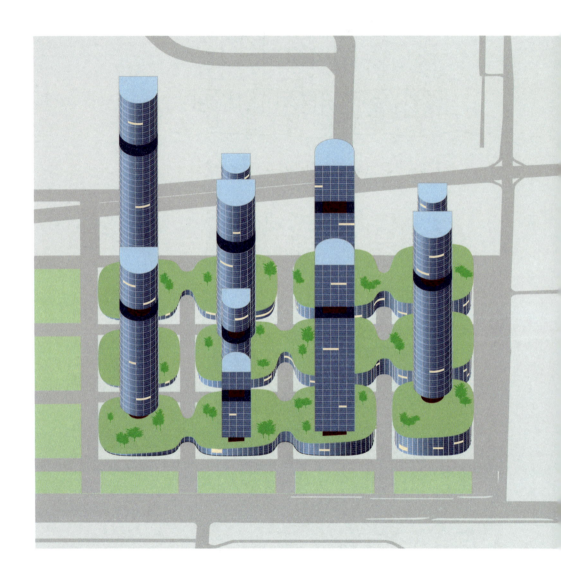

High-rise offices hovering over cultural and commercial programs below

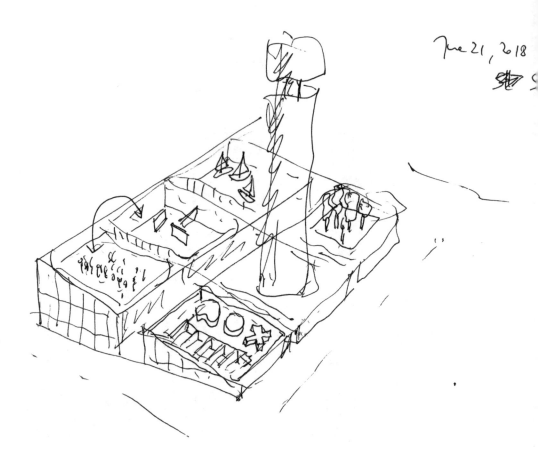

Preliminary concept diagrams

towers on Hanging Gardens

Beijing, 100KM2 City, 2018

BEIJING

389

Cluster Grid

How do you design a type of city aimed at fostering multiple advanced scientific and technological developments while simultaneously accounting for existing historical, topographical, and sociological conditions?

Islands vs. Grids

Historically, cities have taken a number of configurations. Two were often considered antithetical—the Grid and the Cluster (or "Islands"). Both configurations had drawbacks, including the lack of identity for one and the lack of connectivity for the other. Why not combine both to create a research community for the future? In dialogue with the grid, every island community can invent its own logic, nurturing a culture of differences. Each configuration can accommodate nature as well as architecture, the old or existing as well as the new and emerging, but in its own way.

Grid Network

100KM2 City begins with a one-by-one kilometer grid (approximately two-thirds of a mile squared), an abstract network of flows that is partly adjusted to the existing topography and infrastructure of the overall area. This new grid-road network is then adapted further and enlarged to fit the needs of the future science city.

Program-Islands

Each of the approximately one-by-one kilometer squares corresponds to a 15-minute walk. Urban islands are then inserted into each square, occasionally but rarely overlapping another square. Each island has a different shape or configuration. Each island is surrounded by its own local ring road, independent from the main grid roads.

BEIJING
391

Collage of urban islands, infrastructure, and landscape

Concept
Each urban island in 100KM2 City is surrounded by a local ring road and a green belt. Each island has its own character and individual density. The green belt is located between the local ring road and the main city grid.

There are five different types of "islands":
- 45-meter-tall islands (10-12 floors)
- 30-meter-tall islands (6-8 floors)
- 15-meter-tall islands (3-4 floors)
- Mixed-height islands (15-45 meters tall)
- Historical village islands (1-2 floors)

The above typologies are never mixed within the same island. However, there are no restrictions in planning islands, except that individual buildings cannot be closer to each other than the building's height. This low density means that on a 45-meter-tall island, a 45-meter-tall building must be 45 meters away from adjacent buildings. Similarly, on a 15-meter-tall island, a building 15 meters tall must be spaced 15 meters away from the building next to it.

Islands can be specialized: one for research, another for sport. However, a few islands may mix different types of activities. (See "Experimental Islands.")

Program
Each urban island has its own specific character, ready to incorporate an array of activities, from rigorous scientific research to vibrant centers of commerce and education to restorative neighborhoods for residential life.

There are five different types of islands, organized according to function: scientific research islands, mixed-use islands, residential islands, education islands, and green parkland islands. With their own density, characteristics, and functional logic according to existing site conditions, programmatic requirements, and phasing, the islands can adapt to the master plan "game." For example, with a unique and specific architectural language, the science-city research islands lend a distinctive and easily identifiable presence to the city.

Environmental Infrastructure
A global approach to the water cycle, rainwater collection and storage, clean solar- and wind-power generation, and intelligent municipal systems ensure a sustainable future. Green building technology with net-zero consumption serves as the baseline for the architecture of 100KM2 City.

Experimental Islands
A few islands are intentionally mixed both programmatically and socially, while rigorously maintaining their typological integrity.

BEIJING
393

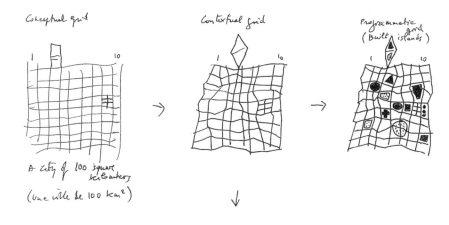

Conceptual grid

A city of 100 square kilometers
(One will be 100 km²)

Contextual grid

Programmatic grid
(Built islands)

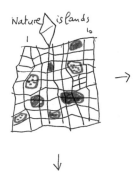

Nature islands

Buildings are buildings (Building islands)
Nature is nature. (Nature islands)
They are generally on separate blocks.

EACH ISLAND OF CONSTRUCTION CONNECTS TO AN ISLAND OF GREEN

BSC
CONTEXTUAL GRID
(FINE GRAIN)

B. NORD-SOUTH = Avenues
   EAST-WEST = STREETS

BT 1/1/2018

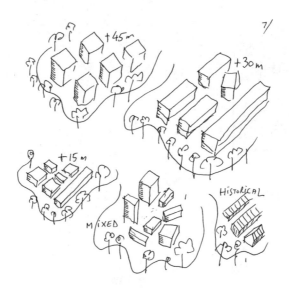

Islands with different characteristics and regulations

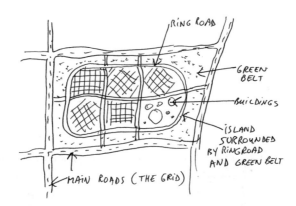

A local ring road and green belt surround each island within the grid.

GRID NETWORK   PROGRAM-ISLANDS

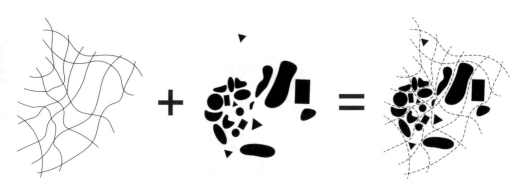

Aerial view

Budapest, Museum of Ethnography, 2016

With Michel Desvigne Paysagiste

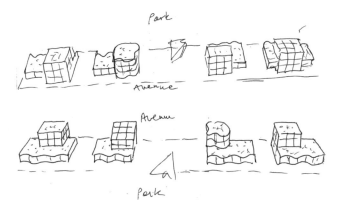

Architectural Landscape

Rather than designing a museum monolith located between and separating an avenue and a park, the proposal articulates the museum into several singular parts so they become a permeable filter and complementary component of nature.

View from the avenue

BUDAPEST
403

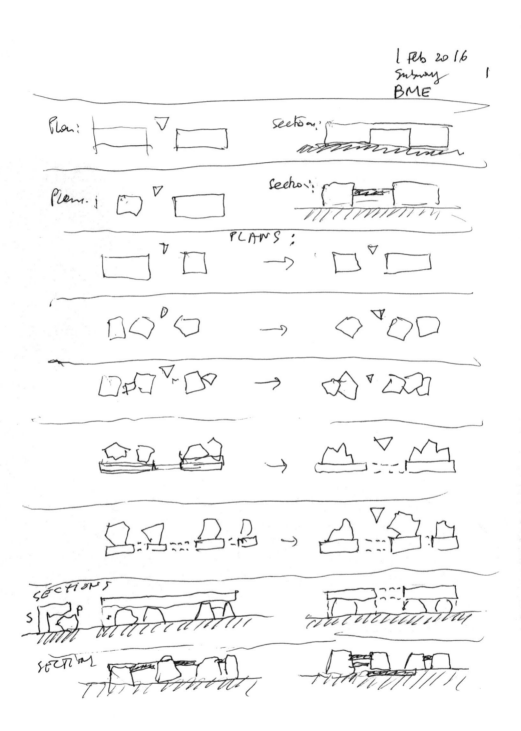

Early massing strategies: fragmenting the program into a series of related objects

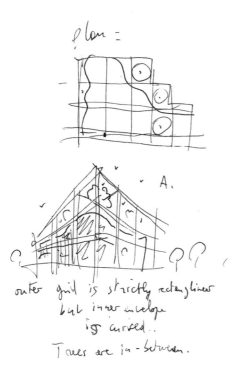
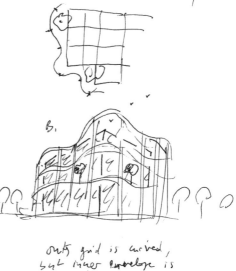
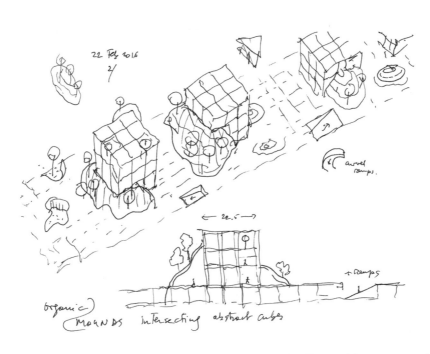

Pavilions: grid vs. nature options

EXISTING CONDITION

RECONFIGURATION OF THE PARK'S FRINGE

ARTICULATION BETWEEN THE CITY AND THE PARK

City vs. Park

The restoration and protection of an important historical park are the starting points for the design proposal for the Museum of Ethnography in Budapest. The museum site is located at the edge of a park created specifically for public use and enjoyment.

The first move was to examine the condition of the park along its longest edge, a major city avenue. To replace the jagged appearance of the existing car park, 1,000 new trees will be planted as a sequence of orchards along the 1,000-meter-long stretch of the park edge. The new museum is intended to appear as if it had emerged from the trees—park, orchard, and museum fuse into a single entity.

The next move ensures that the new museum building does not act as a large object obstructing the park view. Instead of building a single, oversized volume, the mass of the program is divided into four pavilions, leaving large openings between them that offer routes and perspectives along the avenue into the park. The underground connection between the pavilions provides spectacular open storage. The primary exhibition space, which requires no daylight, is nestled just below ground level. Children's spaces and other activities are located in the pavilions that rise up from the orchards along the avenue.

Architecturally, the four pavilions provide an interactive transition between the natural environment of the park and the built environment of the city. The pavilions' curvilinear volumes showcase and expand on the cultural heritage of Budapest.

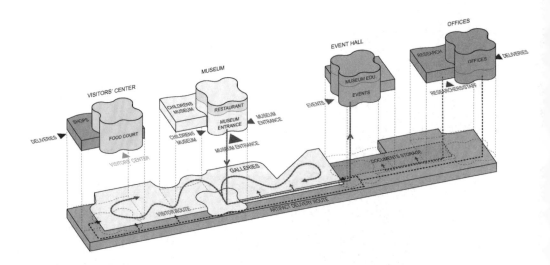

PLANTING PRINCIPLES

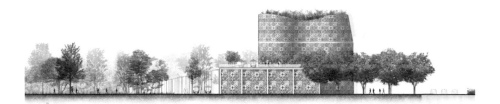

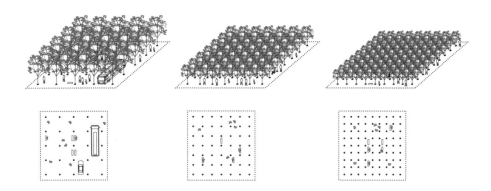

Planting sequences and grids: an orchard of varied ambiances

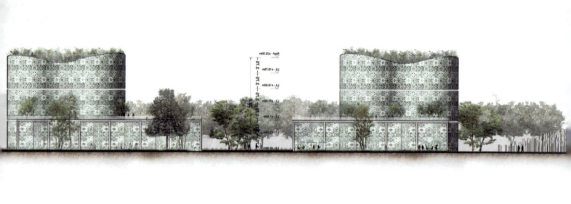

25m HEIGHT LIMIT

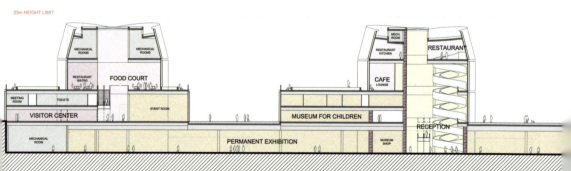

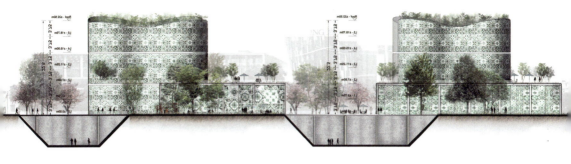

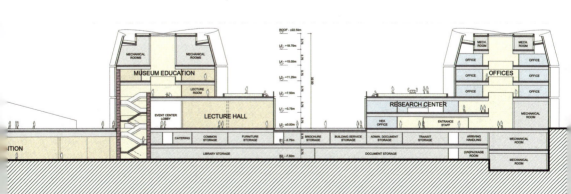

| FIRST PAVILION: VISITORS' CENTER | SECOND PAVILION: ENTRANCE & CHILDREN | THIRD PAVILION: EVENTS & EDUCATION | FOURTH PAVILION: OFFICES & RESEARCH |

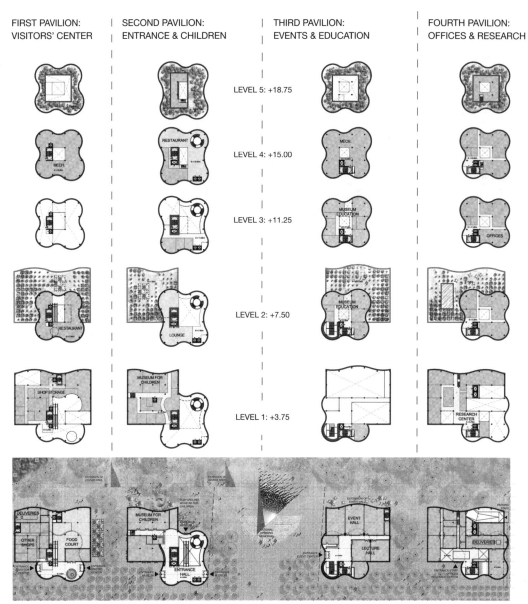

LEVEL 5: +18.75
LEVEL 4: +15.00
LEVEL 3: +11.25
LEVEL 2: +7.50
LEVEL 1: +3.75

LEVEL 0: +0.00

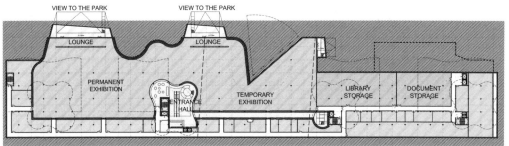

EXHIBITION LEVEL: -7.50

BUDAPEST

413

Top: The shaping of the pavilions echoes the pottery in the museum's collection.
Bottom: Traditional Hungarian patterns applied to fritted glass

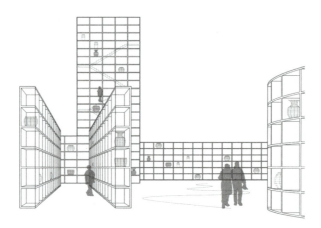
Underground visible storage and exhibition spaces connect the pavilions.

Descending from the park into the galleries

***Paris-Saclay,
Biology-Pharmacy-Chemistry Center,
2015–2022***

With Groupe-6 (laboratories and research spaces)

Interlinked Chain

Conceptual clarity is paramount, no matter the scale of a project. Two main concepts generated this scheme: an urban chain of six buildings connected by flying bridges and a spectacular entrance hall where the major movement vectors intersect.

A gigantic research and educational campus is rising on the immediate outskirts of Paris, concentrating many of the *Grandes Écoles* and national research institutions from the Paris region. A priority of the new Paris-Saclay University is to respond to emerging social challenges by encouraging innovation in the fields of energy and health. The development totals over 1.3 million square meters (approximately 14 million square feet). Within a rigid official master plan, numerous architectural interventions mark the area.

2.4 km (1.5 miles)

The Henri Moissan site (outlined in white), named after the Nobel Prize-winning French chemist and pharmacist, was inaugurated in 2023. Planning and construction of the Biology-Pharmacy-Chemistry Center on the Henri Moissan site were led by Bouygues Construction as part of a public-private partnership following a two-and-a-half-year international competition. Rather than designing a single set piece, the BPC Center is conceived as an urban typological sequence.

Travel distances and potential connections across the Henri Moissan site

The new BPC complex is one of the largest educational projects in France and is dedicated to critical scientific research and education. Located opposite the future Orsay-Gif Metro station on the Grand Paris Express, the building offers the outward face of the university and the gateway to its science and research facilities.

The complex is made up of three major components—two independent educational and research wings linked by a central atrium, the *"Coeur de Pôle"*—and includes research laboratories, classrooms and auditoria, social spaces, restaurants, offices, logistical areas, and underground parking. Bernard Tschumi *urbanistes* Architectes oversaw the overall urban and architectural coordination as well as the design of the *Coeur de Pôle* and teaching facilities; Groupe-6 Architectes was responsible for the research units with their laboratories and technical infrastructure. The site will accommodate more than 4,500 people, with 3,300 students and 1,300 teacher-researchers.

A generator of dynamic exchanges
The *Coeur de Pôle* (or "galleria") is the main entry point as well as a crossroads for the different users of the university. This dynamic generator of exchange is extended through the clarity of circulation and the distribution of spaces along the two continuous internal "streets," which encourages scientific collaboration by putting research and education in a direct relationship with each other and stimulating interdisciplinary overlaps among the otherwise separate disciplines of biology, chemistry, and pharmacy.

Design Concepts
The architectural and urban strategy, designed by Bernard Tschumi, consists of a chain of six buildings connected to each other by a continuous "street" and glazed pedestrian bridges. The complex spans the vehicular streets below while forming an elevated, nearly kilometer-long artery that serves as a common denominator for the whole. At its center, the atrium of the *Coeur de Pôle* links the two wings. To the west, along the *Rue de l'Enseignement*, are teaching facilities and the southern access to the site.

The research area, designed by Groupe-6, opens to the east of the atrium. The *Rue de la Recherche* hosts state-of-the-art laboratories, workspaces for researchers, and pleasant meeting places. The openings between floors visually connect the building and its four patios. The research street is accessible 24 hours a day, unlike conventional laboratories whose entry is strictly controlled.

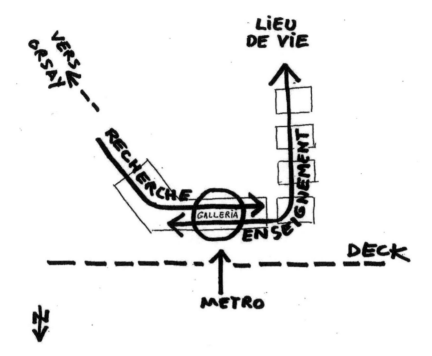

INTERACTION (CONCEPT)

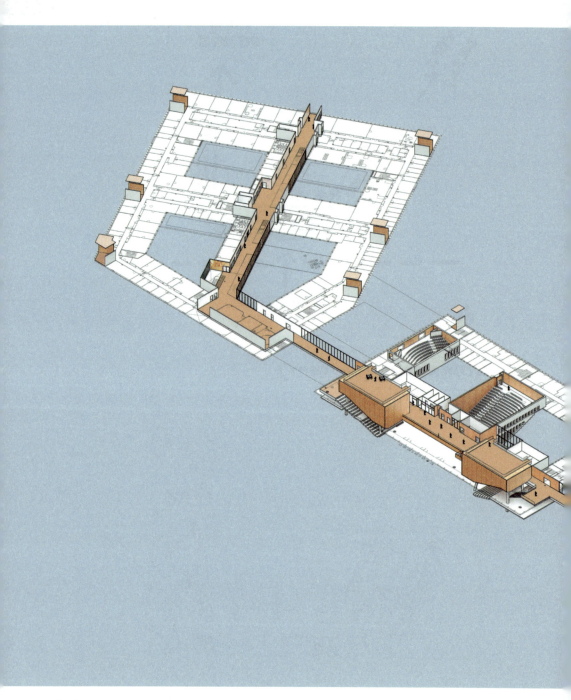
A primary movement vector links all parts of the scheme.

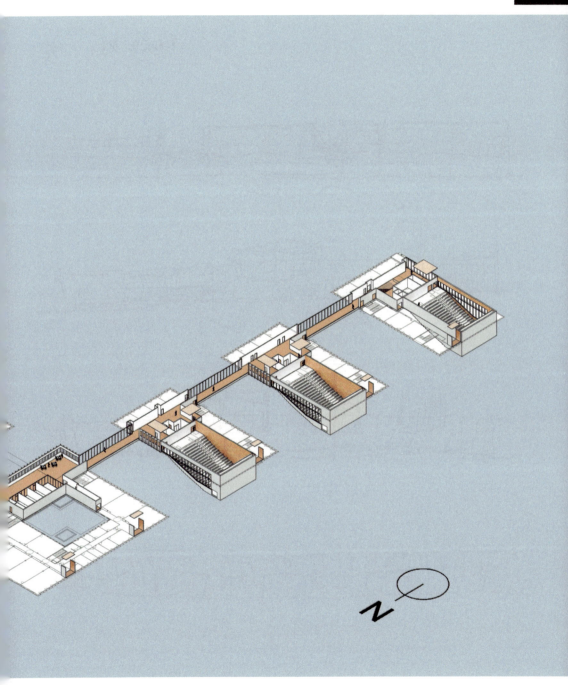

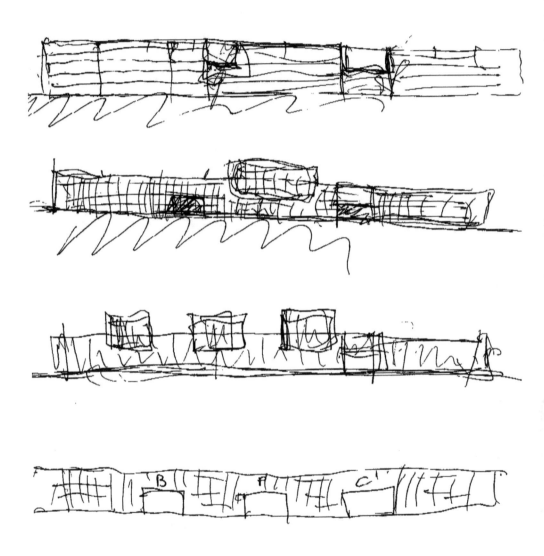

Early conceptual diagrams: The volumes are intuitive at first.

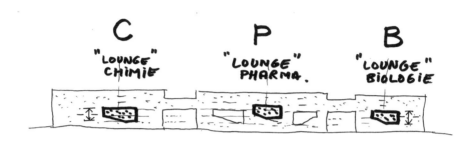

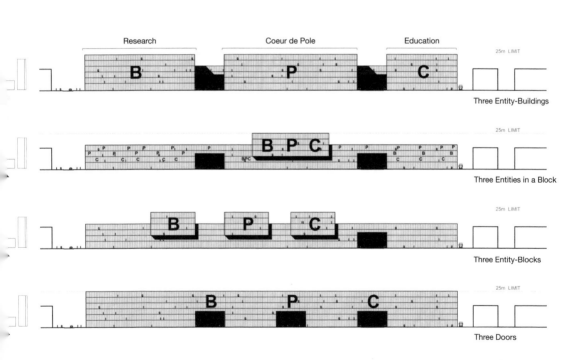

How to identify Biology (B), Pharmacy (P), and Chemistry (C) on the 300-meter-long (1,000-foot) facade?

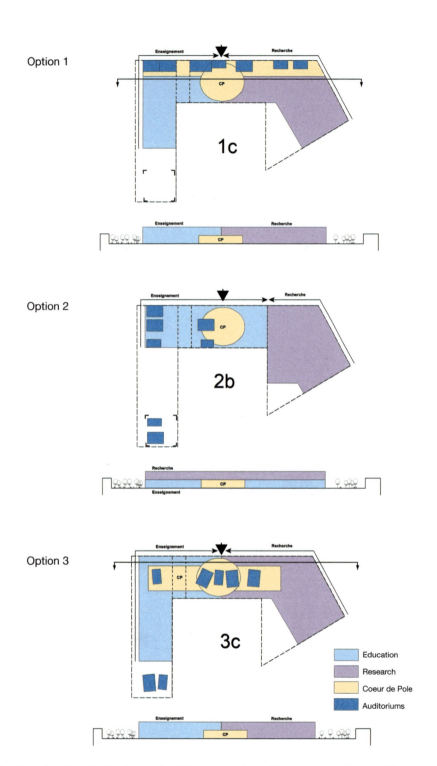

Families of options to distribute education, research, and interchange with amphitheaters

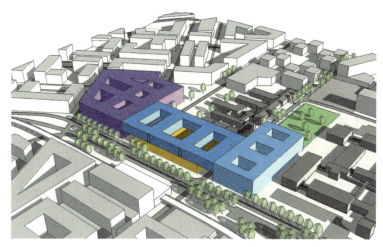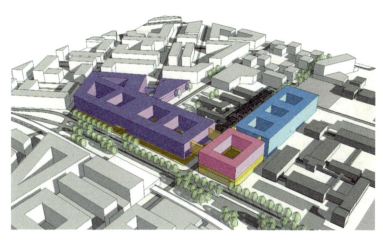

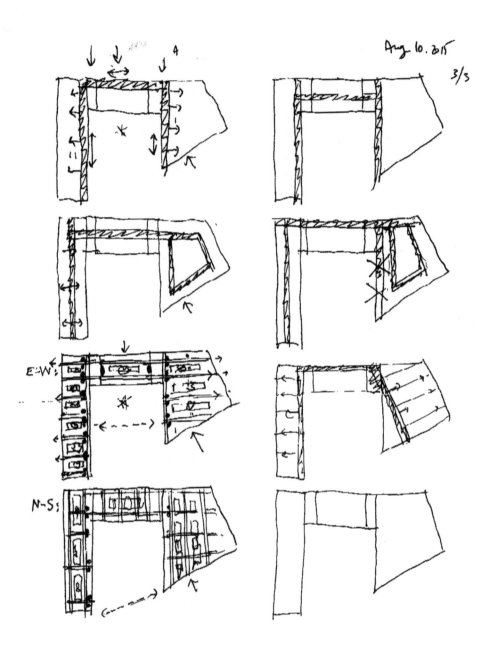

First movement vector diagrams

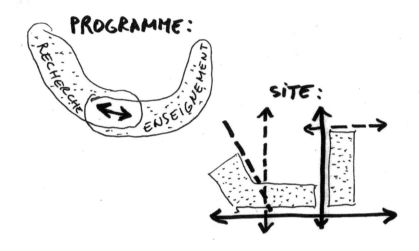

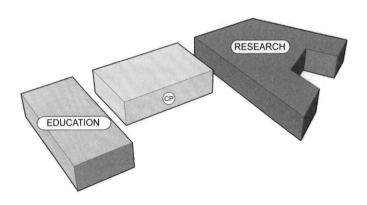

Overall distribution strategy: Education (west), *Coeur de Pôle* (center), Research (east)

Multiple options were studied urbanistically, functionally, and architecturally....

Option 1

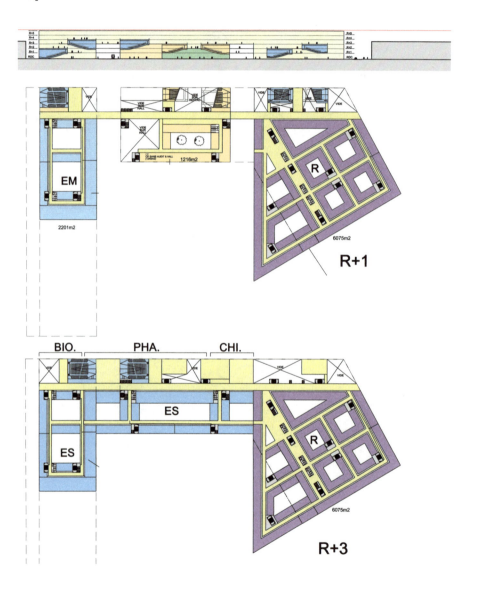

Option 1: The "Galleria" is a continuous glazed meeting space along the north elevation, forming a link between teaching labs and research labs.

Option 2

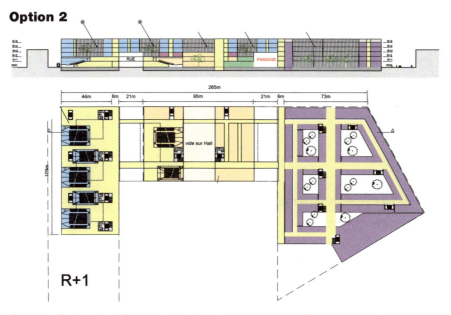

Option 2: The "Hyphen" organizes the site into three parts: Education (west), Research labs (east) with teaching labs, and central meeting space in between.

Option 3

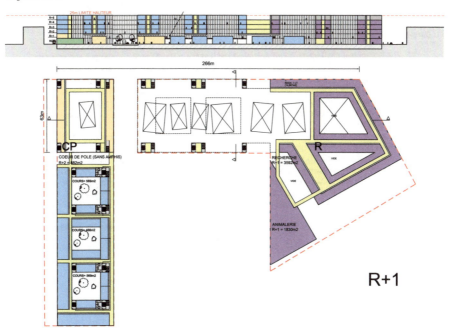

Option 3: The "Spine" locates all the amphitheaters along the north avenue, while the teaching labs are immediately adjacent to or above the research labs.

19 November 2015

Some thoughts about BPC
Let's discuss:

Saclay

What is this project about?

What does it do?

Does it really bring Research and Teaching together?

How does it make interaction visible?

How does interaction become a symbol of sorts?

What is the idea? The Galleria

Is it a programmatic idea or an urban idea?

How do we reconcile the urban and the programmatic?

But what is the concept?

Recherche/Enseignent Spécialisé = Continuities?

Urbanité?

i.e., retroactively, what have we been trying to say?

We appear to have been trying to say the following:

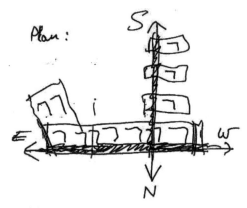

Our project reconciles the programmatic and the urban. It is made of two routes and a symbol:

1.) The first route is the Galleria. It runs East-West and is at the scale of the Saclay Campus and connects all major institutions along the Deck. For BPC, it acts as a common denominator and as the meeting ground for professionals from Biology, Pharmacy, and Chemistry involved in research and the students learning to do so. This major covered route connects all three and contains lounges, conference spaces, auditoriums, and teaching zones, chat areas, a small café, etc. We call it the Galleria along the Deck; it is the interaction vitrine of the project. It is also the vitrine of Paris Sud and it is distinctly urban in character.

2.) The second route is the Arcade. It runs North-South and is at the scale of the neighborhood. For BPC, it acts as a friendly connection between the Galleria with its Cœur de Vie and the neighborhood's Place du Lieu de Vie. It is composed of a chain (or sequence) of the "salles d'enseignement banalisés" and includes three large 400 seat amphitheaters. Some shops or services are along this route. It is in the middle of trees all visible from the classrooms and the auditoriums. It is distinctly "nature"-oriented.

3.) The symbol of the interaction between Research and Teaching is given by the Galleria and its suspended auditoriums and meeting spaces, overlooking the Deck.

Together the East West Galleria and the North South Arcade define the character of the new Université de Paris Sud:

"URBANITÉ ET CONTINUITÉ" INTERACTION

Early memo from Bernard Tschumi clarifying the concepts

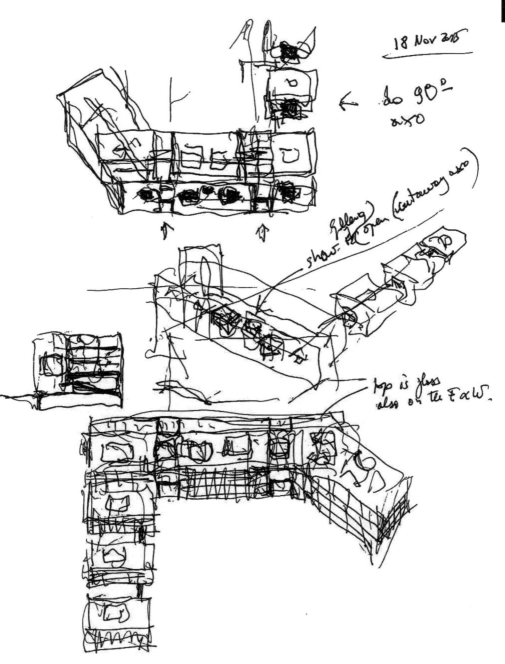

Concept 1: The Interlinked Chain

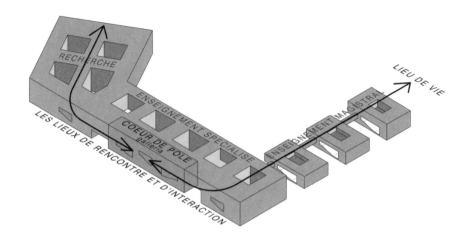

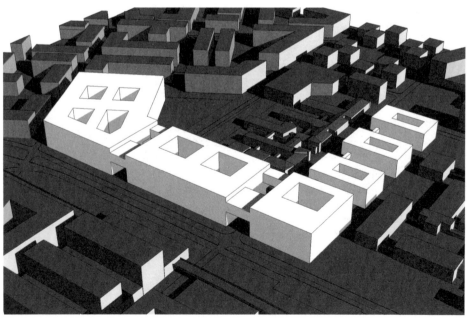

View from the North

Movement vectors and urban volumes

Concept 2: The Galleria

The central *Coeur de Pôle* is where circulation paths distribute and overlap users. Floating auditoria are legible from inside and outside.

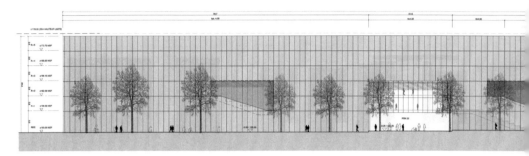

NORTH ELEVATION GALLERIA (DECK)

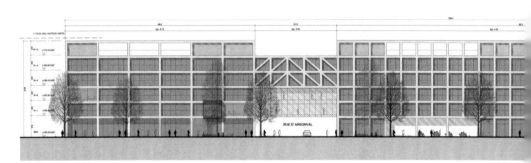

SOUTH ELEVATION

Two elevation types, simultaneously
The project's urban siting determined two principles for the facades: transparent glass for the north and opaque concrete for the south, east, and west.

PARIS-SACLAY
437

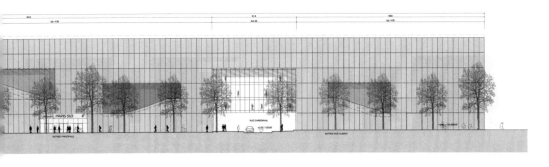

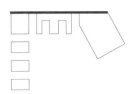

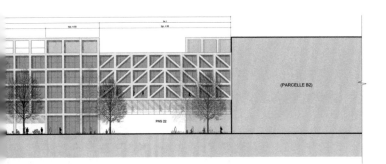

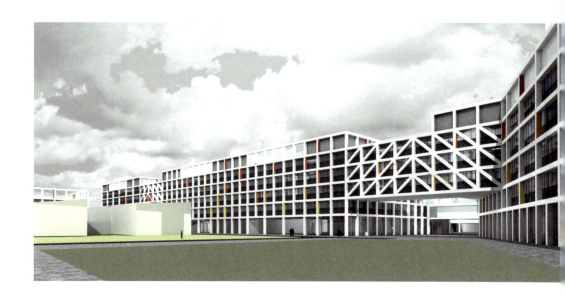

South elevation tests (precast concrete structure)

North elevation tests (glazed envelope)

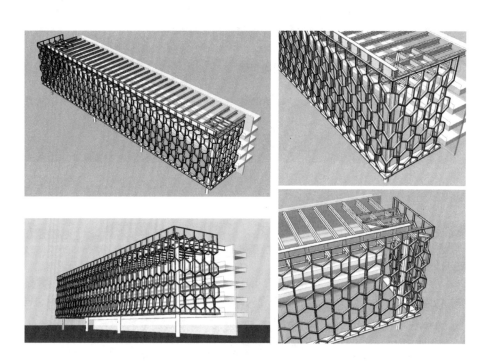

North elevation structural tests (hexagons rejected by the client)

PARIS-SACLAY
441

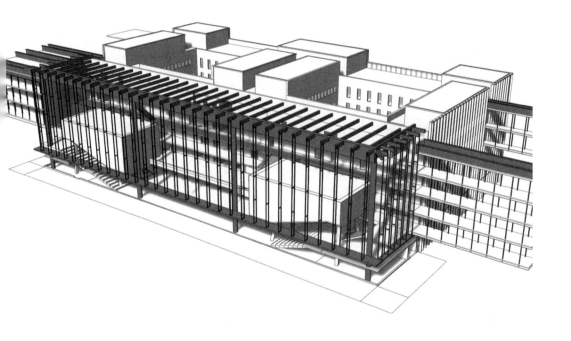

Perspective views (final competition stage)

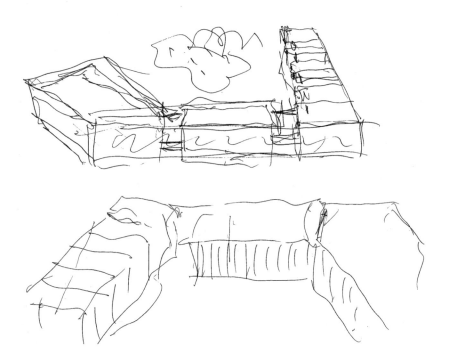

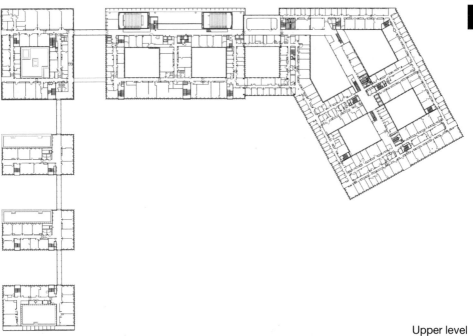

Upper level

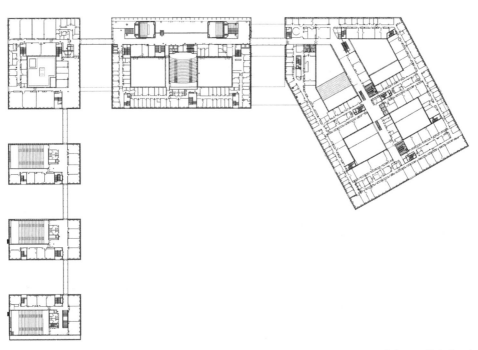

Intermediate level

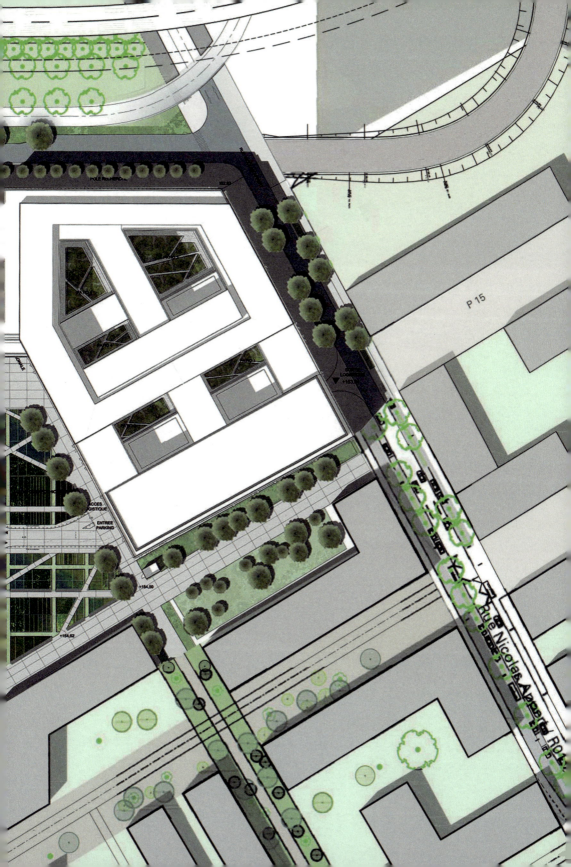

The *Coeur de Pôle* under construction

Suspended weights stretch the steel structure in order to install the glass panels.

South, west, and east elevations: precast structural concrete
White precast concrete ribs articulate the building's mass. The verticality of the structural concrete is echoed in the large glass surfaces of the windows punctuating the white facades and reflecting the surrounding landscape.

PARIS-SACLAY
461

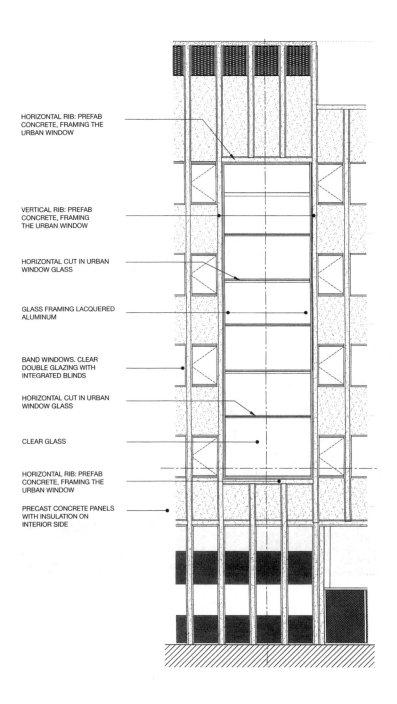

- HORIZONTAL RIB: PREFAB CONCRETE, FRAMING THE URBAN WINDOW
- VERTICAL RIB: PREFAB CONCRETE, FRAMING THE URBAN WINDOW
- HORIZONTAL CUT IN URBAN WINDOW GLASS
- GLASS FRAMING LACQUERED ALUMINUM
- BAND WINDOWS. CLEAR DOUBLE GLAZING WITH INTEGRATED BLINDS
- HORIZONTAL CUT IN URBAN WINDOW GLASS
- CLEAR GLASS
- HORIZONTAL RIB: PREFAB CONCRETE, FRAMING THE URBAN WINDOW
- PRECAST CONCRETE PANELS WITH INSULATION ON INTERIOR SIDE

North elevations: structural glass and curtain walls
To the north along the main campus avenue, a fully glazed vitrine showcases the internal activities of encounter and exchange. Glass bridges provide transparent connectors to subdued curtain walls.

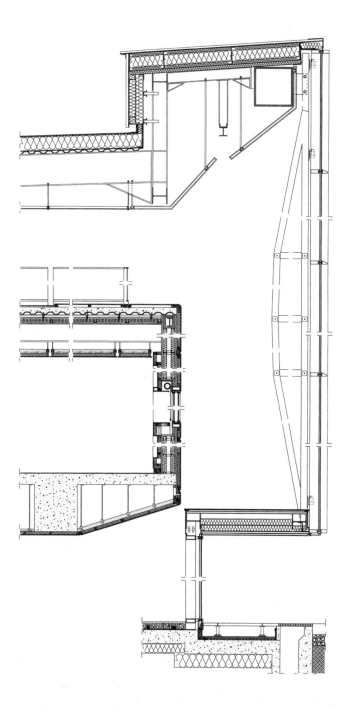

1   RECHERCHE

0⁵   ASSOCIATIONS ÉTUDI

0   ACCUEIL

VACHERON CONSTANTIN HEADQUARTERS EXTENSION, GENEVA (2011-15)

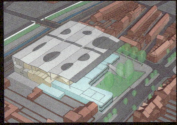

LE FRESNOY EXTENSION, TOURCOING (2019)

FOLIE P7 CAFE, PARC DE LA VILLETTE, PARIS (2011)

FOLIE L4 HYPERTENT, PARC DE LA VILLETTE, PARIS (2021)

MICRO-FOLIES, FRANCE (2015-)

E. Self-Preservation

Occasionally an architect is asked to design an extension, programmatic modification, or simple technical updates to a project they constructed several years earlier. How does an author respond to their existing building (sometimes already protected by landmark status) without negating its architectural singularity?

Geneva, Vacheron Constantin Headquarters Extension, 2011–15

GENEVA
485

Thematic Variation

The manufacturer's original building complex by Bernard Tschumi Architects was based on the idea that administrators ("white collar") and watchmakers ("blue collar") should work under the same continuous roof. When a large extension became necessary, a new question arose: How should the original concept be extended without contradicting its intent?

Photograph of the original building

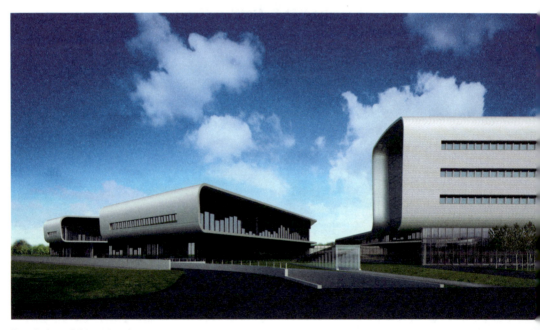
Rendering of the extension

Original building (2001-2005) (see *Event-Cities 3*)
This building serves as the manufacturing and administrative headquarters of Switzerland's oldest watchmaking company. The concept for the project is based on the idea of a thin, flexible, continuous envelope. The exterior surface is formed from a metallic sheet that unrolls over the structure's geometry, lifting to create the larger multistory portion of the building. The interior is clad with wood veneer. The resulting space is sleek and precise outside and warm and inviting inside. The logic of unrolling makes the building appear almost unenclosed. The envelope opens to welcome workers and visitors, admitting ample direct light on the north side and filtered light on the south.

In contrast to the wood-and-metal material palette, major movement vectors are made of glass. In the multistory part of the building, for example, a glass atrium contains several circulation elements—walkways, stairs, and an elevator—all made of glass. The continuity of the metal cladding lends the building a visual and functional coherence and suggests a fluid relationship among management, design, and production in the company's operations.

Extension (2011-2015)
The original Headquarters and Manufacturing Center required additional facilities to meet the company's increasing demands for state-of-the-art watch production. Although the new program is more than double the size of the original four-story building situated on the outskirts of Geneva, the client insisted on preserving untouched the original building's iconic and symbolic presence.

The new building is located so as to open up a cone of vision toward the existing building. Anticipating potential construction in the future, the extension is conceived as part of a campus in which all buildings differ in configuration but belong to the same conceptual and material family.

The manufacturing spaces have been oriented on the north side of the extension to achieve the best natural light for the skilled watchmakers, with skylights providing comfortable working conditions. A large restaurant opens onto a generous lawn. A ground-level service court allows for truck deliveries, while the car park and small delivery depot occupy the basement level. For the extension, a two-story variation on the original roof supports 15,000 square feet (1,500 square meters) of continuous solar panels for energy conservation and efficiency.

A key feature of the extension is a glazed stepped ramp that serves as a vestibule and leads to the watchmakers' changing rooms. The sloped entrance provides an articulation between the original and new buildings.

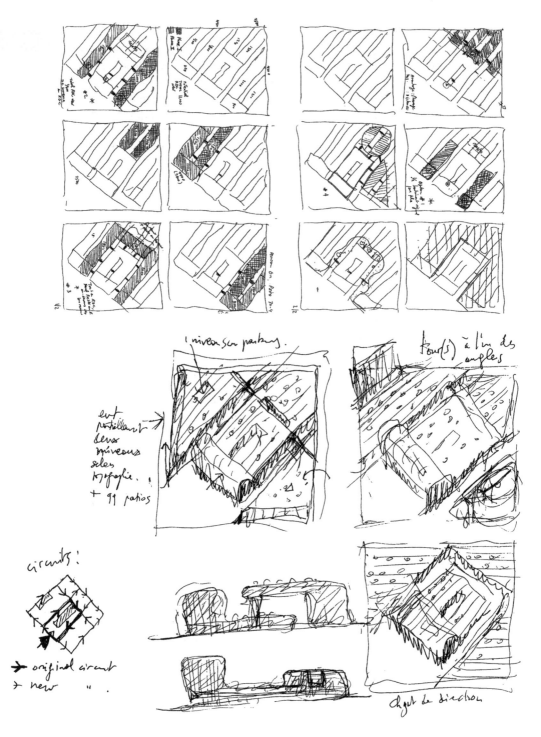

Testing various options for the extension's placement

MAY 2011

GENEVA
489

Extruding the existing building's profile was conceptually true to the original project, but did not meet the client's evolving spatial needs.

Aerial view of the new (left) and old (right) buidings

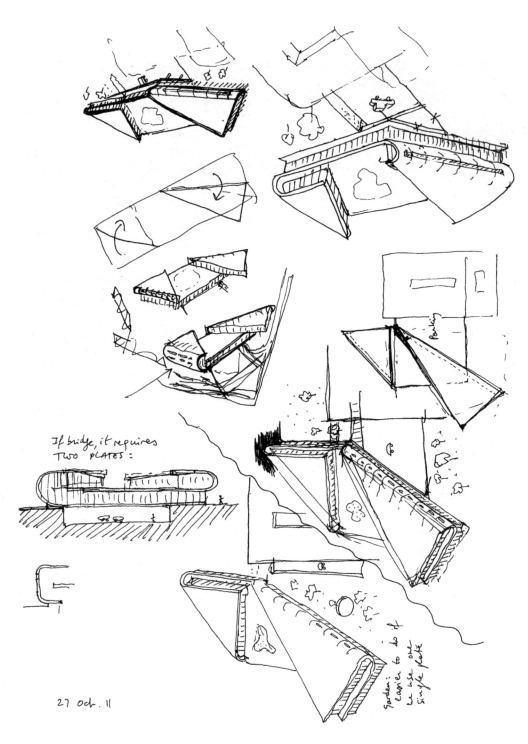

Exploring options to fold the extension's envelope

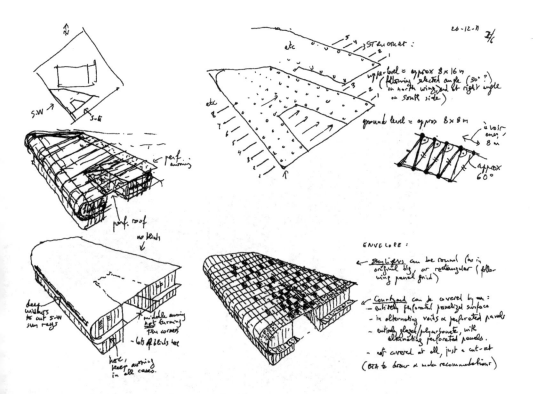

Final massing: Relations between envelope and structure, roof panels and skylights

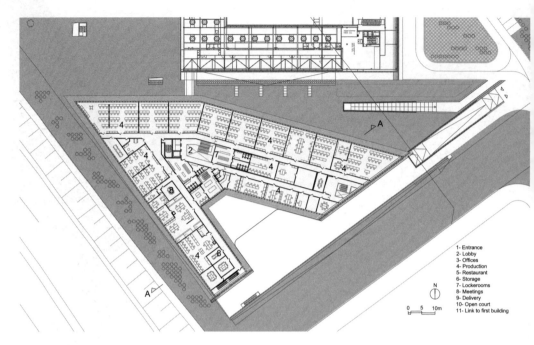

Upper level

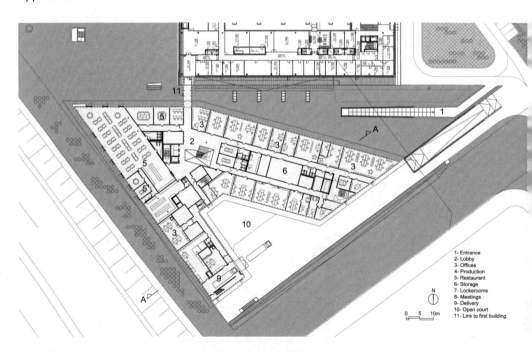

Ground floor

Structural diagram

Tourcoing, Le Fresnoy Extension, 2019

TOURCOING

505

Material Continuations

"We would therefore like to ask you for a small piece of work, which is obviously not the architectural project that you would be called upon to design, but rather an artist's improvisation, a sketch, an image that will make people dream..."

(Excerpt from Alain Fleischer's letter to Bernard Tschumi, December 2018)

Early 20th century (1920-30s)

Late 20th century (1990s)

TOURCOING
507

The In-Between (1990s)

Case History

Won by Bernard Tschumi Architects in 1991 (see *Event-Cities*), the competition for the National Studio for the Contemporary Arts aimed to create an interdisciplinary facility with exhibition, performance, and production spaces for practices in film, video, and electronic media. The pedagogical intention of combining multiple disciplines in a single project was to foster experimentation at the interstices of individual fields.

Located in Tourcoing, an aging industrial town in northern France, the site was an abandoned leisure complex from the 1920s that once housed cinema, ballroom dancing, skating, and horseback riding, among other activities. Neither of the two easy options—a costly and exhaustive renovation or a *tabula rasa* demolition—presented an interesting architectural solution.

Working within a constrained budget, the design focused on the conservation of the majestic elements from the existing Le Fresnoy buildings and their incorporation into a larger complex suitable for the contemporary arts.

"You think about unusual juxtapositions, collage, montage, Marcel Duchamp, preservation, and the old versus the new. The program is about multimedia and crossovers. Why not keep the old buildings and put a technologically advanced new roof over the old roofs to keep out the rain and snow, but also add contemporary electrical wiring, heating, ventilation, and air conditioning, with all the necessary pipes and ducts?

The new roof, while totally utilitarian, will also add something else: An "in-between" or new interstitial space will be created between the old and the new roof. This in-between space, which artists can appropriate, is the result of a strategy instead of formal composition. Finally, the roof will fold back and become one of the facades, thereby suppressing the historical articulation between roof and facade. The concept of the architectural envelope is born." (Excerpt from *Bernard Tschumi. Architecture: Concept & Notation* (2014))

Request

The request in 2019 to consider an expansion to the original project was challenging. The questions posed by the architect in 1991 were: What if, instead of designing a new building, one keeps the building slated for demolition? How do you insert a unique and original program inside the old and new structures? Can architecture be achieved without resorting to "design"?

TOURCOING 509

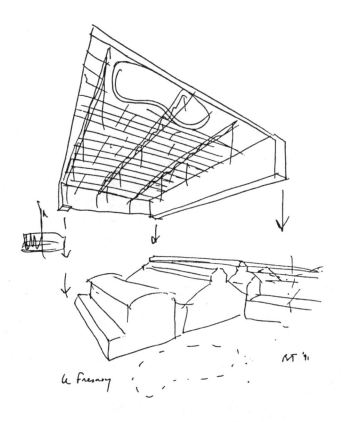

le Fresnoy

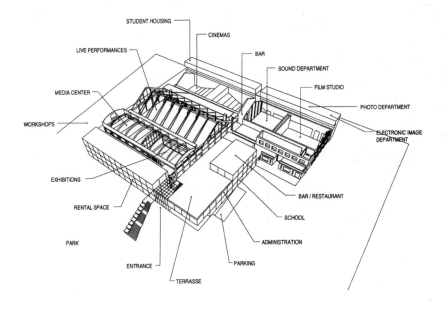

Le Fresnoy Studio National des Arts Contemporains (photo 1990s)

A New Question for the 21st Century

How do you enlarge an already-famous building without distorting it and exceeding the rules established during its design? The design process from the early 1990s contemplated the possibility of other volumes sheltered under the large roof of Le Fresnoy and seemed to anticipate an extension such as the new "StudioLab."

Le Fresnoy StudioLab
For the historical site of the Fresnoy building, the problem is simple. It involves extending the facilities by 32,000 square feet, distributed on a narrow residual strip of land adjoining the existing building and a more substantial surface on its main facade. This extension allows for an easily identifiable volume as a new phase in the development of the institution.

In designing these new volumes, it seemed preferable to remain as simple as possible, for budgetary reasons and for the dialogue established with the existing building. In order not to blur the now-iconic reading of Le Fresnoy, the only materials considered were the steel and glass of the original building, allied with two potential strategies.

The first strategy uses the ribbed metal vocabulary of the roof and rear facade of Le Fresnoy to form a rectangular steel volume with rounded edges, like a "negative" of the existing geometry of the skylights in the roof. This volume reads as separate from the 1990s complex.

The second strategy continues in glass the massing that was originally planned for a future extension of Le Fresnoy, extending and enlarging the glazed building in a large organic curve that is capable of housing the new programmatic requirements. This is the recommended solution.

Total new buildings on the Le Fresnoy site   **approx. 2642 m2**

A StudioLabs: Artistic and Scientific Production   approx. 1450 m2
B Workshop Construction and Large Scale Protoypes   approx. 300 m2
C FabLab and Expertise Installations   approx. 460 m2
D Lounge and Pedagogy Team, Production and Technique   approx. 432 m2

E to K Existing parts built in the 1991 project

Note: Part (A) is a possibility without being mandatory (around 260 m2).

METAL VERSION
First strategy

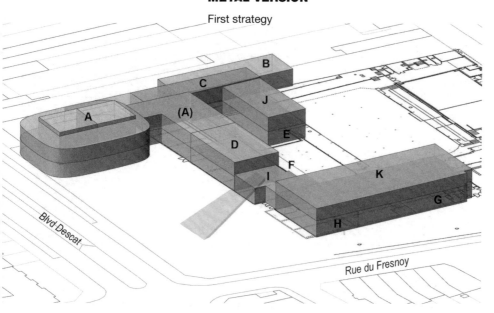

Elements (A) and D use the same glazed facade expression as Element K.
The new element A uses the same metal as the 1990s rear facade.

GLASS VERSION
Second strategy (recommended)

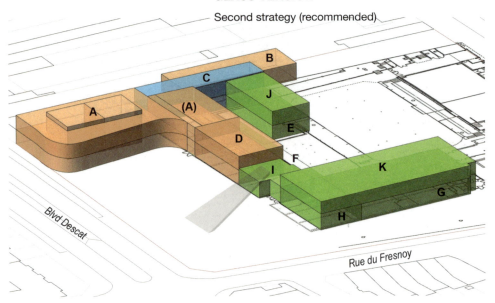

Elements A, (A), and D use the same glazed facade expression as the 1990s Element K.

Aerial view of the extension (Glass Version)

Photograph of existing 1990s building

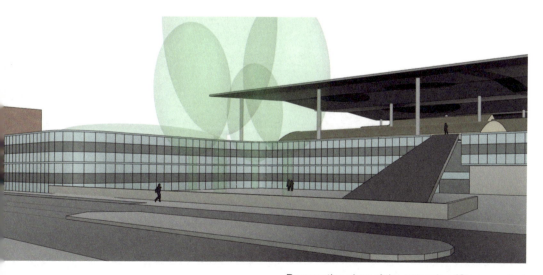

Perspective view of the extension (Glass version)

Paris,
Folie P7 Café, Parc de la Villette, 2011

Material Hypervigilance

How do you carefully enlarge an existing construction that is protected by its historical landmark status?

ORIGINAL

EXPANSION

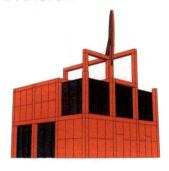 

About a quarter century after its construction, the Folie Café at the Parc de la Villette (1982-98) (see *Event-Cities 2*) needed expansion to cater to increased numbers of visitors. A minimalist strategy of black-tinted transparent glass was devised for the partially enlarged enclosure on the upstairs level.

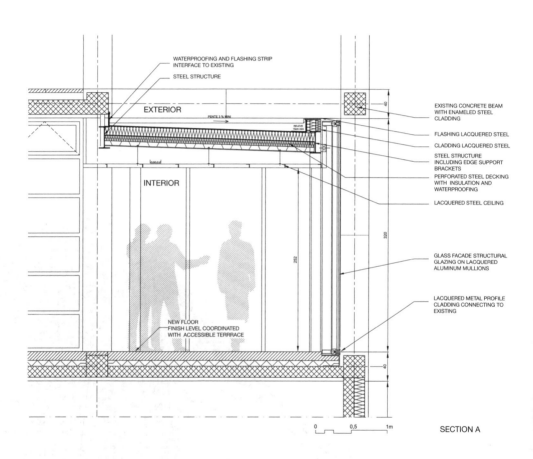

Paris,
Folie L4 HyperTent, Parc de la Villette, 2021

PARIS
525

Material Difference

How do you establish a dialogue between old and new when the older part is protected by its historical landmark status? How do you design a complementary element without altering the existing structure?

Case History

In conjunction with the opening of spaces for circus arts in the northwest sector of the Parc de la Villette (1982-1998) (see *Event-Cities 2*), Bernard Tschumi Architects was asked to design a ticket booth located on the podium of Folie L4, which was originally a music venue. The booth needed to have an iconic presence and to meet strict functional and budgetary requirements, while taking into account the constraints of context.

How does an architect approach a project to extend a building they designed—one protected by landmark status—without altering it? According to specifications from the 1980s, any additional elements had to be able to be added or removed without interfering with the original structure. Hence, the hyperbolic paraboloid of the tent sheltering the booth was conceived so as not to touch the "megabeam" of the existing *folie*.

A company specializing in custom tents carried out the project, following the architect's instructions. The primary materials are a durable architectural PTFE membrane and transparent polycarbonate for the vertical envelope. The typographic design for the screen-printed pattern on the exterior was also part of the specifications.

The HyperTent is the smallest building realized by Bernard Tschumi Architects.

Note: The use of the original bandshell designed in the early 1980s to host musical performances was ironically outlawed when residents who had moved to the park neighborhood, attracted by its landscape and culture, lodged noise complaints.

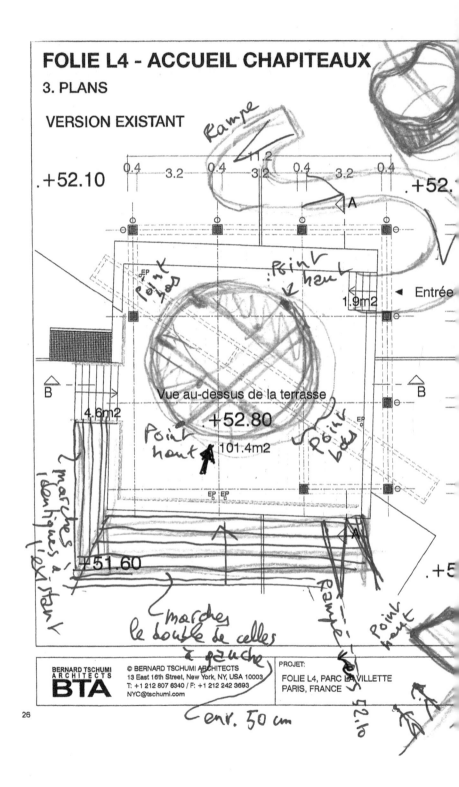

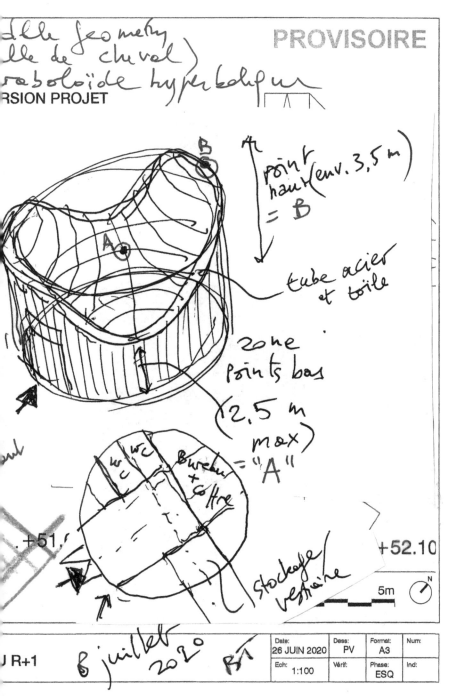

PROVISOIRE

...elle geometry
...lle de cheval)
...raboloïde hyperbolique
RSION PROJET

point haut (env. 3,5 m) = B

tube acier et toile

zone points bas (2,5 m max) = "A"

WC · Bureau + coffre · Stockage vestiaire

5m

+52.10
+51.

R+1   8 juillet 2020   BT

Date: 26 JUIN 2020   Dess: PV   Format: A3   Num:
Ech: 1:100   Vérif: Phase: ESQ   Ind:

= d = 7.20 (r = 3.60) = 40 m²

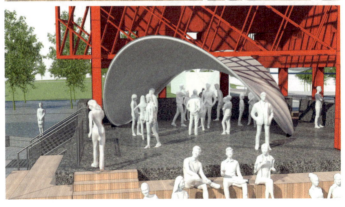

Studies

PARIS
531

Realization

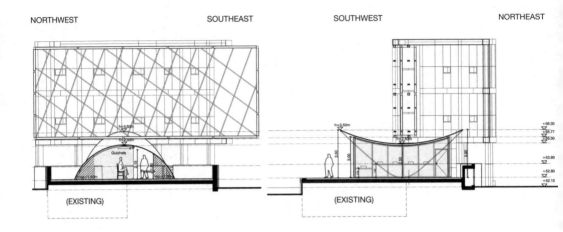

Section AA

Section BB

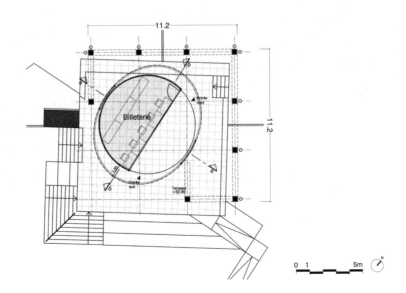

Plan

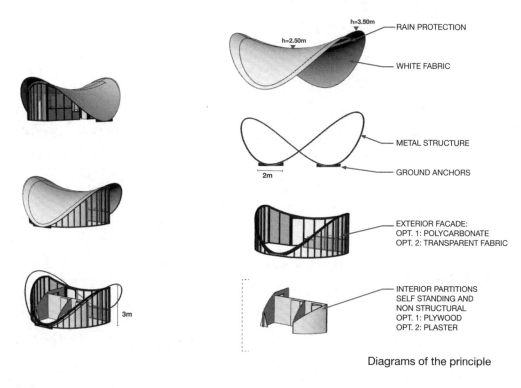

Diagrams of the principle

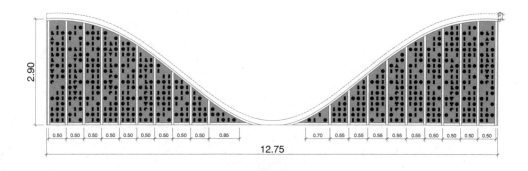

Exterior facade pattern

France, Micro-folies, 2015–

Combinatory Games

Inspired by the *folies* in the Parc de la Villette, this initiative—supported by the French Ministry of Culture and coordinated by La Villette, in partnership with various institutions—is intended to share national culture democratically and to support creativity through localized interventions.

The primary project components are a digital museum bringing together artworks from French national institutions, displayed via screens and interactive tablets; a café, library, and performance area for children with educational workshops, film screenings, and other events organized by artists, cultural organizations, and local associations; and a FabLab/DIY corner, supporting designers and anyone who wants to explore creativity through tools like 3D printing. Other spaces can be imagined, depending on the activities already in place and the needs of the area.

As of 2024, "*micro-folies*" have been realized in dozens of small towns throughout France and beyond. The structures were designed and built by a range of authors based on a set of guidelines established by Bernard Tschumi Architects.

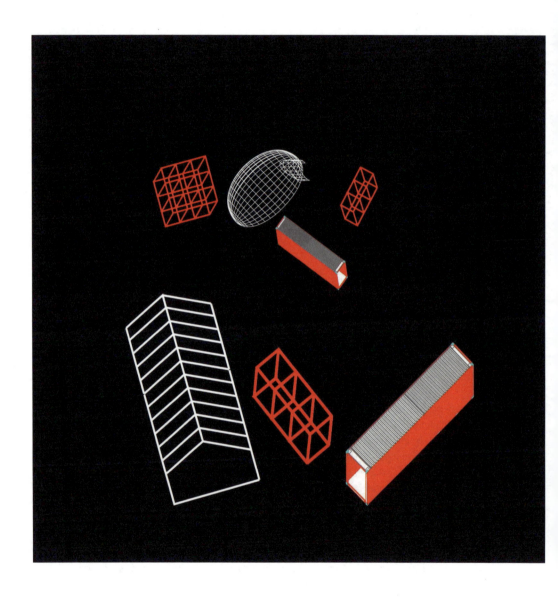

A *micro-folie* is a temporary cultural space organised around three units—a digital museum, a café, and a FabLab. Each element is adaptable to local demands.

FRANCE
539

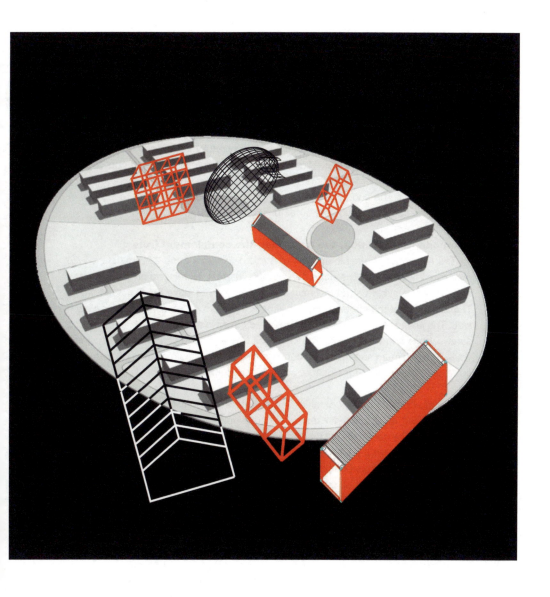

Micro-folie Specifications (excerpts from 2016 report)

The ambition is to promote cultural activities on an ad hoc basis but at a national scale. Taking as a starting point the concept of the *folies* at the Parc de la Villette, this new project is not intended for the park, but for all of France. The *micro-folies* offer points for gathering, activity, and interaction that can be carried out with moderate budgets. These constructions are designed generally to be mobile or ephemeral.

Definitions

Folie: Historically, small constructions in nature, designed for the pleasure of their users. Also, madness, unreason. Grid of small red buildings characterizing the Parc de la Villette in Paris. *Micro-folie*: Small *folie*, generally less than 200 square meters, including extensions and outbuildings. *Macro-folie*: Large *folie*, generally more than 200 square meters, including extensions and outbuildings. The rules governing *micro-* and *macro-folies* must be distinguished carefully from those governing the *folies* at the Parc de la Villette. *Micro-folies* and *macro-folies* are made up of three inseparable constituent elements (the "red cube," the "red container," and the "complement"). The cube and the container are part of the entrance, reception, or signage; the complement meets other functional requirements.

Components: the cube, the container, the complement (rules)

1.) The red cube: The minimum unit of a *micro-folie* is a cube 2.26 meters x 2.26 meters x 2.26 meters. The cube can be built in steel, aluminum, or wood. It may consist of the simple structure marking its six sides or have several solid sides. The thickness of the cube structure will be a minimum of 5.5 centimeters on each side. The juxtaposition or superposition of red cubes is authorized, while respecting safety norms and regulations. The cubes can be equipped with rotating or sliding walls. The minimum number of red cubes is three; there is no maximum. A single red cube can be a support for signage, possibly electronic.

2.) The red container: The container serves both as a useful space for the duration of events and as a container during the transport of the elements of the *micro/macro-folie*. The container will be a standard container: 6.05 meters or 12.19 meters (l) x 2.43 meters (w) x 2.59 meters (h). The interior dimensions are 2.33 meters (w) x 2.38 meters (h). Juxtaposition of containers, opening and closing, signage: The combining or stacking of containers is authorized, while respecting safety and accessibility standards. The container can be enclosed or have openings. The number of containers is a minimum of one, or as many as needed. Signage on the container is permitted, but it must be white, and the red color must be retained on 80% of each side.

3.) The complement: The complement is the element that will host the programmatic and functional requirements and must be added to the cube(s) and container(s) to form a complete trio. The complement is free in both its shape and its dimensions. It could be an inflatable structure, a tent, a metal or polycarbonate shelter, etc. It could also be an existing construction, to which the red cube(s) and the red container(s) would be associated. Note: The color red is not allowed for the complement.

Scenarios

The *micro/macro-folie* can easily be moved from one location to another. All the elements of the project would be packaged in the container(s) and loaded onto trucks. The elements must be designed in such a way as to limit the labor required for assembly and dismantling. The three main components can each be increased or reduced according to programmatic needs and/or site characteristics.

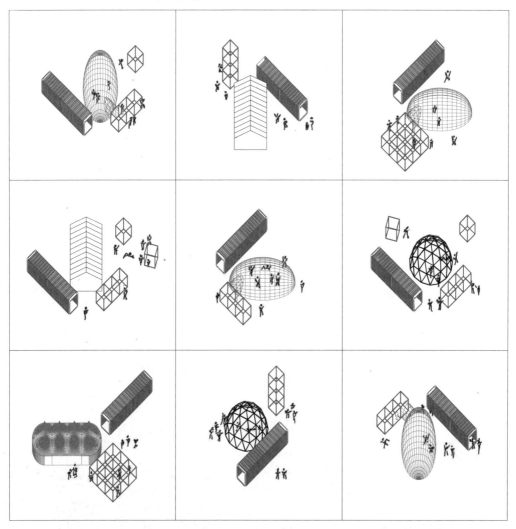

Different configurations can be invented, depending on the site: For example, horizontal deployment on a first site and, after moving, vertical installation, superimposing the red cubes. One can also imagine the *micro/macro-folie* installed in a factory or an abandoned church. In this case, one can keep only the red cube(s) and the red container(s) and consider that the existing shelter plays the role of the complement.

Micro-folie in Sevran, France (2017), realized by h2o architectes

ARCHITECTURE AND EVENT, MOMA, NEW YORK (1994)

CHRONOMANIFESTES 1950-2010, FRAC CENTRE, ORLÉANS (2013-14)

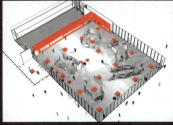

CONCEPT & NOTATION, CENTRE POMPIDOU, PARIS (2014)

CONCEPT & NOTATION, SWISS ARCHITECTURE MUSEUM, BASEL (2015)

CONCEPT & NOTATION, POWER STATION OF ART, SHANGHAI (2016)

F. Retrospective Concepts

Books and exhibitions conceived by architects on their own work are important. They do not inevitably serve as propaganda for their author's designs or ideological beliefs. In the following examples, each of these exhibitions, conceived and developed in tandem with books, aims to foreground architectural thinking. Significantly, these installations often provide a means for the architect to access an overview of what they are trying to achieve. To put it another way, as critic Susan Sontag once explained: "I write in order to find out what I think."

Simultaneously, these installations become pieces of architecture in themselves: Volumes, enclosures, sequences, loops are all parts of the narrative.

*New York, Thresholds/Bernard Tschumi,
Museum of Modern Art, 1994*

NEW YORK

549

Architecture and Event

Exhibition documenting Bernard Tschumi's theoretical projects and first built works

An exhibition of the work of the architect Bernard Tschumi was the second in the Museum's Thresholds series devoted to thematic explorations of contemporary issues in architecture and design. *Thresholds/Bernard Tschumi: Architecture and Event* explores the tension between the rational systems by which buildings are designed and the constant transformation of these buildings by the changing events within them.

As an introduction to five major architectural projects, the exhibition begins with Tschumi's theoretical project, *The Manhattan Transcripts*, which serves as a reference for much of his later work. Represented in the exhibition through models and drawings are Parc de la Villette, Paris (1982–98); Bridge-City, Lausanne (1988), an urban project consisting of four inhabited bridges; Kansai International Airport, Osaka (1988); Chartres Business Park, Chartres (1991), an office and leisure development; and Le Fresnoy National Studio for Contemporary Arts, Tourcoing, France (1991–97), an "electronic Bauhaus."

The installation designed by the architect reinforces the uneasy relationship between the precision of architecture and the instability of day-to-day life. Models are suspended from cables, while video images of human activity underscore the importance of events in defining architectural space.

—Adapted from the institutional press release for *Architecure and Event*

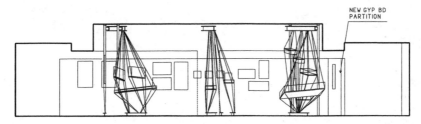

LAYOUT "D" SECTION/ELEVATION "XX"

LAYOUT "D" SECTION/ELEVATION "YY"

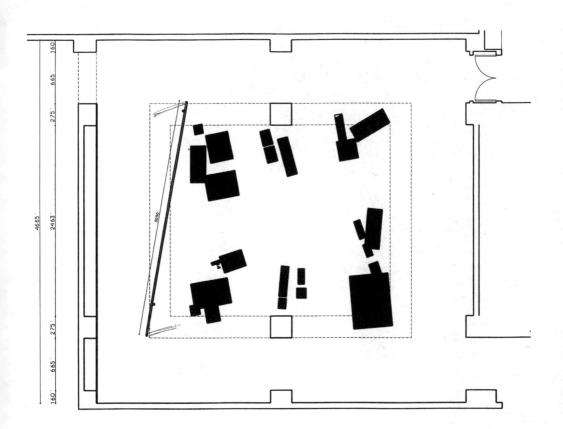

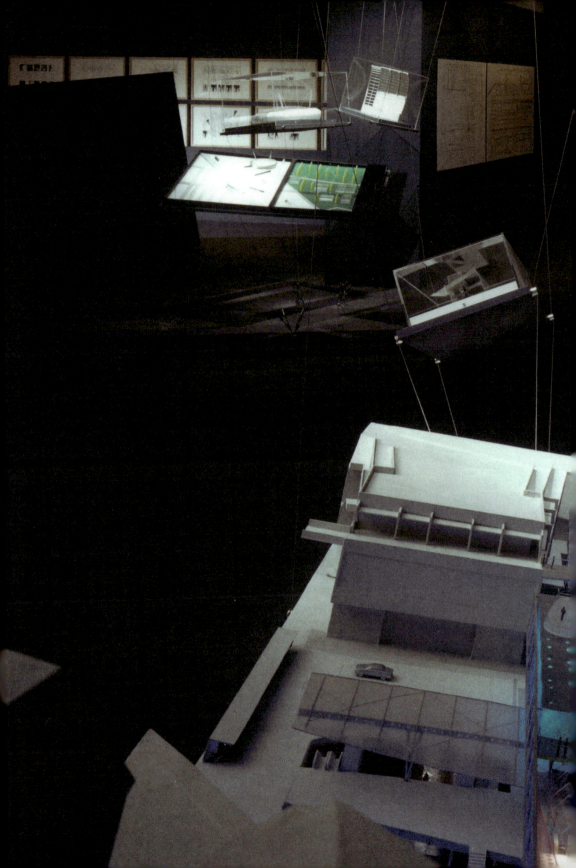

*Orléans, Chronomanifestes 1950–2010,
Frac Centre, 2013–14*

ORLÉANS
557

Avant-Garde Timeline

Chronomanifestes 1950–2010 celebrates six decades of work by radical architects.

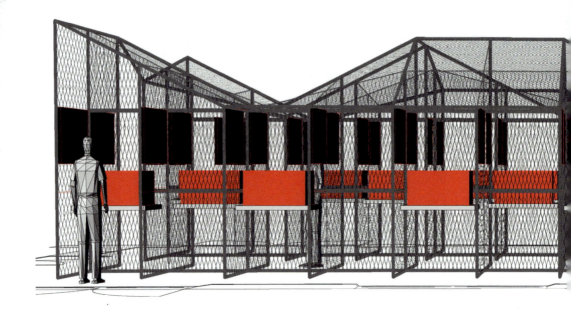
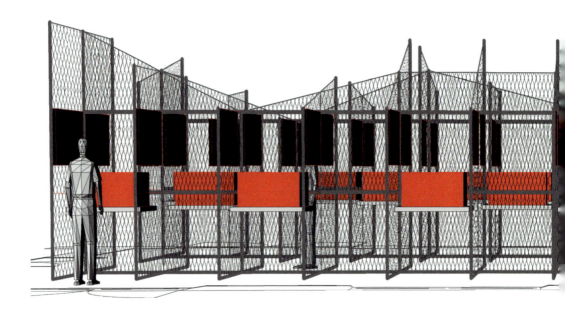

ORLÉANS
559

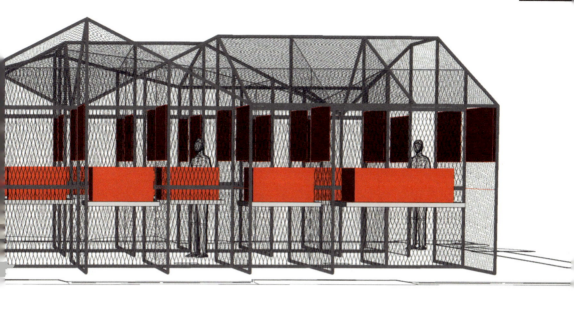
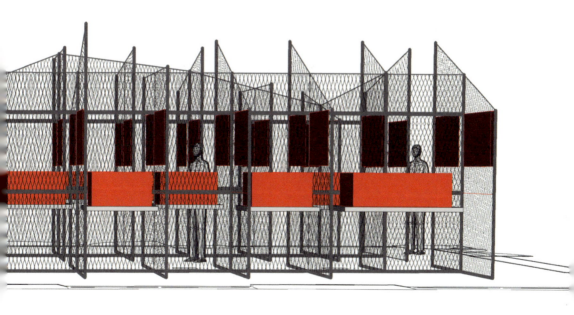

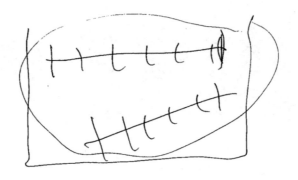

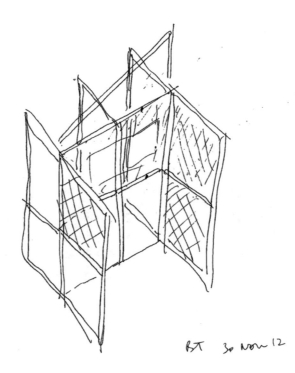

Initial diagrams

An extraordinary collection of 20th- and 21st-century architectural drawings and models has been assembled in the regional collection (Frac) of the French city of Orléans. In 2012, Bernard Tschumi was given carte blanche to design an exhibition of some of the collection's most striking artifacts.

The exhibition layout is a simple linear series of near-transparent mesh partitions. Organized chronologically, the exhibition is deliberately abstract, evading ideological groupings and geographic origins. If there are suggestive juxtapositions, relationships are left open to the viewer's interpretation as transitions from one year to another show different sensibilities that collide and clash as much as they extend the discourse. Starting at the beginning of global communication, many of the protagonists influenced each other either personally or through publications and magazines. The display proposes the evolution of polemics, evoking different times and sensitivities that fed the city and architecture from the 1950s through 2010.

The exhibition and accompanying publication are also a tribute to the Frac Centre's historical role and pay homage to its directors, Frédéric Migayrou and Marie-Ange Brayer, who assembled the collection and facilitated the show.

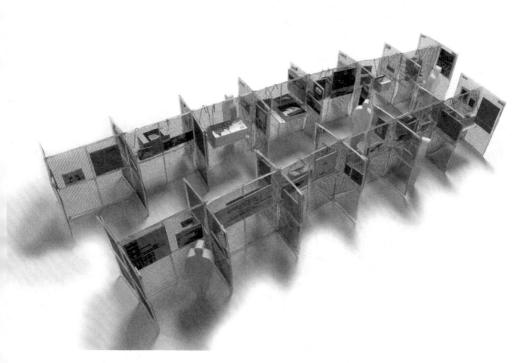

Study model

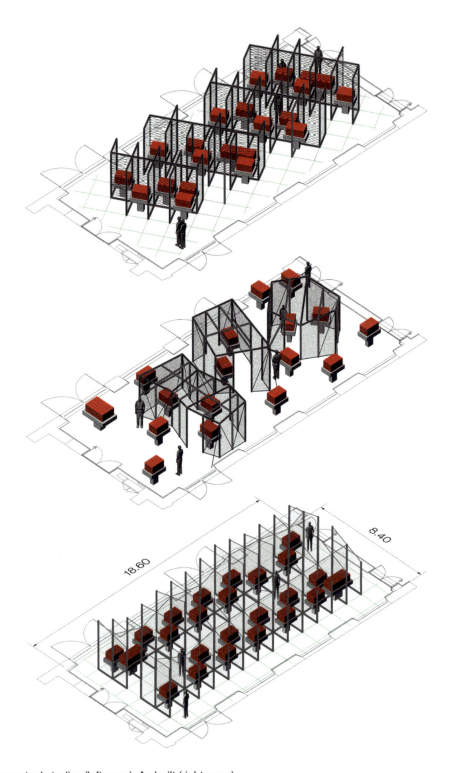

Conceptual studies (left page). As built (right page)

*Paris, Retrospective,
Centre Pompidou, 2014*

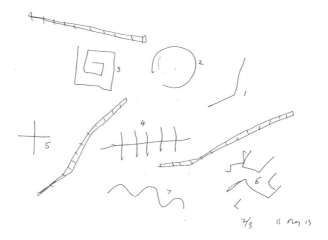

Concept & Notation I

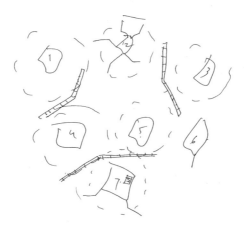

The exhibition and catalogue *Bernard Tschumi. Architecture: Concept and Notation* addresses the architect's thought and work through five themes, starting with theoretical work and extending through built projects.

Following the publication of *Architecture Concepts: Red is Not a Color* in 2012, curators from the Architecture Department at the Centre Pompidou in Paris approached Bernard Tschumi about designing an exhibition based on the material and themes of the book. The result was *Architecture: Concept and Notation*, the first major retrospective of the work of the office in Europe and the first career retrospective of Bernard Tschumi.

Designing the exhibition was a project in itself. As with other projects, Bernard Tschumi Architects wanted to satisfy the requirements of the program while questioning and going beyond them. The project was challenging: As modes of architectural representation have expanded, the architectural exhibition as a form has struggled to accommodate these changes. With a career spanning the analog and the digital, it was clear that a consistent language needed to be developed so that projects and the concepts behind them could be appreciated whether drawn by hand or rendered on the computer, built or unbuilt, as small pavilions or large master plans.

The major aims animating the exhibition were to show the development of the concepts powering both built and unbuilt work; to choreograph the visitor's movement through the exhibition space; and to show the role played by cultural artifacts from many disciplines in the development of architectural thought. The resolution of those aims has been persuasively addressed by the late Anthony Vidler in his 2014 essay "After the Event" (see Bibliography). The following is adapted from the institutional press release for the exhibition:

The exhibition—based on Bernard Tschumi's work as an architect, writer, and educator—explores the making of architecture as a series of arguments, ideas, influences, and responses to the contemporary definition of architecture today. Tschumi's major architectural projects are organized around two primary ideas and five themes. The primary ideas are concept and notation: There is no architecture without an idea or concept, just as there is no architecture without a method of notation to express its content. The five thematic zones in the exhibition each propose a fundamental area in the definition of architecture: Space and Event, Program and Superposition, Vectors and Envelopes, Context and Content, and Concept-Form.

Tschumi illustrates these themes through a series of well-known and lesser-known projects, from the historic Parc de la Villette in Paris to later projects such as the Acropolis Museum in Athens, as well as the new architecture for the redesign for the Paris Zoological Park. Alongside the projects are a series of 18 red reference tables that extend and amplify the main narrative of the exhibition through topics related to architectural thought and production. The exhibition is the most complete display of Tschumi's work to date, including 45 projects with over 350 drawings, sketches, collages, and models, many of them never shown previously. The exhibition was organized by curators Frédéric Migayrou and Aurélien Lemonier.

Density of Material
Dense version
Image dominant

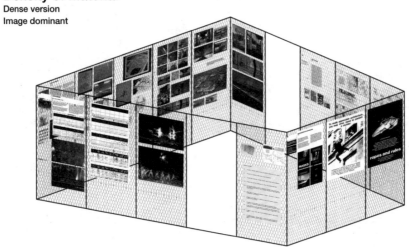

Testing different configurations and content strategies

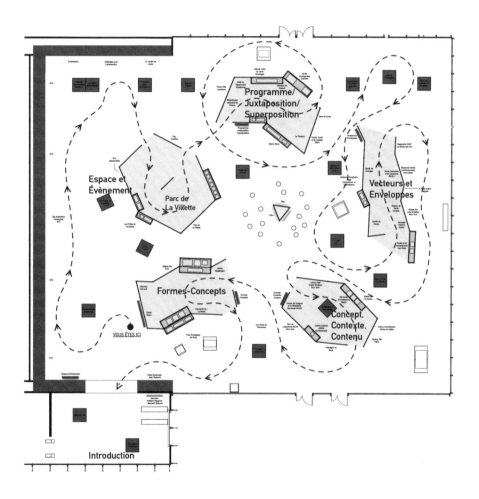

Final installation plan

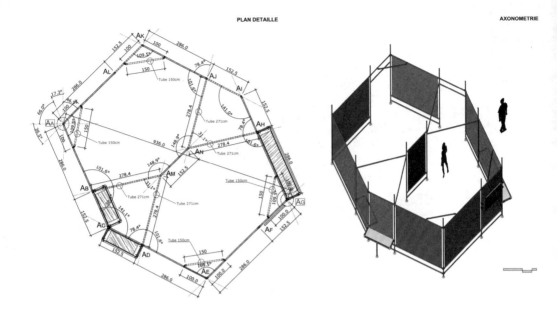

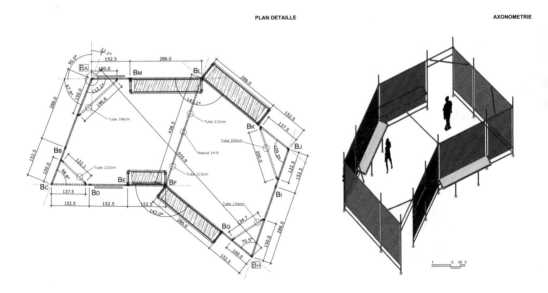

Thematic enclosures: evolving the content and structure simultaneously (for example—built-in model shelves balancing each side and improving lateral stability)

PARIS
573

PLAN DETAILLE

AXONOMETRIE

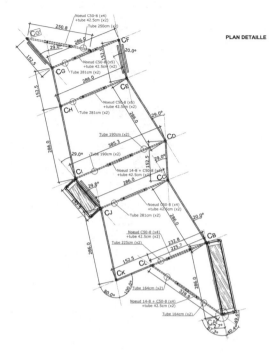
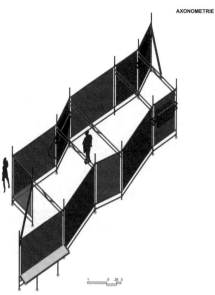

NOTE : TOUTES LES DIMENSIONS SERONT A VERIFIER SUR SITE PAR LES ENTREPRISES

PLAN DETAILLE

AXONOMETRIE

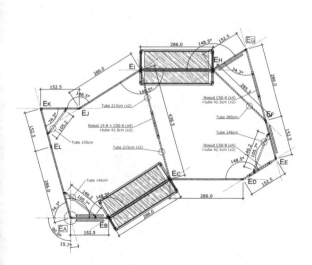
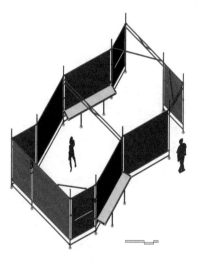

Thematic enclosure: Parc de la Villette

PARIS

579

Basel, Retrospective,
Swiss Architecture Museum, 2015

BASEL

Concept & Notation II

Bernard Tschumi. Architecture: Concept and Notation at the Swiss Architecture Museum in Basel, Switzerland in 2015 was an edited version of the larger exhibition of the same name organized by the Centre Pompidou in Paris the prior year.

*Shanghai, Retrospective,
Power Station of Art, 2016*

SHANGHAI
585

Concept & Notation III

Bernard Tschumi. Architecture: Concept and Notation was redesigned for the Power Station of Art in Shanghai, where it was accompanied by a Chinese-language version of the catalogue.

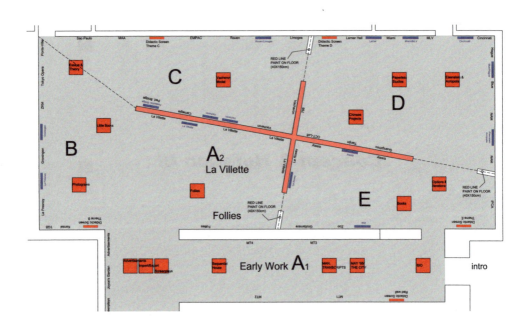

Themes

Manifestos: Space and Event (A), Program/Juxtaposition/Superimposition (B), Vectors and Envelopes (C), Concept, Context, Content (D), and Concept-Forms (E)

SHANGHAI
587

Architecture is a form of knowledge.
建筑是认知的一种形式。

Architecture is the materialisation
of a concept.
建筑是概念的物质化呈现。

Bernard Tschumi
伯纳德·屈米

Project Chronology 1974-2024

Selected Projects 1974–2024

Legend
Projects collected in the *Event-Cities* series

- Event-Cities
- Event-Cities 2
- Event-Cities 3
- Event-Cities 4
- Event-Cities 5

Fireworks
London, 1974

Advertisements for Architecture,
1976–1978

Joyce's Garden
London, 1976–1977

Screenplays
1976–1978

The Manhattan Transcripts,
1976–1981

20th-Century Follies
1979–1982

Sequential House
1981

Parc de la Villette
Paris, 1982–1998

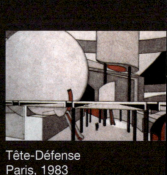

Tête-Défense
Paris, 1983

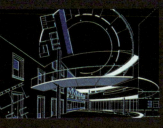
County Hall
Strasbourg, 1986

New National Theater
Tokyo, 1986

Loft
New York, 1987

Future Park, Flushing
Meadows (with SOM)
New York, 1987

Amerika-Gedenkbibliothek
Berlin, 1988

Spoortunnel
Rotterdam, 1988

Deconstructivist Architecture
Exhibition, MoMA
New York, 1988

Kansai Airport
Osaka, 1988

Ponts-Villes
(with L. Merlini)
Lausanne, 1988–2009

Vieux-Port
Montreal, 1988

Bibliothèque nationale
de France (TGB)
Paris, 1989

Center for Art and Media
Technology (ZKM)
Karlsruhe, 1989

New Cité Industrielle
Völklingen, 1989

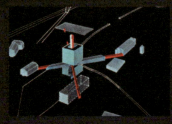
Arbed Headquarters
Esch-sur-Alzette, 1990

Glass Video Gallery
Gröningen, 1990

Art et Publicité Exhibition
Paris, 1990

New Berlin
Berlin, 1990

Kyoto JR Railway Station
Kyoto, 1991

Zénith Concert Hall
Tours, 1991

Business Park
Chartres, 1991

Le Fresnoy
Tourcoing, 1991–1997

Quartier des États-Unis
Lyon, 1991

Kongresshaus
Salzbourg, 1991

Fireworks, La Villette
Paris, 1992

Spartan Villa
The Hague, 1992

World Meteorological Organization
Geneva, 1993

EPFL Extension
Lausanne, 1993

Alfred J. Lerner Student Center, Columbia University
New York, 1994–1999

École d'architecture
Marne-la-Vallée
1994–1999

Renault, Ile Seguin
Boulogne-Billancourt
(Paris), 1994

Franklin Furnace Gallery
New York, 1994

Space and Event Exhibition, MoMA
New York, 1994

Department Store K-Polis
Zurich, 1995

Flon Railway Hub
(with Merlini + Ventura)
Lausanne, 1995

MoMA Expansion
New York, 1997

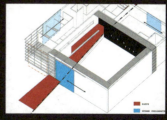
Frac Pays-de-la-Loire
Nantes, 1997

French Embassy
Pretoria, 1998

Zénith Concert Hall and
Exhibition Center
Rouen, 1998–2001

Contemporary Art Center
Cincinnati, OH, 1998

FIU School of Architecture
Miami, FL, 1999–2003

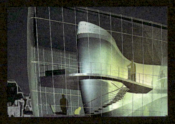
Urban Glass House
New York, 1999

Centre omnisports
Metz, 1999

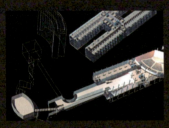
World Intellectual Property
Organization
Geneva, 1999

Cité internationale
Lyon, 1999

Vélodrome
Aulnay-sous-Bois, 2000

Italian Space Agency
Rome, 2000

Museum aan de Stroom
Antwerp, 2000

Downsview Park
Toronto, 2000

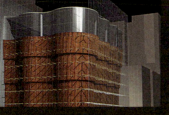
Museum for African Art
New York, 2000

Carnegie Science Center
Pittsburgh, PA, 2000

Ponte Parodi
Genoa, 2000

Exhibition Center
Angoulême, 2000

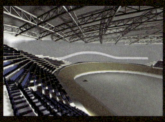
Opera House/Vélodrome
Vendée, 2000

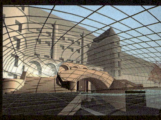
South Entrance, American
Museum of Natural History
New York, 2000

Acropolis Museum
Athens, 2001–2009

Electronic Media and
Performing Arts Center
Troy, NY, 2001

Cité Euroméditerranée
Marseille, 2001

Palais des sports
Issy-les-Moulineaux, 2001

Vacheron Constantin
Headquarters and Factory
Geneva, 2001–2004

Museum of Contemporary
Art
São Paulo, 2001

Richard E. Lindner
Athletics Center
Cincinnati, OH, 2001–2006

Expo internationale 2004
Paris, 2001

Tri-Towers of Babel
New York, 2002

Contemporary Art Museum
Yerevan, 2002

MuséoParc
Alésia, 2002–2012; 2015

World Trade Organization
Geneva, 2003

Zénith Concert Hall
Dijon, 2003

Zénith Concert Hall
Limoges, 2003–2007

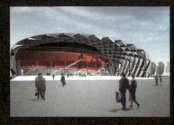
Zénith Concert Hall
Strasbourg, 2003

Metro Station M2
(with Merlini + Ventura)
Lausanne, 2003–2008

BLUE Residential Tower
New York, 2004–2007

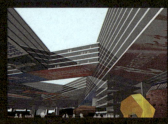
Factory 798
Beijing, 2004

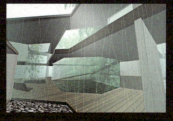

Sophia-Antipolis
Technopolis Extension
Nice, 2004

Facade-Envelope, Ile Seguin
Boulogne-Billancourt (Paris),
2004

Urban Villas
Beijing, 2004

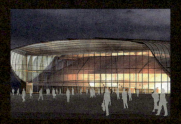
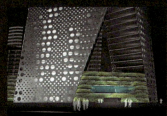

Apartment Interior
Beijing, 2004

Sports and Exhibition
Complex
Montbéliard, 2004

West Diaoyutai Tower
Beijing, 2004

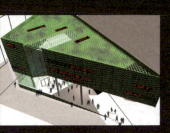

Architecture Foundation
Center
London, 2004

Airbus Delivery Center
Toulouse, 2004

Ceramic Tiles of Italy
Pavilion
Orlando, FL, 2005

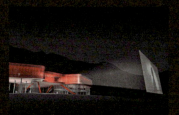

Housing Concept Study
Abu Dhabi, 2005

Surf City
Biarritz, 2005

Busan Film Center
Busan, 2005

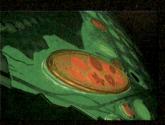

Elliptic City IFCA
Santo Domingo,
2005–2012

Dubai Opera House
Dubai, 2005

New Hague Passage
The Hague, 2005–2014

École cantonale d'art
de Lausanne (ÉCAL)
Renens (Lausanne),
2005–2007

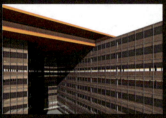

Town Hall
Toulouse, 2006

Swiss Pavilion Exhibition
Venice, 2006

Cultural Center
Cenon (Bordeaux),
2006–2010

Pedestrian Bridge
(with H. Dutton)
La Roche-sur-Yon,
2007–2010

Austerlitz Railway Station
Master Plan
Paris, 2006

Palais de justice
Aix-en-Provence, 2007

Sheikh Zayed
National Museum
Abu Dhabi, 2007

Hospital Antoine-Béclère
Extension
Clamart (Paris), 2007

Musée Jean-Cocteau
Menton, 2007

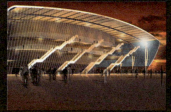
Mega-Hall
Montpellier, 2008

▌Mediapolis
Singapore, 2008

▌Typolounger
2008

▌National Bank of Greece
Athens, 2008

▌University Student Center
Dallas, TX, 2008

▌Media Zone Master Plan
Abu Dhabi, 2008

▌Media Zone Master Plan,
Shabaka Option
Abu Dhabi, 2008

▌Uni-Cité
Lausanne, 2008

Hotel Aphrodite Astir
Athens, 2008

▌Parc zoologique de Paris
(with V. Descharrières +
J. Osty)
Paris, 2008–2014

Prince George's African-
American Museum
North Brentwood, MD, 2009

Carnal Hall,
Institut Le Rosey
Rolle, 2009–2014

EDF Headquarters
Saclay (Paris), 2009

Atmosphere Park
Santiago, 2010

Tianjin Cultural Center
Master Plan
Tianjin, 2010

Musée Cantonal
des Beaux-Arts
Lausanne, 2010

OCT-LOFT Master Plan
and Museum
Shenzhen, 2011

LAIFEX Office Building
Santo Domingo, 2011

Vacheron Constantin
Headquarters and
Factory Extension
Geneva, 2011–2015

Zénith Concert Hall in La
Martinique
Lamentin, 2011

A.N.I.M.A. Cultural Center
Grottammare, 2012–2014

Cité Musicale de l'Ile
Seguin,
Boulogne-Billancourt (Paris),
2012

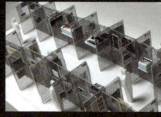
Chronomanifestes 1950–
2010, Frac Centre
Orléans, 2013–2014

Presidential Hotel
Doha, 2013

Campus HES-SO Valais
Sion, 2013

Binhai Science Museum
Tianjin, 2013–2019

Retrospective Exhibition,
Centre Pompidou
Paris, 2014

Guangzhou Museum
Guangzhou, 2014

Retrospective Exhibition,
Swiss Architecture Museum
Basel, 2015

Biology-Pharmacy
Chemistry Center,
Paris-Saclay University
Saclay (Paris), 2015–2022

Retrospective Exhibition,
Power Station of Art
Shanghai, 2016

Petite Maison,
Villa le Corbusier
Corseaux, 2016

Honoria Tower
Monaco, 2016

Museum of Ethnography
Budapest, 2016

Université-Cité d'Entreprises
Cannes, 2016

Cité de la Musique
Geneva, 2017

ArcelorMittal Headquarters
Luxembourg, 2017

Pompeii and the Greeks
Exhibition
Pompeii, 2017

Center for Science and
Entrepreneurship,
Institut Le Rosey
Rolle, 2017–2025

Bank Lombard-Odier
Geneva, 2017

100KM2 City
Huairou (Beijing), 2018

Xiangmihu Area
Shenzhen, 2018

World Health Museum
Geneva, 2018

Grid House
Jinhua, 2019

Yinxu Ruins Museum
Anyang, 2019

Palais des Congrès
Nîmes, 2019

Le Fresnoy Extension
Tourcoing, 2019

 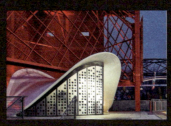 

Finance Culture Center
Shenzhen, 2020

Folie L4 HyperTent,
Parc de la Villette
Paris, 2021

Caran d'Ache Headquarters
Geneva, 2021

Guangming Scientists Valley
Shenzhen, 2022

Carthage National Museum
Carthage, 2022

Untitled House
Beacon, New York, 2023–

Selected Publications 1974–2024

The Manhattan Transcripts (1981)

Architecture and Disjunction (1994)

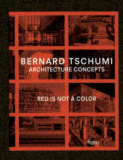
Architecture Concepts: Red is Not a Color (2012)

Bernard Tschumi. Architecture: Concept & Notation (2014)

Cinégramme folie: le Parc de la Villette (1987)

Tschumi Parc de la Villette (2014)

Questions of Space (1990)

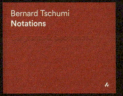
Notations: Diagrams and Sequences (2014)

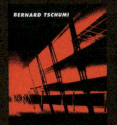
Event-Cities (1994)

Event-Cities 2 (2001)

Event-Cities 3: Concept vs. Context vs. Content (2005)

Event-Cities 4: Concept-Form (2010)

Le Fresnoy: Architecture In/Between (1999)

Glass Ramps/Glass Wall: Deviations from the Normative (2004)

Bernard Tschumi: Zénith de Rouen (2003)

ECAL by Tschumi (2009)

Tschumi on Architecture: Conversations (2006)

The New Acropolis Museum (2009)

Architecture Zoo (2014)

Chronomanifestes 1950-2010 (2013)

Bernard Tschumi (2003)

Bernard Tschumi (2008)

The State of Architecture at the Beginning of the 21st Century (2003)

INDEX Architecture: A Columbia Architecture Book (2003)

Grid House, 2019

"The city is like a great house, and the house in its turn a small city."

—Leon Battista Alberti, ca. 1442

Project Teams

Carthage, Carthage National Museum
Bernard Tschumi, Joel Rutten, Tina Marinaki, Valeria Paez Cala, Wenjun Yu
Landscape: Michel Desvigne Paysagiste; *Structural*: Hugh Dutton Associés; *Exhibition Design*: scenevolution

Alésia, MuséoParc
New York: Bernard Tschumi, Joel Rutten, Kim Starr, Adam Dayem, Jane Kim, Kyungjune Min, Adrien Durrmeyer, Matthew Stofen, Paula Tomisaki, Nefeli Chatzimina
Paris: Bernard Tschumi, Véronique Descharrières, Antoine Santiard, Jean-Jacques Hubert, Rémy Cointet, Alice Dufourmantelle, Sarah Gould, Agnes Winiarzska, Christina Devizzi, Adrien Del Grande
Exhibition Design: G.C. François with J.H. Manoury and Pascale Guillou; *Landscape*: Michel Desvigne with Sophie Mourthé; *Structural*: ACI; *Mechanical*: Choulet

Geneva, World Health Museum
Bernard Tschumi, Christopher Ball, Wenjun Yu

Shenzhen, Shenzhen Finance Culture Center
Bernard Tschumi, Joel Rutten, Sonia Grobelny, Christopher Ball, Wenjun Yu, Valeria Paez Cala, Nianlai Zhong, Guillermo Hevia Garcia, Alex Hudtwalcker Rey, Kai Blatt
Local Architects: Tianjin Architecture Design Institute

Rolle, Le Rosey Center for Science and Entrepreneurship
Bernard Tschumi, Joel Rutten, Christopher Ball, Sonia Grobelny, Valeria Paez Cala, Wenjun Yu, Tina Marinaki, Kai Blatt, Clement Laurencio, Mikail Gün, Pauline Viennot-Bourgin, Alissa Lopez Serfozo, Susie Steinfield
Executive Architects: Fehlmann Architectes SA (Serge Fehlmann, Nicolas Engel, Christophe Faini, Pascal Visinant, Samuel Nugues, Jerome Hoffmann)
Structural: Arup; Alberti Ingénieurs SA; *MEP*: SRG Engineering (Dominique Gori, Renaud Kocher, Thomas Perpina, Dario Aiulfi); *Facade Consultant*: BCS

Doha, Presidential Hotel
Bernard Tschumi, Joel Rutten, Kate Scott, Sung Yu, Bart-Jan Polman, Jerome Haferd, Nianlai Zhong, Jake Matatyaou, Colin Spoelman

Monaco, Tour Honoria
Bernard Tschumi, Joel Rutten, Pierre-Yves Kuhn, Pedro Camara, Jerome Haferd, Nianlai Zhong, Cecil Barnes, Clement Laurencio, Ruoxi Yang
Engineers: Arup (Ray Quinn, David Farnsworth, Michelle Roelofs)
Perspectives: ByEncore (Guillaume Paturel); *Cost Estimator*: BMF

Luxembourg, ArcelorMittal Headquarters
Bernard Tschumi, Joel Rutten, Cecil Barnes, Jerome Haferd, Pierre-Yves Kuhn, Pedro Camara, Clement Laurencio, Fiona Caselli
Structural, Mechanical: Arup (Ray Quinn, David Farnsworth, Michelle Roelofs, Brian Streby); *Cost Estimator*: BMF; *Renderings*: ByEncore (Guillaume Paturel)

Anyang, Yinxu Ruins Museum
Bernard Tschumi, Christopher Ball, Wenjun Yu, Valeria Paez Cala, Sonia Grobelny
Local Architects: ArchiFED

Lausanne, Musée Cantonal des Beaux-Arts
Bernard Tschumi, Bart-Jan Polman, Clinton Peterson, Emmanuel Desmazières, Grégoire Giot, Grace Robinson-Leo, Jocelyn Froimovich, Joel Rutten, Jerome Haferd, Kate Scott, Paul-Arthur Heller, John Eastridge

Shenzhen, OCT-LOFT Master Plan
Bernard Tschumi, Christopher Lee, Nianlai Zhong, Kim Starr, Bart-Jan Polman, Jerome Haferd

Guangzhou, Guangzhou Museum
Bernard Tschumi, Christopher Lee, Nianlai Zhong, Joel Rutten, Pierre-Yves Kuhn, Bart-Jan Polman, Jerome Haferd, Dora Felekou, Pedro Camara, Shayi Liang, Nate Oppenheim
Local Architects: Guangzhou Urban Planning & Design Survey Research Institute

Paris, Cité Musicale, Ile Seguin
New York: Bernard Tschumi, Christopher Lee, Nianlai Zhong, Bart-Jan Polman, Dustin Brugmann, Jocelyn Froimovich, Jake Matatyaou, Joel Rutten, Jerome Haferd, Sung Yu
Paris: Bernard Tschumi, Véronique Descharrières, Rémy Cointet, Emmanuel Desmazières, Catherine Rambourg

Tianjin, Binhai Master Plan and Binhai Science Museum
Master Plan:
Bernard Tschumi, Kim Starr, Jerome Haferd, Clinton Peterson, Bart-Jan Polman, Christopher Lee, Jocelyn Froimovich, Kate Scott, Joel Rutten, Colin Spoelman, Taylor Burgess, John Eastridge, Grace Robinson-Leo
Local Architects: KDG Group
Science Museum:
Bernard Tschumi, Joel Rutten, Nianlai Zhong, Christopher Lee, Pierre-Yves Kuhn, Jerome Haferd, Bart-Jan Polman, Dora Felekou, Pedro Camara, Shayi Liang, Nate Oppenheim, Kate Scott, Clinton Peterson, Olga Jitariouk, Sung Yu
Local Architects and Engineers: Tianjin Urban Planning and Design Institute
Facade Consultant: Inhabit

Geneva, Caran d'Ache Headquarters
Bernard Tschumi, Joel Rutten, Sonia Grobelny, Valeria Paez Cala, Wenjun Yu

Grottammare, A.N.I.M.A. Cultural Center
Bernard Tschumi, Joel Rutten, Chris Lee, Bart-Jan Polman, Jerome Haferd, Nianlai Zhong, Eleonora Flammini, Jake Matatyaou, Dustin Brugmann, Olga Jitariouk, Colin Spoelman, Alison McIlvride, Ruben Gutierrez
Local Collaborators and Consultants: Alfonso Giancotti, Michele Tiberi, Enrico Moretti, Alessandro Federici, Giuseppe Puglia, Fabio Giannini, Vittorio Marucci, Antonio Morganti, Marco Brizzi

Shenzhen, Xiangmihu Area
Bernard Tschumi, Christopher Ball, Wenjun Yu
Local Collaborators: HHDesign and iDEA

Beijing, 100KM2 City
Bernard Tschumi, Christopher Ball, Wenjun Yu
Local Collaborators: ArchiFED

Budapest, Museum of Ethnography
Bernard Tschumi, Joel Rutten, Pierre-Yves Kuhn, Pedro Camara, Jerome Haferd, Cecil Barnes, Christopher Lee, Nate Oppenheim, Nianlai Zhong
Landscape: Michel Desvigne Paysagiste; Újirány Landscape Architects
Engineering: Arup

Paris-Saclay, Biology-Pharmacy-Chemistry Center
Coeur de Pôle and teaching spaces, urban design and architectural coordination:
New York (Competition and Project Development): Bernard Tschumi, Joel Rutten, Cecil Barnes, Sebastian Cilloniz, Karen Berberyan, Christopher Ball, Jerome Haferd, Christopher Lee, Nate Oppenheim, Nianlai Zhong, Pedro Camara, Pierre-Yves Kuhn, Clement Laurencio, Fiona Caselli, Ruoxi Yang
Paris (BTuA) (Project Coordination and Supervision): Bernard Tschumi, Véronique Descharrières, Rémy Cointet, Vincent Prunier, Emmanuel Desmazières, Thomas Sanson, Florence Festa, Valentina Garreton
Research spaces and laboratories: Groupe-6 architectes: Alain Eyraud, Denis Bouvier, Nathalie Pierre; *Landscape:* Sophie Mourthé
Construction and Engineering: Bouygues Construction

Geneva, Vacheron Constantin Headquarters Extension
New York: Bernard Tschumi, Paul-Arthur Heller, Clinton Peterson, Nicolas Grillet, Pierre-Yves Kuhn, Joel Rutten, Dustin Brugman, Sung Yu
Paris: Bernard Tschumi, Véronique Descharrières, Rémy Cointet, Emmanuel Desmazières
Associate Architects: Glauco Lombardi Architectes Associés
Engineers: MDI Ingénieurs; *Facade Consultant*: BCS

Tourcoing, Le Fresnoy Extension
Bernard Tschumi, Christopher Ball, Wenjun Yu

Paris, Folie P7 Café, Parc de la Villette
Bernard Tschumi, Paul-Arthur Heller, Taylor Burgess
Local Architects: h2o architectes (Antoine Santiard, Jean-Jacques Hubert)

Paris, Folie L4 HyperTent, Parc de la Villette
Bernard Tschumi, Sonia Grobelny, Pauline Viennot-Bourgin, Valeria Paez Cala
Fabrication: Irmafer

France, Micro-folies (Guidelines)
Bernard Tschumi, Jerome Haferd, Cecil Barnes

New York, Thresholds: Architecture and Event, MoMA
Bernard Tschumi, Yannis Aesopos, Henning Ehrhardt, Mark Haukos, Tom Kowalski, Eric Lifton, Jordan Parnass, Robert Young
Museum of Modern Art Curator: Terence Riley

Orléans, Chronomanifestes 1950-2010, Frac Centre
Bernard Tschumi, Jerome Haferd, Olga Jitariouk, Ruben Gutierrez

Paris, Architecture: Concept & Notation, Centre Pompidou
New York: Bernard Tschumi, Kate Scott, Bart-Jan Polman, Jerome Haferd, Greg Barton, Olga Jitariouk, Pierre-Yves Kuhn, Nicolas Grillet, Nianlai Zhong, Sarah Rafson, Alison McIlvride, Jess Myers, Erin Shreiner, Joel Rutten, Christopher Lee, Colin Spoelman
Paris: Bernard Tschumi, Vincent Prunier, Catherine Rambourg
Centre Pompidou Curators: Frederic Migayrou, Aurélien Lemonier

Basel, Architecture: Concept & Notation, Swiss Architecture Museum
Bernard Tschumi, Bart-Jan Polman, Greg Barton, Sarah Rafson, Kate Scott, Pierre-Yves Kuhn
Swiss Architecture Museum Curator: Hubertus Adam

Shanghai, Architecture: Concept & Notation, Power Station of Art
Bernard Tschumi, Bart-Jan Polman, Nianlai Zhong, Alison McIlvride, Pierre-Yves Kuhn
Power Station of Art Director and Curators: Gong Yan, Xiang Liping, Hong Yuxi

Project List

2023
    Untitled House, Beacon, New York

2022
    Carthage National Museum, Carthage, Tunisia (*competition*)
    Guangming Scientists Valley, Shenzhen, China (*competition*)

2021
    Caran d'Ache Headquarters, Geneva, Switzerland (*competition*)

2020
    Folie L4 HyperTent, Parc de la Villette, Paris, France *(completion 2021)*
    Shenzhen Finance Culture Center, Shenzhen, China (*competition*)

2019
    Le Fresnoy Extension, Tourcoing, France (*study*)
    Palais des Congrès, Nîmes, France (*competition*)
    Yinxu Ruins Museum, Anyang, China (*competition*)
    Musée National d'Archaeologie et des Sciences de la Terre, Rabat, Morocco (*competition*)
    Grid House, Jinhua, China

2018
    World Health Museum, Geneva, Switzerland (*study*)
    Shenzhen Xiangmihu Area, Shenzhen, China (*competition*)
    100KM2 City, Beijing, China (*competition*)

2017
    Restaurant Luberon, Gordes, France (*study*)
    Clamart Sports Complex, Clamart, France (*competition*)
    Bank Lombard Odier, Geneva, Switzerland (*competition*)
    Le Rosey Center for Science and Entrepreneurship, Rolle, Switzerland *(completion 2025)*
    Pompeii and the Greeks, Pompeii, Italy (*exhibition design*)
    ArcelorMittal Headquarters, Luxembourg City, Luxembourg (*competition*)
    Cité de la Musique, Geneva, Switzerland (*competition*)

2016
    Université-Cité d'Entreprises, Cannes, France (*competition*)
    Tour Honoria, Monaco
    Museum of Ethnography, Budapest, Hungary (*competition*)
    Architecture: Concept & Notation, Power Station of Art, Shanghai, China (*exhibition*)

2015
    Petite Maison, Villa le Corbusier, Corseaux, Switzerland (*study*)
    Biology-Pharmacy-Chemistry Center, Paris-Saclay University, Saclay, France
        (*competition: first place; completion 2022*)
    Alésia MuséoParc (revision), Alise-Sainte-Reine, France
    Architecture: Concept & Notation, S AM Basel, Basel, Switzerland (*exhibition*)

2014
    Guangzhou Museum, Guangzhou, China (*competition*)
    Radio Television Suisse (RTS), Ecublens, Switzerland (*competition*)
    Architecture: Concept & Notation, Centre Pompidou, Paris, France (*exhibition*)

2013
    Doha Media Headquarters Building, Doha, Qatar (*competition*)
    Binhai Science Museum, Tianjin, China (*completion 2019*)
    Campus HES-SO Valais-Wallis, Sion, Switzerland (*competition*)
    Presidential Hotel, Doha, Qatar (*competition*)
    Chronomanifestes 1950-2010, Frac Centre, Orléans, France (*exhibition*)

2012
    A.N.I.M.A. Cultural Center, Grottammare, Italy
    Ozeanium Basel, Basel, Switzerland (*competition*)
    Roland Garros, Paris, France (*competition*)
    Cité Musicale, Île Seguin, Paris, France (*competition*)

2011
    Zénith du Lamentin, Le Lamentin, Martinique (*competition*)
    Folie P7 Café Renovation, Parc de la Villette, Paris, France (*completion 2013*)
    OCT-LOFT Master Plan, Shenzhen, China (*study*)
    Vacheron Constantin Headquarters Extension, Geneva, Switzerland (*completion 2015*)

2010
    Binhai Cultural Center (master plan), Tianjin, China (*competition: first place*)
    Musée Cantonal des Beaux-Arts, Lausanne, Switzerland (*competition*)
    Onassis Cultural Center Extension, New York, United States (*study*)
    Laifex Building, IFCA, Santo Domingo, Dominican Republic
    Atmosphere Park, Santiago, Chile (*study*)

*Project and bibliographic information prior to 2010 is included in the first four volumes of *Event-Cities*.

Books, Catalogs, and Selected Articles by Bernard Tschumi

2010

Acropolis Museum, Athens. Barcelona: Ediciones Poligrafa, 2010.

Event-Cities 4: Concept-Form. Cambridge, MA and London: MIT Press, 2010.

"Materialization of Concepts." In *Solid States: Concrete in Transition*. New York: Princeton Architectural Press, 2010, pp. 209-17.

2012

Architecture Concepts: Red is Not a Color. New York: Rizzoli, 2012.

Hardingham, Samantha and Kester Rattenbury. *SuperCrit #4: Parc de la Villette*. Abingdon: Routledge, 2012.

"Iconism and Kitsch." *Artforum* (New York), September 2012, pp. 464-66.

2013

Chronomanifestes 1950-2010. Collection Frac Centre. Orléans: Éditions Hyx, 2013.

"Sanctuaries." (1973) In *Everything Loose Will Land: 1970s Art and Architecture in Los Angeles*. Nürnberg: Verlag für modern Kunst, 2013, pp. 181-97.

2014

Architecture et disjonction (French edition). Paris: Editions Hyx, 2014.

Architecture Zoo: Parc Zoologique de Paris. Paris: Somogy Editions d'Art, 2014 (with Véronique Descharrières).

"Architectural Manifestos." In *After the Manifesto*. New York: GSAPP Books, 2014, pp. 173-81.

Bernard Tschumi. Architecture: Concept & Notation. Paris: Éditions du Centre Pompidou, 2014.

"Ce n'est pas un hasard…" ("This is no accident…"). In *Cher Corbu…*. Paris: Bernard Chauveau, 2014, pp. 30-1, 46.

"Designing a Pompidou Exhibition." *The Plan* (Bologna), November 2014, pp. 7-10.

"Eine Frage?" *Werk, Bauen + Wohnen* (Zurich), November 2014, pp. 66, 71.

Notations: Diagrams & Sequences. London: Artifice, 2014.

Notations: Diagrammes & Séquences. Paris: Éditions Somogy, 2014.

Tschumi Parc de la Villette. London: Artifice, 2014.

2015

"A Planet in its Own Orbit – On Being Zaha." *uncube* (Berlin), no. 37 (2015), pp. 24-27.

"Advertisements for Architecture." In *Transgression: Towards an Expanded Field of Architecture*. Abingdon: Routledge, 2015.

"Architecture and Concept." *Domus* (Milan), July-August 2015, pp. 6-9.

"Montage: Deconstructing Collage." In *Reckoning with Colin Rowe*. New York: Routledge, 2015, pp. 139-51.

"Some Notes on Architectural Theory." In *2000+: The Urgencies of Architectural Theory*. New York: GSAPP Books, 2015, pp. 220-28.

2016

Bernard Tschumi. Architecture: Concept & Notation. Shanghai: China Academy of Fine Arts Press, 2016.

"Building Concepts (Why Schools?)." In *The Building*. Zurich: Lars Müller Publishers, 2016, pp. 388-91.

"On Being Zaha." *Artforum* (New York), June 2016.

Urban Environment Design Magazine (China), Issue 99 (February 2016).

2017

"Préface." In Luca Merlini. *Le XIQ: dits et dessins d'architecture*. Geneva: MetisPresses, 2017, p. 8.

"Témoignage." In *La Nouvelle relation public-privé: Pour une coproduction de l'investissement public*. Paris: Eyrolles, 2017, p. 185.

"The Making of a Generation: How the Paperless Studios Came About." In *When Is the Digital in Architecture?*. Montreal: Canadian Centre for Architecture; Berlin: Sternberg Press, 2017, pp. 405-419.

2021

"L'Architecture dans l'Architecture." In *Jean Tschumi, architecte*. Paris: Cité de l'architecture et du patrimoine and Bernard Chauveau Édition, 2021, pp.15-23.

"Architecture, limites et programme." (1983) In *Architecture 1. Postmodernités*. Paris: Artpress, 2021, pp. 64-75.

2022

Architecture and Disjunction (Chinese edition). Shanghai: Tongji University Press, 2022.

"Leçons d'architecture." In *Le Cèdre. Jean Tschumi 1951-1956*. Gollion: Infolio, 2022, p. 25.

Selected Criticism, Reviews, Published Interviews on Bernard Tschumi

2010

Alison, Jane and Mary Ann Caws. *The Surreal House*. London: Yale University Press, 2010, pp. 228-31, 324.

Atanasov, Todor. "Acropolis Museum, Athens." *Architektura*, no. 4 (2010), pp. 58-63.

Defontaines, Cécile and Élodie Lepage. "Qui a volé la cuisse de Jupiter?" *Le Nouvel Observateur* (Paris) 5-11 August 2010, pp. 22-25.

Fajardo, Julio. *Starchitects: Visionary Architects of the Twenty-First Century*. New York: Collins Design, 2010, pp. 108-19.

Franci, Francesco. "Under a Reflective Steel Dome." *Abitare* Blog, 22 July 2010.

Garcia, Mark. "The Diagrams of Bernard Tschumi." In *AD Reader: The Diagrams of Architecture*. New York: Wiley, 2010, pp. 194-203.

Guislain, Margot. "Une boîte à musique polivédrique." *Le Moniteur* (Paris), 1 October 2010, pp. 58-59.

Hubert, Christian and Ioanna Theocharopoulou. "Musée imaginaire." *Log* (New York), no. 18 (Winter 2010), pp. 37-50.

Hawaleshaka, Dan. "Detour: Athens, Greece." *Dwell* (San Francisco), vol. 11, no. 1 (November 2010), pp. 70-78.

Kimmelman, Michael. "Who Draws the Borders of Culture?" *The New York Times* (New York), 5 May 2010.

Lang, Jon and Walter Moleski. *Functionalism Revisited: Architectural Theory and Practice and the Behavioral Sciences*. Farnham: Ashgate, 2010, p. 18.

Li Wang. "Questions of Sustainable Urban Form and Structure: Tschumi and Koolhaas at the Parc de la Villette." *World Architecture, Ecological Urbanism*, no. 235 (January 2010), pp. 85-89.

Lindstedt, Katherine. "Unveiled: Carnal Hall." *The Architect's Newspaper* (New York), no. 16 (6 October 2010), p. 14.

Makstutis, Geoffrey. *Architecture: An Introduction*. London: Laurence King Publishing Ltd., 2010.

Malone, Alanna. "Snapshot." *Architectural Record* (New York), vol. 198, no. 6 (June 2010), p. 232.

Maillard, Carol. *Les Zénith en France*. Paris: Archibooks, 2010.

Moskow, Keith and Robert Linn. *Small Scale: Creative Solutions for Better City Living*. New York: Princeton Architectural Press, 2010.

Naidoo, Ridhika. "Bernard Tschumi Architects and HDA: La Roche sur Yon." *Designboom*, 16 March 2010.

"New Acropolis Museum." In *Architecture Now! Museums*. Cologne: Taschen, 2010, pp. 366-75.

"Parc de la Villette." In *Städtebau und Architektur: Das 20. Jahrhundert*. Potsdam: H.F. Ullman Publishing, 2010, p. 297, 342-43.

"Parque Atmosfera." in *SCL 2110: arte, arquitectura, performance*. Santiago, Chile: Uqbar, 2010, pp. 260-69.

Peeters, Benoît. *Derrida*. Paris: Flammarion, 2010, pp. 463-64.

Rubini, Constance. *La Ville mobile, Biennale internationale de design Saint-Étienne*. Saint-Étienne: Cité du design, 2010.

Scaramiglia, Viviane. "Carnal Hall, prestige culturel." *Bâtir* (Brussels), 1 September 2010.

Spector, Nancy. *Contemplating the Void: Interventions in the Guggenheim Museum*. New York: Guggenheim Museum, 2010.

"The Blue Tower by Bernard Tschumi." In *Manhattan Skyscrapers*. New York: Princeton Architectural Press, 2010.

Théodoropoulos, Takis. "L'Acropole: En compagnie des belles Hellènes." *Hors-Série Geo* (2010), pp. 126-31.

Zoppi, Mariella. "The Modern-Day Garden." In *Storia del giardino europeo*. Italy: Alinea Editrice, 2009, pp. 252-3, 259.

2011

Angélil, Marc and Jørg Himmelreich (eds.). *Architekturdialoge: Positionen – Konzepte – Visionen*. Zurich: Verlag Niggli AG, pp. 574-93.

Bassoleil, Franck. "J-163 Le compte à rebo." *Le Bien Public* (Dijon), 15 October 2011, pp. 2-3.

Catsaros, Christophe. "Athènes." *L'Architecture d'Aujourd'hui*, no. 386 (November 2011).

Davidson, Justin. "The Greatest Building: 'If I Had To Pick One Tower, It Wouldn't Be the Empire State Building.'" *New York Magazine* (New York), 17 January 2011.

Drevon, Jean-François (ed.). *EDF sur le plateau de Saclay. Un concours pour intégrer le campus*. Paris: Éditions Bookstorming et Cité de l'architecture et du patrimoine, 2011.

Eekhout, Mick. *Tubular Structures in Architecture*. Geneva: CIEDCT/TU Delft, 2011.

Evin, Florence. "Zoo de Vincennes: le projet contesté." *Le Monde* (Paris), 18 February 2011.

Gilsoul, Nicolas. *La Ville fertile. Vers une nature urbaine*. Paris: Cité de l'architecture et du patrimoine, Paysages Actualités - Éditions du Moniteur, 2011.

Hartoonian, Gevork. "Bernard Tschumi Draws Architecture!" *Footprint*, no. 7 (Autumn 2011), pp. 29-44.

"Interface Flon Railway and Bus Station + M2 Metro Station." *A+U* (Tokyo), vol. 484 (January 2011), pp. 94-97.

Kristal, Marc. "Swiss Movement." *Surface* (New York), 1 February 2011.

Miljacki, Ana. "The Logic of the Critical and the Dangers of 'Recuperation' or Whatever Happened to the Critical Promise of Tschumi's Advertisements for Architecture." In *Critical Tools: International Colloquium on Architecture and Cities #3*. Bruxelles: NeTHCA, 2011, pp. 141-53.

"New Acropolis Museum, Athens." In *Museums*. Hong Kong: Design Media, 2011, pp. 181-88.

"Nuovo Museo dell'Acropoli, Atene." *L'Arca International* (Monte Carlo), no. 265 (January 2011), pp. 72-79.

Pedersen, Martin. "Living History: Deconstructivism." *Metropolis* (New York), vol. 30, no. 9 (April 2011), pp. 80-85.

Souza, Eduardo. "AD Classics: Parc de la Villette/Bernard Tschumi Architects." *ArchDaily*, 9 January 2011.

van Uffelen, Chris. *Contemporary Museums: Architecture, History, Collections*. Salenstein: Braun Publishing AG, 2011, pp. 314-17.

Walker, Enrique. "Special Prize." *Bauwelt* (Berlin), vol. 102, no. 1-2 (7 January 2011), pp. 58-61.

Wang, Michael. "Into Thin Air." *Artforum* (New York), vol. 49, no. 9 (May 2011), pp. 230-37.

2012

"Acropolis Museum." In *2011 European Union Prize for Contemporary Architecture – Mies van der Rohe Award*. Barcelona: Actar, 2012, pp. 91-97.

"Acropolis Museum, Athens." In *Detail in Contemporary Concrete Architecture*. London: Laurence King, 2012, pp. 14-17.

"Alésia Museum." *Architecture and Detail Magazine*, no. 5 (October 2012), pp. 702-705.

"Alésia Museum." *Archiworld* (Seoul), no. 206 (2012), pp. 44-53.

Barba, José Juan. "Alésia Museum and Archaeological Park." *Metalocus* (Madrid), 23 March 2012.

Barbaccia, Annie. "Le temps d'une pause à Alésia." *Le Figaro* (France), 27 June 2012.

Bailey, Spencer. "Caesar's Palace." *Surface* (New York), vol. 94 (May 2012), pp. 58-59.

Bennes, Crystal. "Alésia Centre." *Icon* (London), no. 105 (March 2012), p. 40.

Bingham, Neil. *100 Years of Architectural Drawing 1900-2000*. London: Laurence King Publishing, 2012.

Chipperfield, David (ed.). *Common Ground: 13th International Architecture Exhibition*. La Biennale di Venezia, 2012.

Crysler, C. Greig, Stephen Cairns and Hilde Heynen (eds.). "Architectural Theory in an Expanded Field." In *The Sage Handbook of Architectural Theory*. London: Sage, 2012, pp. 1-20.

Curtis, William Jr. "Circular Reasoning. Architects: Bernard Tschumi Architects." *Architectural Review* (London), vol. 231, no. 1384 (June 2012), pp. 34-43.

de Bure, Gilles. "L'ami américain." *Le Journal des Arts* (Paris), no. 362 (3 February 2012), p. 22.

Descombes, Mireille. "Alésia: La revanche des gaulois." *L'Hebdo* (Lausanne), no. 8, 23 February 2012, pp.42-45.

Eisenschmidt, Alexander. "Importing the City into Architecture: An Interview with Bernard Tschumi." *City Catalyst: Architecture in the Age of Extreme Urbanisation*, AD, no. 219 (September-October 2012), pp. 130-35.

Flouquet, Sophie. "Bernard Tschumi: Alésia MuseoParc." *L'Oeil* (Paris), 1 February 2012, pp. 42-47.

Geraki, Palmyra. "A Building's Building: The New Acropolis Museum." *Log* (New York), no. 24 (Winter-Spring 2012), pp. 63-70.

Hartoonian, Gevork. *Architecture and Spectacle: A Critique*. Farnham: Ashgate, 2012.

Lucan, Jacques. "Formalism and Linguistic Paradigm." In *Composition, Non-Composition: Architecture and Theory in the Nineteenth and Twentieth Centuries*. Abingdon: Routledge, 2012, pp. 522-41.

Maillard, Carol. "Une insertion tout en 'Retenue.'" *ARCHISTORM* (Paris), vol. 55 (August 2012), pp. 16-24.

Martinez de Guerenu, Laura. "Material World." *Architectural Record*, vol. 200, no. 7 (July 2012), pp. 51-89.

Maxwell, Robert. *A Few Years of Writing Interspersed with Some Facts of Life*. London: Artifice, 2012, pp. 99, 148-49.

McDonough, Tom. "The Manhattan Transcripts." In *Urban Design Ecologies Reader*. New York: Wiley, 2012, p. 248.

Pagliari, Francesco. "Alésia Museum Park." *The Plan* (Bologna), vol. 58 (June 2012), pp. 54-68.

Redecke, Sebastian. "Alésia? Ich kenne kein Alésia (Alésia? I Know Nothing of Alésia)." *Bauwelt* (Berlin), vol. 103, no. 23 (8 June 2012), pp. 24-31.

Salle, Caroline. "Au zoo de Vincennes, la future serre tropicale émerge." *Le Figaro* (Paris), 16 October 2012.

Stephens, Suzanne. "Au naturel: A concrete drum wrapped in a larch wood screen provides a distinctive orientation center for a historic battlefield." *Architectural Record* (New York), vol. 200, no. 7 (July 2012), p. 51, 62-67.

Sunwoo, Irene. "From the "Well-Laid Table" to the "Market Place:" The Architectural Association Unit System." *Journal of Architectural Education*, vol. 65, no. 2 (March 2012), pp. 24-41.

Teixeira, Carlos. "Interview with Bernard Tschumi." In *Entre: Architecture from the Performing Arts*. London: Artifice, 2012, pp. 236-49.

2013

"Alésia Museum Visitor Center." *Details* (New York), no. 32 (April 2013), pp. 92-99.

"ANIMA Cultural Centre – Grottammare, Italy." *HINGE* (Hong Kong), no. 213 (June 2013), p. 28.

"Anima Kultur Merkezi/Anima Cultural Center." *YAPI* (Istanbul), no. 380 (July 2013), pp. 122-24.

"Architecture and Transgression: An Interview with Bernard Tschumi." In *Architectural Design: The Architecture of Transgression*. New York: Wiley, 2013, pp. 32-37.

"Architecture et entreprise unies dans la 'Corporate Identity.'" *Le Temps* (Geneva), 2 October 2013.

Abbasy-Asbagh, Ghazal. "A Conversation with Bernard Tschumi, FAIA." *AIArchitect Newsletter*. September 2013.

Amiguet, Lluis. "Bernard Tschumi." *La Vanguardia* (Barcelona), 12 March 2013.

"Bernard Tschumi: Alésia Museum (First Phase)." *GA Document* (Tokyo), no. 125 (October 2013), pp. 86-93.

"Bernard Tschumi: 'L'architecture invente des concepts et les matérialise.'" *Ductal Solutions*, no. 14 (October 2013).

"Bernard Tschumi/Rem Koolhaas." In *Spatial Design: Gespräche über Architekturen, Ausstellungen, Bühnenbilder und Urbane Interventionen*. Zurich: Zurich University of the Arts, Institute für Design Research, 2013, pp. 36-60.

Bollack, Francoise Astorg. "Le Fresnoy National Studio for Contemporary Art." In *Old Buildings, New Forms: New Directions in Architectural Transformations*. New York: Monacelli Press, 2013, pp.116-21.

Bollmann, Benjamin. "L'intellectuel: Bernard Tschumi." *Dadi* (Lausanne), no. 5 (2013), p. 98.

"BTUA Bernard Tschumi Urbanistes et Architectes." *ARCHISTORM* (Paris), no. 58, (January-February 2013), p. 75.

Buss, Bastien. "Vacheron Constantin sur le point de franchir le cap des 1000 employés." *Le Temps* (Geneva), 12 October 2013.

Coen, Lorette. "La belle brique de Bernard Tschumi." *Le Temps* (Geneva), 15 January 2013.

"Conversation entre Bernard Tschumi et Marie-Ange Brayer, directrice Frac Centre." In *Les Pléiades: 30 ans de création dans les Fonds régionaux d'art contemporain*. Paris: Flammarion, 2013, pp. 68-75.

Di Francia, Cristiano Toraldo. "Bernard Tschumi Architects. ANIMA a Grottammare." *MAPPElab* (Italy), no. 2 (July 2013), pp. 18-25.

Etwareea, Ram. "Le British Museum doit restituer la frise du Parthénon à la Grèce." *Le Temps* (Geneva) 14 October 2013.

Harlambidou, Penelope. *Marcel Duchamp and the Architecture of Desire*. Farnham: Ashgate, 2013.

"I do not mind people being innocent, but I hate when they're naive. Interview with Bernard Tschumi and Peter Eisenman." *Log*, no. 28 (June 2013), pp. 99-108.

"Interview with Bernard Tschumi." In *AoD Interviews: Architecture of Deconstruction, The Specter of Jacques Derrida*. Belgrade: University of Belgrade – Faculty of Architecture, 2013, pp.144-49.

Luo Bin and Haiying Xie. "Two Poles, One Scene: Interprative Center of Alésia Museum, France." *Time+Architecture* (Shanghai), issue 3, no. 131 (May 2013), pp. 110-15.

Menking, William. "Studio Visit." *Architect's Newspaper* (New York), 6 March 2013.

Merz, Yves. "Le Rosey bâtit un centre culturel unique en Europe." *24 heures* (Lausanne), 5 July 2013.

Navarro, Pedro. "ANIMA. The first project by Bernard Tschumi in Italy." *Metalocus* (Madrid), 28 February 2013.

"New Acropolis Museum." In *World Architecture 14: Art Museum II*. Guangdong: Jtart Publishing, 2013.

"Notice Board: ANIMA." *MARK* (Amsterdam) no. 45 (August/September 2013), p. 13.

Pasquale, Joseph. "Bernard Tschumi Alésia Museum." *L'Arca International* (Monte Carlo), no. 112 (May-June 2013), pp. 18-27.

Quinton, Maryse. "Bernard Tschumi en Italie." *The Good Life*, no. 8 (May-June 2013), p. 74.

Stephens, Suzanne. "Artes Polioceticas." *Arquitectura Viva* (Madrid), 1 February 2013.

Togni, Mario. "Le futur tram ravive les luttes au Flon." *Le Courrier* (Geneva), 26 September 2013.

Tzortzi, Kali. *Museum Space: Where Architecture Meets Museology*. Farnham: Ashgate, 2013, pp. 338-44.

"Un café de Folie au Parc de la Villette!" *Le Moniteur* (Paris), 7 July 2013.

2014

Albert, Marie-Douce. "Bernard Tschumi, architecte réfléchi." *Le Moniteur* (Paris), 13 June 2014.

Albert, Marie-Douce. "Jaqueline Osty/Bernard Tschumi, Parc Zoologique, Paris 12e." *AMC* (Nanterre), no. 232 (April 2014), pp. 36-43.

Alonso, Xavier. "Bernard Tschumi: 'L'architecture est la matérialisation d'une idée.'" *Tribune de Genève* (Geneva), 12 May 2014.

Balbo, André. "Au Centre Pompidou, l'architecte Bernard Tschumi, de La Villette au Zoo de Vincennes." *Evous*, 29 April 2014.

Beesley, Ruby. "Realigning Architecture." *Aesthetica Magazine* (York), 1 April 2014.

Betsky, Aaron. "Paris Zoological Park." *Architect Magazine*, May 2014, pp. 100-11.

Blaisse, Lionel. "Quel zoo pour le 21e siècle?" *Architecture Intérieure Crée* (Saint-Ouen), no. 366 (May-June 2014), pp. 68-77.

Catling, Charlotte. "Damned if You Do, Damned if You Don't: What is the Moral Duty of the Architect?" *The Architectural Review* (London), 22 September 2014.

Chenal, Matthieu. "La nouvelle salle du Rosey s'offre le Royal Philharmonic Orchestra." *24 Heures* (Lausanne), 4 October 2014.

Clément, Catherine. "J'ai voulu dialoguer avec Pythagore." *L'Un* (Paris), no. 16, 23 July 2014.

Coen, Lorette. "Bernard Tschumi: 'Je bâtis pour savoir ce que je pense.'" *Le Temps* (Geneva) 10 May 2014.

Coissy, Emmanuel. "Une nouvelle salle de spectacles voit le jour." *20 Minutes* (Lausanne), 11 September 2014.

Coissy, Emmanuel. "Vaisseau culturel flambant neuf sur le campus huppé." *20 Minutes* (Lausanne), 12 September 2014.

Deitz, Paula. "The Classical View: The Parthenon Marbles at Home in the World." *The Weekly Standard* (Washington D.C.), vol. 20 (10 November 2014).

Descombes, Mireille. "L'Habitat en Bois du Rosey Concert Hall." *Tracés* (Switzerland), vol. 22 (21 November 2014).

Di Carlo, Tina. "Avant la lettre." *Log* (New York), no. 32 (Fall 2014), pp. 25-30.

Di Carlo, Tina. "Bernard Tschumi's Retrospective." *Artforum* (New York), November 2014.

Didelon, Valéry. "Une exposition d'architecture, pour quoi faire?" *D'Architectures* (Paris), 1 July 2014.

Fèvre, Anne-Marie. "Architecture: Tschumi en toutes Folies." *Libération* (Paris), 23 May 2014.

Finch, Paul. "Interview: Bernard Tschumi." *The Architectural Review* (London), 10 September 2014.

Fixsen, Anna. "Snapshot: Parc Zoologique de Paris." *Architectural Record* (New York), 16 May 2014.

Fuksas, Massimiliano. "Acuto Francese." *L'Espresso* (Rome), 15 May 2014.

Gautier, Christophe. "Urban Jungle, Il nouveau zoo de Vincennes. " *Aéroports de Paris*, no. 84 (April 2014).

Grandjean, Emmanuel. "Un ovni au Rosey." *Le Matin Dimanche* (Lausanne), 28 September 2014.

Grenon, Thomas, Sonia Henry, and Véronique Descharrières. "L'architecture du XXIe siècle: Une dissociation entre l'enveloppe visuelle & l'enveloppe fonctionnelle." *La Revue de la Terre*, no. 15, pp. 31-33.

Guifré, Maurizio. "Lo spazio sognato è anche percorribile." *Il Manifesto* (Rome), 19 July 2014.

Hays, K. Michael and Peggy Kamuf. "Rereading: Jacques Derrida's 'Point de folie – maintenant l'architecture' (1986)." *Harvard Design Magazine* (Cambridge, MA), no. 38 (Spring-Summer 2014), pp. 95-101.

Hill, John. "Book Review: Two Tschumi Titles." *A Daily Dose of Architecture*, 23 July 2014.

Hill, John. "So You Want to Learn About: Bernard Tschumi." *A Daily Dose of Architecture*, 14 December 2014.

Hollenstein, Roman. "Konzepte statt Fassaden." *Neue Zürcher Zeitung* (Zurich), 25 June 2014.

Katz, Ariela and Tricia Meehan "Hindsight Is 20/20: Bernard Tschumi at the Centre Pompidou." *Journal of Architectural Education*, 2 October 2014.

Kim, Dave. "Bernard Tschumi." *Surface* (New York), 1 June 2014.

Kipnis, Jeffrey. "Let Architecture Speak." *Domus* (Milan), 19 August 2014.

Kipnis, Jeffrey. "Our Chances. How Bernard Tschumi's retrospective quietly reaffirmed the case for architectural conjecture during the summer of fundamentalism." *Log* (New York), no. 32 (Fall 2014), pp. 31-38.

"La Mémoire des Images." *L'Hebdo Suisse* (Lausanne), 25 September 2014.

Laurent, Jocelyne. "Rolle: Le Rosey devient un nouvel acteur culturel." *La Côte* (Nyon), 12 September 2014.

Leonetti, Antoine. "La forme suit le movement." *Artpassions* (Geneva), 1 July 2014.

Leuschel, Klaus. "Maintenant – Bernard Tschumi im Centre Pompidou." *Architonic*. 3 May 2014.

Lunder, Samantha. "Le Carnal Hall dévoile son dôme high-tech et futuriste." *La Côte* (Nyon), 15 September 2014.

Mainimann, Joseph. "Die Bewegung eines Skateboards auf der Strasse." *Süddeutshe Zeitung* (Munich), 30 May 2014.

Merlini, Luca. *L'archipel Tschumi: Cinq îles*. Paris: Éditions B2, 2014.

Petit, Emmanuel. "Bernard Tschumi Retrospective." *Harvard Design Magazine* (Cambridge, MA), no. 39 (Fall-Winter 2014), pp. 171-73.

Pouthier, Adrien and Julie Nicolas. "Pimpant octogénaire, le zoo de Vincennes rouvre ses portes." *Le Moniteur* (Paris), 4 April 2014.

Querrien Gwenaël. "Le nouveau zoo de Vincennes." *Archiscopie* (Paris), no. 131 (May 2014), pp. 14-17.

Rose, Julian. "Digital Post-Modernities: From Calculus to Computation." *Constructs* (New Haven), vol. 17, no. 1 (Fall 2014), pp. 6-8.

Roulet, Sophie. "Bernard Tschumi, architecte conceptuel." *Architecture Intérieure Crée* (Saint-Ouen), 1 February 2014.

Ryan, Raymund. "Tschumi in the Capital of Modernity." *Architect's Newspaper* (New York), 23 July 2014.

Sels, Geert. "De bouwhonger van de anti-architect." *De Standaard* (Brussels), 19 July 2014.

Simenc, Christian. "Ces animaux qui cachent les zoo." *L'œil* (Paris), no. 670 (July-August 2014), pp. 70-73.

Sykes, Julian. "Le Rosey, ovni futuriste." *Le Temps* (Geneva), 12 September 2014.

Sykes, Julian. "Une acoustique en devenir." *Le Temps* (Geneva), 4 October 2014.

Trelcat, Sophie. "Rétrospective: Les concepts de Tschumi." *Le Journal des Arts* (Paris), 23 May 2014.

Trétiack, Philippe. "Bernard Tschumi: L'architecte qui déconstruit en couleurs." *BeauxArts Magazine* (Paris), no. 369 (June 2014), pp 96-99.

van Uffelen, Chris. *The Book of Drawings + Sketches of Architecture*. Salenstein: Braun Publishing, 2014, pp. 340-47.

Vidler, Anthony. "After the Event: Bernard Tschumi Retrospective at the Pompidou Centre." *The Architectural Review* (London), 3 September 2014, pp. 87-95.

2015

Angelidou, Ioanna. "The Three States of the Transcripts, or: Archives, Narratives and Bricolage." *Graz Architecture Magazine* (Graz), issue 11 (April 2015), pp. 206-27.

"Architecture of Difference." *Neue Zürcher Zeitung* (Zurich), 4 June 2015.

Atlas of European Architecture. Salenstein: Braun Publishing, 2015, pp. 450-51.

Bailey, Spencer. "Gallery: Vacheron Constantin's Christian Selmoni shows us around the watchmaker's newly extended Geneva headquarters." *Surface* (New York), September 2015, pp. 144-59.

Barnes, Cecil and Wade Cotton. "Around the Mountain or Though the Mountain." *Colon* (New York), vol. 3, no. 1, January 2015.

Belogolovsky, Vladimir. "Bernard Tschumi: I believe in placing architecture in the realm of ideas and invention (2004)." *Conversations with Architects: In the Age of Celebrity*. Berlin: DOM Publishers, 2015.

"Bernard Tschumi: The first European retrospective exhibition of the work of architect, educator, and theorist Bernard Tschumi is now on view at the Swiss Architecture Museum in Basel, Switzerland." *Domus* (Milan), 23 May 2015.

"Carnal Hall, Rolle, Switzerland." *L'Arca International* (Monte Carlo), no. 124 (May–June 2015), pp. 48-55.

"Camouflage: Zoo von Tschumi in Paris." *BauNetz* (Berlin), 9 April 2015.

Chupin, Jean-Pierre, Carmela Cucuzzella and Bechara Helal (eds.). *Architecture Competitions and the Productions of Culture, Quality, and Knowledge: An International Inquiry*. Montreal: Potential Architecture Books, 2015, pp. 93-109.

"Cinq réalisations emblématiques de 2014." *Le Moniteur* (Paris), 5 January 2015.

Clemence, Paul. "Modernism Reloaded: Hadid, Libeskind, and Tschumi Riff off a Le Corbusier Gem." *Metropolis* (New York), 23 July 2015.

Coates, Nigel. "Nigel Coates on teaching with Bernard Tschumi in the 1980s." *Architectural Research Quarterly* (London), vol. 19, no. 3, pp. 196-97.

Derrida, Jacques, Ginette Michaud, Joan Masó and Cosmin Popovici-Toma. *Les arts de l'espace: écrits et interventions sur l'architecture*. Paris: Editions de la Différence, 2015.

Désveaux, Delphine. "Passage à ciel couvert." *Architecture Intérieure Crée* (Saint-Ouen), March-April 2015, pp. 92-97.

Dwyre, Cathryn and Chris Perry. "Architecture Beyond Architecture: Cathryn Dwyre and Chris Perry in conversation with Bernard Tschumi." *A Journal of Performance and Art* (Cambridge, MA), vol. 109 (January 2015), pp. 8-15.

"Equipement culturel. La philharmonie entre à l'internat." *Le Moniteur* (Paris), no. 5815 (8 May 2015), pp. 60-61.

Giancotti, Alfonso. "A Conversation with Bernard Tschumi." In *Re-Start: Dai luoghi dell'ex produzione alla città*. Melfi: Casa Editrice Libria, 2015.

Hartoonian, Gevork. "Bernard Tschumi Interviewed by Gevork Hartoonian." In *Global Perspectives on Critical Architecture*. Surrey: Ashgate, 2015, pp. xii, 153-59.

Havik, Klaske. *Urban Literacy: Reading and Writing Architecture*. Rotterdam: Nai010 Publishers, 2015.

Hensel, Michael and Jeffrey Turko. *Grounds and Envelopes: Reshaping Architecture and the Built Environment*. Abingdon: Routledge, 2015, pp. 189-94.

Hosch, Alexander. *Architekturführer Schweiz – Die besten Bauwerke des 21. Jahrhunderts*. Munich: Callwey, 2015, pp. 180-81, 186-87.

Ijeh, Ike. "Carnal Hall." *Building Design* online, 27 February 2015.

Jamieson, Claire and Rebecca Roberts-Hughes. "Two modes of a literary architecture: Bernard Tschumi and Nigel Coates." *Architectural Research Quarterly* (London), vol. 19, no. 2, pp. 110-22.

Jodidio, Philip. "Alésia Museum and Archaeological Park." In *100 Wood Buildings*. Cologne: Taschen, 2015, pp. 566-73.

La Torre, Vincenzo. "Built to last." *Prestige* (Malaysia), January 2015, pp. 122-25.

Lelong, Guy. "Les appareillages mixtes ou la double recusation du réductionisme. Lichtenstein/LeWitt, Berio/Stockhausen, Perec/Emet Williams, Venturi/Tschumi." *Les Cahiers du Musée national d'art moderne* (Paris), no. 131 (Spring 2015), pp. 3-25.

Leuschel, Klaus. "Doppeldeutiges und Subjektives." *Werk Bauen+Wohnen* (Zurich), no. 7/8 (July-August 2015), pp. 66-67.

"Manufacture Vacheron Constantin." In *L'architecture à Genève XXIe siècle, 2000 – 2013*. Gollion: Infolio, 2015, pp. 142-43.

"Mais à quel usage ce bâtiment est-il destiné?" *D'architectures* (Paris), no. 237 (July 2015), p. 114.

Marjanovic, Igor and Jan Howard. *Drawing Ambience: Alvin Boyarsky and the Architectural Association*. Saint Louis: Mildred Lane Kemper Art Museum, 2014.

Millioud-Henriques, Florence. "Le dôme de Bernard Tschumi couronné." *24 heures* (Lausanne), 21 April 2015.

Mun-Delsalle, Y-Jean. "Bernard Tschumi's Architecture is Not Just About Space and Form, But Also the Events Happening Inside." *Forbes*, 7 September 2015.

"Power 100: Bernard Tschumi." *Surface* (New York), issue 119 (June-July 2015), p. 169.

Rappaport, Nina. *Vertical Urban Factory*. New York: Actar Publishers, 2015, p. 302.

Renault, Gilles. "La Villette, champ de cultures." *Libération* (Paris), 18 September 2015.

Risen, Clay. "Paul and Henri Carnal Hall at Institut Le Rosey, Rolle, Switzerland, Bernard Tschumi Architects." *Architect Magazine* (Washington D.C.), vol. 104, issue 8 (August 2015), pp. 108-17.

Steiner, Evelyn. "Inventing Questions: An Interview with Bernard Tschumi." *uncube* (Berlin), 18 June 2015.

Terragni, Emilia (ed.). *Architizer A+ Awards 2015*. New York: Phaidon, 2015, p. 98-9.

Yunis, Natalia. "Classical Architecture: Parc de la Villette/Bernard Tschumi Architects." *Plataforma Arquitectura*, 3 June 2015.

2016

Banou, Sophia. "Drawing the Digital: From 'Virtual' Experiences of Spaces to 'Real' Drawings." In *Drawing Futures*. London: UCL Press, 2016.

Bodart, Céline. "À propos de conservation." *A+ Architecture en Belgique* (Brussels), no. 2 (April–May 2016), pp. 60-64.

Colomina, Beatriz and Mark Wigley. *Are We Human? Notes on an Archaeology of Design*. Zurich: Lars Müller Publishers, 2016.

De Caters, Adélaïde and Rosa Ferré (eds.). *1000m2 of Desire*. Barcelona: Centro de Cultura Contemporaneá, Barcelona, 2016.

Dumbadze, Peter. "Why Tschumi Matters." *TL Magazine* (Brussels), 2 September 2016.

Fontana-Giusti, Gordana. "The Landscape of the Mind: A Conversation with Bernard Tschumi." *Architecture and Culture: Journal of the Architectural Humanities Research*, vol. 4, issue 2 (2016), pp. 263-80.

Girot, Christophe. *The Course of Landscape Architecture: A History of our Designs on the Natural World, from Prehistory to the Present*. London: Thames and Hudson, 2016.

Gooden, Mario. "Space as Praxis as Identity." *Dark Space: Architecture, Representation, Black Identity*. New York: Columbia Books on Architecture and the City, 2016, pp. 42-96.

Hougaard, Anna. *The Animate Drawing*. Copenhagen: Royal Danish Academy of Fine Arts, 2016.

Klimentov, Mikhail. "Lerner is a (Quintessential) Columbia Building." *Columbia Spectator* (New York), 27 April 2016.

Manaugh, Geoff. *A Burglar's Guide to the City*. New York: Farrar, Straus and Giroux 2016.

Manaugh, Geoff. "Committing Crime is Just Another Way to Use a City." *Fast Company Co.Design*, 2 May 2016.

Roberts, Bryony (ed.). *Tabula Plena: Forms of Urban Preservation*. Zurich: Lars Müller, 2016, pp. 98-101.

Stavrakakis, Emmanouil. "A Reflection or a Freestanding Object?" In *The Building*. Zurich: Lars Müller Publishers, 2016, pp. 240-47.

Stephens, Suzanne. "Time Warp." *Architectural Record*, vol. 204, no. 8 (August 2016), pp. 56-61.

Terra-Salamão, Mark. "Bernard Tschumi, the Pittsburgh Transcripts." *Inter.punct*. Pittsburgh: Carnegie Mellon University, vol. 2 (2016), pp. 82-93.

Waldheim, Charles. *Landscape as Urbanism. A General Theory*. Princeton and Oxford: Princeton University Press, 2016, p. 7, 35, 153-54.

White, Aaron. "Ambivalence as Agency." In *The Building*. Zurich: Lars Müller Publishers, 2016, pp. 202-9.

2017

"Richard E. Linder Athletics Center, Cincinnati, USA, 2006." *World Architecture Magazine* (Beijing), no. 327 (September 2017), pp. 86-87.

Banerjee-Din, Chloé. "L'ECAL, de l'avant-garde à l'âge de raison." *24 Heures* (Lausanne), no. 220-37 (16 September 2017), p. 4.

Benjamin, David (ed.). *Embodied Energy and Design: Making Architecture Between Metrics and Narratives*. New York: Columbia University GSAPP and Lars Müller Publishers, 2017, p. 22, 87.

Buck, David Nicholas. *A Musicology for Landscape*. Abingdon: Routledge, 2017.

Czerniak, Julia. "Parc de La Villette: Bernard Tschumi." In *Companions to the History of Architecture*. Chichester, West Sussex; Malden, MA: John Wiley & Sons, 2017.

Evangelou, Angelos. *Philosophizing Madness from Nietzsche to Derrida*. Cham, Switzerland: Palgrave Macmillan, 2017.

Keller, Benjamin. "6 Swiss Architects Who Conquered the World." *House of Switzerland*. 26 October 2017.

Merwood-Salisbury, Joanna. "This is Not a Skyscraper." *AA Files* (London), no. 75 (2017), p. 137.

Stathaki, Ellie. "Jean Tschumi: Architecture at Full Scale." *Wallpaper** (London), 25 May 2017.

The Now Institute. *100 buildings: 1900-2000*. New York: Rizzoli International Publications, 2017, pp. 142-43, 243.

2018

Branciaroli, Paola. "Bernard Tschumi Architects, Il Nuovo Museo Dell'Acropoli." *Thema* (Montesilvano), 30 November 2018.

Comberg, Ella. "How the Parc de la Villette Kickstarted a New Era for Urban Design." *ArchDaily*, 10 August 2018.

"Entornos compartidos: Paris Zoological Park (France)." *Arquitectura Viva* (Madrid), no. 206 (July-August 2018), pp. 16-21.

Gullbring, Leo. "Bernard Tschumi." *What I've Learned: Twenty-eight creatives share career-defining insights*. Amsterdam: FRAME, 2018, pp. 212-21.

Gullbring, Leo. "Post Paper." *Frame Magazine* (Amsterdam), no.124 (September-October 2018), pp. 62-66.

Hannah, Dorita. *Event-Space: Theatre Architecture and the Historical Avant-Garde*. Abingdon: Routledge, 2018.

Lambert, Guy and Eleonore Marantz. *Architectures Manifestes: Les Écoles d'Architecture en France Depuis 1950*. Geneva: MetisPresses, 2018.

Lus-Arana, Luis Miguel. "Comics and architecture: a reading guide." *The Routledge Companion on Architecture, Literature and The City*. Abingdon: Routledge, 2018, pp. 347-84.

McLeod, Virginia (ed.). *Red: Architecture in Monochrome*. London: Phaidon, 2018.

Perroud, Sandrine and Bernard Tschumi. "Mediocre tools lead to mediocre thinking." *EPFL News* (Renens), 19 October 2018.

Spiller, Neil. "Introduction: That was Then, This is Now and Next." *Architectural Design* (London), vol. 88 (March-April 2018), pp. 6-15.

Stierli, Martino. *Montage and the Metropolis: Architecture, Modernity, and the Representation of Space*. New Haven: Yale University Press, 2018.

Vidler, Anthony. "Architecture after the Rain." *Architectural Design* (London), vol. 88 (March–April 2018), pp. 16-23.

Violeau, Jean-Louis. "Parc de la Villette: l'hybridation au programme." *AMC* (Nanterre), no. 267 (March 2018), p. 20.

Vitale, Francesco. "Writing Space: Between Tschumi and Derrida." *The Last Fortress of Metaphysics: Jacques Derrida and the Deconstruction of Architecture*. New York: State University of New York Press, pp. 63-78.

2019

Barba, José Juan. *Congreso Anyway*. Barcelona: Fundación Arquia, 2019.

"Bernard Tschumi Architects, Exploratorium museum in Tianjin (China)." *Arquitectura Viva* (Madrid), 28 January 2019.

Brun-Lambert, David. "La Grande Interview: Bernard Tschumi." *Dossiers Publics* (Geneva), September 2019, pp. 12-17.

"Building blocks: new structures around the globe in 2019." *Wallpaper** (Bath), 15 April 2019.

Croset, Pierre-Alain. *Grid Second Life*. Online research project of Polytechnic of Milan, 2019.

Cubillos, Jimena Silva. "Entre pasado y futuro." *El Mercurio* (Valparaiso), 13 April 2019.

D'Souza, Newton. "Verbal/Linguistic Skills: Bernard Tschumi's narrative deconstruction and Maya Lin's prose poetry." *The Multi-Skilled Designer: A Cognitive Foundation for Inclusive Architectural Thinking*. New York: Routledge, 2019, pp. 181-87.

"Die roten Schlote von Tianjin Museum bei Peking von Bernard Tschumi Architects." *BauNetz* (Berlin), 20 February 2019.

"Ein gigantischer Raketenstadl – Binhai Science Museum, Tianjin." *Architektur* (Perchtoldsdorf, Austria), May–June 2019, pp. 72-77.

"El Exploratorium de Bernard Tschumi." *Arquine* (Mexico DF), 12 February 2019.

"Exploratorium." *L'Arca International* (Monte Carlo), no. 150 (September-October 2019), pp. 18-25.

Kafka, George. "The Architectural Folly Attempts a Return at a Brussels Exhibition." *Metropolis* (New York), 27 March 2019.

"Kreisgrundrisse - Kultur-, Sport- und Museumsbauten." *Archithese* (Zurich), no. 4 (December-February 2019), p. 41.

Lavin, Sylvia. "Set Up: A Conversation with Sylvia Lavin." *PRAXIS: Journal of Writing + Building* (Boston), no. 15 (2019), pp. 37-42.

Marani, Matthew. "Bernard Tschumi Architects' Exploratorium Museum bulges with cones of perforated aluminum panels." *The Architect's Newspaper* (New York), 14 March 2019.

Moutarde, Nathalie. "Plateau de Saclay: Le Pôle Biologie-Pharmacie-Chimie ouvrira en 2022." *Le Moniteur* (Paris), 11 October 2019, p. 30.

Norris, Mary. "Should the Parthenon Marbles be Returned to Greece?" *The New Yorker* (New York), 25 November 2019.

Oui, Mathieu. "Le parc de la Villette (Architecture & technique Signé Mitterrand)." *Le Moniteur* (Paris), 16 August 2019, pp. 26-30.

Péricchi, Béatrice. "Le Musée de l'Acropole d'Athènes fête ses dix ans." *AMC* (Nanterre), no. 280 (September 2019), p. 16.

Radoslaw, Stach. "Muzeum Nauki I Techniki Binhai." *Architektura murator* (Warsaw), no. 296 (May 2019), pp. 90-105.

Rafson, Sarah. "Ropes & Rules: Performance & Process in Bernard Tschumi's Advertisements for Architecture." *PRAXIS: Journal of Writing + Building* (Boston), no. 15 (2019), pp. 7-14.

Stevens, Philip. "Bernard Tschumi articulates tianjin exploratorium around a series of immense cones." *Designboom*, 24 January 2019.

"Tianjin Binhai Exploratorium, China by Bernard Tschumi Architects." *Gooood* (Beijing), 20 February 2019.

"Urban Narrator." *Mansion* (Taiwan), no. 35 (March-April 2019), p. 20.

2020

Aubin, Charles and Carlos Minguez Carrasco (eds.). *Bodybuilding: Architecture and Performance*. New York: Performa Publications, 2020.

Buchert, Margitta (ed.). *Entwerfen gestalten/Shaping Design*. Berlin: JOVIS Verlag, 2020.

Charitonidou, Marianna. "Simultaneously Space and Event: Bernard Tschumi's Conception of Architecture." *ARENA Journal of Architectural Research* (London), vol. 5, no. 1 (November 2020).

Chiappone-Piriou, Emmanuelle (ed.). *Superstudio Migrazioni*. Cologne: Walther König, 2020.

Concha, Daniel. "The Architect as an Observant: a Remembrance." *ARQ* (Santiago), no. 105 (August 2020), pp. 62-69.

D'Arcy-Reed, Louis. "Exposing the Unconscious through the Para-Architectural Photo-Essay and Prose." *Architecture and Culture*, vol. 8, no. 2 (June 2020), pp. 215-35.

Hougaard, Anna, "Skizzen von Diagrammen und Diagramme von Skizzen." In *Media Agency - Neue Ansätze zur Medialität in der Architektur*. Bielefeld: transcript Verlag, 2020, pp. 100-19.

Lovett, Sarah Breen. "Architectural Codes in the works of Dan Graham, Bernard Tschumi, and Diller and Scofidio." In *Architecture Filmmaking*. Bristol, UK: Intellect Books, 2020, pp. 25-38.

Marcos, Carlos L. (ed.). *Narrativa gráfica y dibujo de arquitectura*. Alicante: University of Alicante, 2020, pp. 33-35.

Wegener, Gerrit. *Philosophisches Entwerfen: Jacques Derrida und die Architektur*. Berlin: DOM Publishers, 2020.

Yu, Yan. "The Graph of Desire of Space—A Narrative Introduction to Psychoanalytic Cartographies." *Landscape Architecture Frontiers* (Beijing), vol. 8, no. 6 (December 2020).

2021

Avermaete, Tom and Janina Gosseye (eds.). *Urban Design in the 20th Century: A History*. Zurich: gta Verlag, ETH Zurich, 2021.

"Bernard Tschumi cède son agence parisienne à Groupe-6." *Le Moniteur* (Paris), 9 December 2021.

Boyer, Charles-Arthur. "Bernard Tschumi. Un projet sur l'entre-deux." In *Architecture 2. Entre forme et concept*. Paris: Art Press, 2021, pp. 49-53.

Cabral, Bárbara Silva da Veiga. "Performance, Programa e Cidade: Urbanismos do Chão." *Revista Prumo*, vol. 6, no. 9 (December 2021), p. 12.

Giovannini, Joseph. *Architecture Unbound: A Century of the Disruptive Avant-Garde*. New York: Rizzoli, 2021.

González, Carlos. "The Smallest Project. Hyperbolic Paraboloid Tent for the Parc de la Villette by Bernard Tschumi Architects." *Metalocus* (Madrid), 2 February 2022.

Juzwa, Nina and Jakub Swierzawski. *Mysli Marzenia Miejsca. Architektura polska w innowacyjnej współczesnosci*. Warsaw: Narodowy Instytut Architektury i Urbanistyki, 2021, p. 98.

Lang, Jon. "A History of Shifting Manifestoes, Paradigms, Generic Solutions, and Specific Designs." *The Routledge Companion to Twentieth and Early Twenty-First Century Urban Design*. New York and London: Routledge, 2021.

Molinari, Carla. "Sequences in architecture: Sergei Ejzenštejn and Luigi Moretti, from images to spaces." *The Journal of Architecture* (London), vol. 26, no. 6 (2021), pp. 893-911.

Saint-Pierre, Raphaëlle. "Le « 7 familles » de l'archi - Bernard Tschumi, la mémoire du père." *Le Moniteur* (Paris), 3 September 2021.

Sharapov, Ivan A. "The Ornament Concept in the Manifestos of the Architect B. Tschumi." *Articult*, issue 1 (2021), pp. 32-42.

Tschudi, Victor Plahte. *Piranesi and the Modern Age*. Cambridge, MA: MIT Press, 2022.

Vervoort, Stefaan. "Scale Models and Postmodernism: Revisiting Idea as Model (1976–81)." *Architectural Theory Review* (London), vol. 24, no. 3 (August 2021).

2022

"Archi-Folies, le monde de la culture et le monde du sport se mobilisent." Ministère de la Culture (France), 9 December 2022.

Astbury, Jon. "Bernard Tschumi is the deconstructivist architect with big ideas." *Dezeen* (London), 11 May 2022.

Borne, Emmanuelle. "Bernard Tschumi, architecte ès folies." *L'Architecture d'aujourd'hui* (Paris), issue 451 (1 October 2022), p. 82.

Càndito, Cristina and Alessandro Meloni. "Revelations of Folies through Geometric Transformations." *Nexus Network Journal*, vol. 25 (April 2023), pp. 269–76.

Carboni, Christine. "Voir et concevoir l'architecture. Repères chronologiques, 1903-2022. " *Archiscopie* (Paris), no. 31 (October-December 2022), pp. 62-63.

Charitonidou, Marianna. "Bernard Tschumi's Politics of Space." *Drawing and Experiencing Architecture: The Evolving Significance of City's Inhabitants in the 20th Century*. Bielefeld: transcript Verlag, 2022, pp. 307-348.

Cutieru, Andreea. "Bernard Tschumi Architects Designs New Addition for Parc de la Villette." *ArchDaily* (2 Feb 2022).

Dündar, Bilgen. "Play and City Relation as a Social Phenomenon: Rhythmanalysis and Place." *Tasarım+Kuram* (Istanbul), vol. 18, no. 36 (2022), 113-128.

Gannon, Todd. *Figments of the Architectural Imagination and Other Essays*. Novato, CA: Applied Research & Design Publishing, 2022.

Gasperoni, Lidia (ed.). *Experimental Diagrams in Architecture: Construction and Design Manual*. Berlin: DOM Publishers, 2022.

Griffiths, Alyn. "Parc de la Villette is the 'largest deconstructed building in the world.'" *Dezeen* (London), 5 May 2022.

"Interview Bernard Tschumi." *20 Minutes* (Switzerland), 30 June 2022, p. 10.

Kaeser, Eduard and Timothy O. Nissen. *Die Aura des Seriellen*. Basel: Schwabe Verlag, 2022, pp. 48-49.

Kang, Xue. "Spatial narrative research with architecture as the media." *Pollack Periodica: An International Journal for Engineering and Information Sciences* (Hungary), vol. 17, no. 1 (April 2022), pp. 173-77.

Kim, Mal-geum, and Chung Yeon-Shim. "Georges Bataille's Concept of 'Anti-Architecture' and Bernard Tschumi's Architectural Theory in Practice." *Journal of Korean Dance* (Seoul), vol. 59 (30 November 2022), p. 147-170.

Ravenscroft, Tom. "The legacy of deconstructivism 'makes me want to retreat to the back of the room' says Bernard Tschumi." *Dezeen* (London), 23 May 2022.

van Uffelen, Chris and Markus Sebastian Braun (eds.). *Contemporary Architecture: Masterpieces around the World.* Salenstein: Braun Publishing, 2023.

Yamasaki, Yasuhiro and Jin Motohashi. *Critical Words for Contemporary Architecture.* Tokyo: Film Art Inc., 2022, p. 230.

2023

Albert, Marie-Douce. "Enseignement: Les chercheurs expérimentent leurs nouveaux campus." *Le Moniteur* (Paris), 20 June 2023. pp. 60-63.

Astbury, Jon. "Glazed 'street' cuts through university science centre in Paris by Bernard Tschumi Architects." *Dezeen* (London), 11 July 2023.

Ball, Christopher and Elyjana Roach. "In Conversation with Bernard Tschumi." *Harvard GSD UD:ID*, 13 September 2023.

Barandy, Kat. "Bernard Tschumi and groupe-6 deliver one of the largest university buildings in france." *Designboom* (Milan), 11 May 2023.

"Biology-Pharmacy-Chemistry Center, Paris-Saclay University by Bernard Tschumi + Groupe-6. One of the largest university buildings in France." *Gooood* (Beijing), 12 October 2023.

Catsaros, Christophe. "Saclay: gigantisme à la française." *TRACÉS* (Écublens). 12 June 2023.

Charitonidou, Marianna. *Architectural Drawings as Investigating Devices: Architecture's Changing Scope in the 20th Century.* Abingdon: Routledge, 2023.

Ciangola, Manuela, "The Imprint of Bodies and Threshold in Interior Architecture: Heterotopias between body and space." *OFFICINA** (Italy), no. 41 (2023), pp. 26-33.

Davis, Lawrence. *Rewriting Exurbia: New People in Aging Sprawl.* Tento and Barcelona: List Lab, 2023.

Dulguerova, Elitza (ed.). *La biennale internationale des jeunes artistes: Paris (1959-1985).* Dijon: Les Presses du réel; Paris: Institut national d'histoire de l'art, INHA, 2023, pp. 570-71.

Fabris, Luca Maria Francesco. "A Positive 'Obsession' with pathways—Polo di Biologia, Farmacia e Chimica Université Paris-Saclay, Parigi, Francia: Bernard Tschumi Architects, Groupe-6 architects." *The Plan* (Bologna), September 2023, no. 148, pp. 48-58.

Gasperoni, Lidia. "Negotiating the Legacy of the Diagram in Contemporary Architecture." In *Handbook of Research on Historical and Modern Approaches to Architectural Drawing and Design*. Newcastle upon Tyne: Cambridge Scholars Publishing, 2023.

Haddad, Elie G. *Modern Architecture in a Post-Modern Era*. London: Lund Humphries, 2023.

Heathcote, Edwin. "When French theory shaped high-minded buildings." *Apollo Magazine* (London), September 2023.

Lelong, Guy. *Déductions de l'art — Un récit transverse partant de Mallarmé: Buren, Grisey, Danielewski, Rahm, Noé*. Liège: Les Presses universitaires de Liège, 2023.

Li, Mengyixin. *Large-Scale Urban Parks on Post-Industrial Sites in Contemporary Urban Landscape Conceptions*. Basel: MDPI, 2023, pp. 84-89.

Maillard, Carol. "Les Passerelles en acier." *MATIÈRES* (Paris), no. 19 (28 July 2023), pp. 32-41.

Orr, Will and Ricardo Ruivo. "Die Pyramide und das Labyrinth." *ARCH+* (Berlin), no. 251 (March 2023), pp. 148-55.

Patrão, André. "What architects do with philosophy: Three case studies of the late-twentieth century." *ARENA Journal of Architectural Research* (London), vol. 8, no. 1 (2023).

Piccoli, Cloe. "Tschumi, l'architetto del museo dell'Acropoli di Atene: "Ora restituite i marmi del Partenone." *La Repubblica* (Rome), 29 May 2023.

"Plateau de Saclay: une nouvelle phase d'aménagement débute." *Le Moniteur* (Paris), 10 May 2023.

Ray, Nicholas. *Thinking Through Twentieth-Century Architecture*. Abingdon: Routledge, 2023, pp. 239-43, 252.

Schoonderbeek, Marc. *Mapping in Architectural Discourse Place-Time Discontinuities*. Abingdon: Routledge, 2023.

Vincent, Amanda Shoaf. *Constructing Gardens, Cultivating the City: Paris's New Parks, 1977-1995*. Philadelphia: University of Pennsylvania Press, 2023.

Violeau, Jean-Louis. *Petites histoires d'architecture – De 1965 à aujourd'hui*. Paris: Éditions du Moniteur, 2023.

2024

Betsky, Aaron. *The Monster Leviathan: Anarchitecture*. Cambridge, MA: The MIT Press, 2024.

Murphy, Jack. "A memorial for Anthony Vidler and a celebration of 40 years of Parc de la Villette offer reasons for reflection." *The Architect's Newspaper* (New York), 9 February 2024.

Photography Credits

All images are courtesy of Bernard Tschumi Architects, with the following exceptions:

p. 44-45/152-153/200-201/260-261/342/372-373/418/480-481 Google Earth **p. 50/54-55/406/409** Michel Desvigne Paysagiste **p. 57** Hugh Dutton Associés **p. 62-63/66-67/68-69** Iwan Baan **p. 64-65/70-71/452/453/454-455/456-457/460/462/465/468-469/473/474-475/478/486 (top)/510-511** Christian Richters **p. 148-149** Michel Santos/Perrin Frères **p. 230 (top)** Russian State Archive for Literature and Art **p. 230 (bottom)** Arata Isozaki **p. 310-311/314-315/316/318-319/322-323** Kris Provoost **p. 312/313** Tianjin Urban Planning Design Institute **p. 317/321** Changheng Zhan **p. 448-449** Bouygues Batiment Grand Ouest **p. 458-459** EPA Paris-Saclay/Carlos Ayesta **p. 464/466-467/470-471/472/476-477/479/531/534-535** Fred Delangle **p. 494-495/498/500-501/502/503/506 (bottom)/507/515/544-545/550-551/554-555** Peter Mauss/ESTO **p. 518/526** Sophie Chivet **p. 542** Jody Carter **p. 543 (top)** h2o architectes **p. 543 (middle)** Mairie de Toulouse/OT Bastides de Lomagne/Parc de la Villette/Ministère de la Culture **p. 543 (bottom)** Ville de Monteux/ER/Jean-Noël Portmann **p. 563** Frac Centre-Val de Loire/Diane Arques © Adagp, Paris, 2024 **p. 582-583** S AM Swiss Architecture Museum/Tom Bisig **p. 587/588-589** Power Station of Art

Architecture is the materialization of concepts.

Concept, not form, is what distinguishes architecture from mere building.

Architects don't choose contexts;
they choose concepts.

Architecture is not so much a knowledge of form
as a form of knowledge.

Architecture is not about the conditions of design,
but about the design of conditions.

Architecture is not only what it looks like,
but also what it does.

Vectors activate; envelopes define.

(In architecture, theory and practice are inseparable.)